THE ETERNAL MESSAGE OF MUḤAMMAD

# The Eternal Message of Muḥammad

by

Abd al-Rahman Azzam

translated from the Arabic by Caesar E. Farah

introduction by Vincent Sheean

The Islamic Texts Society

This edition published by The Islamic Texts Society 1993
5 Green Street
Cambridge CB2 3JU.

UK
British Library Cataloguing in Publication Data
A catalogue record of this book is available from the British Library

ISBN 0 946621 48 9



Printed by The Alden Press, Oxford

# *Foreword*

*

That the name of Abd al-Rahman Azzam should be associated with the Arab League is historically inevitable. In countless articles and books, stretching back to the inception of the League in 1945, the description 'father of the League' or 'founder of the League' has tended to follow his name. Nevertheless the very fact that Azzam's name has been so closely associated with the Arab League has tended to obscure a fundamental point: for him the League was the beginning and not the culmination of a much greater unity. In short, while Azzam spoke about Arab unity, he thought about Islam.

*The Eternal Message of Muḥammad* is neither a historian's history of the origins of Islam, nor a theological study of its tenets. Rather, through the divergent chapters of the book, Azzam attempted to build the framework, based on the Qur'an and the Sunna of the Prophet, which support the moral and spiritual basis of civilization. For him, Islam was a religion and a means to salvation, but it was also a set of principles to which Muslims and non-Muslims can adhere and which can regulate society and harmonize relations. That Azzam felt that such a book was necessary was a consequence of his realization, confirmed by the ravages of the Second World War, that man in the West had forgotten that he is God's vice-regent on earth. Awareness of this responsibility had kept him in control and society had been governed by dictates which maintained a balance. However, once unleashed from this position of responsibility and fear of God, where his actions held eternal repercussions, man had set about destroying his fellow man as well as the world in which he lives. Since the world could no longer look towards the West to provide the spiritual or moral leadership necessary, it had to look elsewhere. For Azzam there was no need to look further than the spiritual values and virtues inherent in the Islamic message.

Today, fifty years after its first publication, the insidious dangers of atheism are for all to see. Traditional societies which had existed for centuries in spiritual harmony have been swept away in the face of encroaching secularism, and it is for this reason, if for no other, that the appearance of *The Eternal Message of Muḥammad* half a century after it first appeared, and on the occasion of the centenary of the author's birth, is both timely and valuable.

Abd al-Rahman Omar Azzam
The Islamic Texts Society 1993

# *Introduction*

*

The author of this book occupies a very special position in the eyes of Arabs and in the Islamic world. As father and first secretary-general of the Arab League, he gave an impetus toward unity and strength which, during the years at the end of the Second World War, brought new life into old lands. Indeed, it is memorable that the years of 'Azzām Pasha's leadership in the League (1945-1952) were a time of energetic hope and wide and true aspiration, and something has gone out of it since then. He brought an age-old promise, ever new, of which this book is another expression in its way: that is, the promise of universalism in Islam, unity and equality and brotherhood.

'Azzām has many more claims to the gratitude of his own people than the creation of the Arab League, however. He has had an immensely active life in the service of the Islamic countries around the Mediterranean, and there is more than one state or region to acknowledge it. Indeed, 'Azzām may be said to exemplify in his own life one of the principles expounded in this book, which is that a citizen of any Islamic state is a citizen of them all. This universalism within the fold—Islam as world and as world community—seems to have inspired his extraordinary range of effort for decades, although perhaps he would have been less explicit about it than he is today. He was only a boy when he ran away to fight for the Turks (that is, for Islam) in the Balkan wars; he fought the Italians in the deserts of Libya for eight years; he served Egypt in the diplomatic service and in parliament; he is today a representative of the King of Saudi Arabia in some delicate negotiations. In Damascus as in Djakarta, Istanbul, and Baghdad, this man is known for valor of spirit and elevation of mind. For it seems that no matter how urgent the affairs of the day, no matter how critical the fight, 'Azzām always had time to reflect upon his own religious heritage, to read the Koran and the commentaries, and to meditate upon the mission of the Prophet Muḥammad (upon whom be peace!). Thus he combines, in the best Islamic mode, the aspects of thought and action, like the Muslim warriors of another time who are typified for us Westerners by the figure of Saladin.

'Azzām Pasha—although such titles are now abolished, it is thus that we think of him by habit—was born into an Egyptian land-owning family which originated centuries ago in the Arabian peninsula. His family had taken to parliamentary government from the earliest days, and there was always an 'Azzām in the Egyptian chamber. 'Azzām emphasizes the strength and vitality of Egyptian parliamentary democracy because, as he feels, it is too often forgotten that this institution had been well established and had become a natural political expression for Egyptians a century ago. For that democracy, hampered and oppressed as it was by the British occupation, he was driven to the sword, the camel, and the desert—open rebellion. His exploits in former years are well remembered in Libya, and that country is one of the Arab states in which he feels especially at home. His contribution to its national emergence, as to that of some others, has never yet been fully recounted.

It was some twenty-seven years ago that I first encountered 'Abd-al-Raḥmān 'Azzām. It was in Cairo, by the kind offices of our old friend George Antonius (author of *The Arab Awakening*), who told me then and always believed that

'Azzām represented a new hope for the Arab world. 'Azzām then—a dashing figure, easy to imagine leading a charge of camels—was leaving parliament for a new life in diplomacy, and had just been named Egyptian ambassador to Baghdad and Tehran. It was there that he began those explorations of the possible and the probable which led him into thoughts of unity, not as an immediate objective but as an ultimate aim—thoughts which would in time find expression in the constitution of the Arab League.

Since then, at various times and places, it has been my privilege to talk with 'Azzām, sometimes for hours on end. Every such conversation has been illuminating; as Jefferson said of Franklin, I never leave his presence unrefreshed. The practical details of administration may have taken up a great deal of 'Azzām's time when he directed the League offices, but he was always ready to abandon them for the sake of more general considerations, reflections, and observations. His mind was never bogged down; it could rise at will. Often I used to think that the study of the Koran and the commentaries, leading him to the analysis of distinctly Islamic ideas and forms of thought, had given him this power of abstraction, which is not too common among men in public affairs. Readers of his book will see that although he quotes texts and is soundly based upon them, he makes his own probe into their meaning and constructs a coherent thesis of Islam in the modern world. As he says, it is not always easy to analyze or describe in English concepts for which we do not possess the vocabulary or, conversely, for which our vocabulary is too precise. Ideas of the state, of nationality, of citizenship, even of law have a defined sense and connotation in English which do not correspond to Muslim modes of thought, all impregnated with the spirit of universal community in one faith. In conveying this spirit through modern terminology 'Azzām has rendered, once again, a service all his own.

Now, in the afternoon of a great life, this noble Arab and deeply Islamic citizen of the world has time to share with us the fruits of his experience and study, the garland of his wisdom. Ours is the benefit—and it has been years since this subject reached us so cogently—but we can feel sure that 'Azzām has worked above all in the service of the faith that has inspired his whole life.

VINCENT SHEEAN

# *Translator's Note*

*

In this translation of a work that is regarded throughout the Muslim world as a classic study of the Prophet's Message and its meaning for all men today, I have tried to preserve the literary wealth of the classical Arabic. To this end, I have reviewed the entire translation with 'Azzām Pasha to make certain that I have accurately portrayed his views in English, particularly in regard to terminology.

Non-Muslim readers need to hold in mind the fact that the various writings which 'Azzām Pasha consolidated in this book were aimed exclusively at a Muslim audience. As he says in his Preface, these essays were intended as an exposition of Islam to its adherents, not as a sermon to Westerners, and the book therefore presumes a cultural orientation that is foreign to English-speaking people. It is always extremely difficult to translate Muslim terms and concepts into Western languages. Professor Bernard Lewis explains this difficulty in these words:

> The European writer on Islamic history labours under a special disability. Writing in a Western language, he necessarily uses Western terms. But these terms are based on Western categories of thought and analysis, themselves deriving in the main from Western history. Their application to the conditions of another society formed by different influences and living in different ways of life can at best be only an analogy and may be dangerously mis-

leading. To take an example: such pairs of words as Church and State, spiritual and temporal, ecclesiastical and lay, had no real equivalent in Arabic until modern times, when they were created to translate modern ideas; for the dichotomy which they express was . . . unarticulated in the mediaeval Muslim mind. The community of Islam was Church and State in one, with the two indistinguishably interwoven; its titular head, the Caliph [imām], was at once a secular and a religious chief. . . . Such words as "religion," "state," "sovereignty," "democracy," mean very different things in Islamic context and indeed vary in meaning from one part of Europe to another.[1]

For the translation of the verses of the Koran, I have relied heavily on Marmaduke Pickthall's *The Meaning of the Glorious Koran,* and certain changes have been made in the wording, spelling, and punctuation of that translation by ʿAzzām Pasha. Pickthall is aware of the difficulties in translating the Koran into English, for he frankly acknowledges that "The Koran cannot be translated. . . . The Book is here rendered almost literally and every effort has been made to choose befitting language. But the result is not the Glorious Koran. . . . It can never take the place of the Koran in Arabic, nor is it meant to do so." [2]

The reader will notice that many quotations stand without source notes. These quotations are almost exclusively part of Arabic oral tradition—sayings of the Prophet Muḥammad,[3] events in his life, reports and parables of famous Islamic scholars and writers—which may be found printed in many different places. So familiar are Muslims with these and the words of the Koran that in the original edition of the present

1 Bernard Lewis, *The Arabs in History* (2nd ed., reprinted; New York: Harper & Brothers, 1960), pp. 19-20.

2 Mohammed Marmaduke Pickthall, *The Meaning of the Glorious Koran* (reprinted; New York: The New American Library, 1961), p. vii.

3 Says Pickthall (*ibid.,* p. xi): "The words which came to [Muḥammad] when in a state of trance are held sacred by the Muslims and are never confounded with those which he uttered when no physical change was apparent in him. The former are the Sacred Book [Koran]; the latter the *Hadīth* or *Sunnah* of the Prophet."

work, as in all Arabic scholarly books, no source notes were given; for the English edition, however, Koranic references have been supplied. Other footnotes, approved or written by 'Azzām Pasha, have also been added in explanation of terms or data with which Western readers might be unfamiliar.

In the interest of correct pronunciation, the linguistically preferred transliterations of Arabic names and words have been adopted rather than generally accepted English usage (where such exists); hence, Muḥammad instead of Mohammed. Exceptions have been made in cases where the English pronunciation accords with the preferred transliteration, as Mecca (instead of Makka), Koran (instead of Qur'ān), and the like.

I am grateful to the American Council of Learned Societies for its kind cooperation in making this translation possible. The first part was written directly in English by the author, and Part IV, "The Islamic State," was translated by the late Professor Husein Kamil Selim of Cairo University from the second Arabic edition.[4]

*Caesar E. Farah*

*Los Angeles State College*

[4] 'Abd-al-Rahmān 'Azzām, *al-Risālah al-Khālidah* (2nd ed.; Cairo: The House of Arabic Books, 1954).

# Contents

*

## *Author's Preface*

*

I did not plan to write *The Eternal Message of Muḥammad* as a book. My intention in writing the original essays was to clarify for Muslims some of the principles and origins of their society, faith, and revealed Law, and to speak of the life of their Prophet. It was not my intention to apologize or preach to non-Muslims.

I may have been inspired also by fear of the onslaught of materialistic ideologies to which some older cultures in many European lands already have succumbed.

"Islam," writes a Christian historian, "is at once a culture and a religion, and in which the culture can hardly be conceived of as existing apart from religion." [1] Consequently, if the Muslims lose their religion, they lose with it their culture and undergo a process of social dissolution. Moreover, the Arab nation (to which I belong), itself a creation of Islamic culture, would also cease to exist through the inevitable process of disintegration.

It therefore seems vital to defend our society against the impact of alien cultures, particularly those consumed by a materialistic outlook.

The nineteenth and twentieth centuries have seen Muslim society and institutions exposed to the impact of European

1 Christopher H. Dawson, *The Dynamics of World History,* ed. John J. Mulloy (reprinted; New York: The New American Library, 1962), p. 105.

culture, which has been influencing Muslim ways and thought and not always advantageously. European culture derives from older creeds and cultures of the same general background from which Muslim society draws its inspiration and strength. Christianity and Judaism are both recognized by the Koran as having a similar origin to that of Islam, and this gives them a common meeting ground.

In the twentieth century, Europe, both East and West, has been gradually losing the religious culture it inherited from previous centuries, and it has become proud and cynical in its scientific achievement and technological success. Today, a large part of the modern world worships its own image. On the other hand, Marxian socialism and welfare capitalism are alike creating rituals for the new materialistic creeds and philosophies in the West as well as in the Communist East.

The God of the universe, of Jews, Christians, Muslims, and all, is being dethroned in favor of an idol to which all kneel and offer sacrifices; that idol is called "a high standard of living." It is becoming the object of unanimous reverence in our material age. In spite of the tug and attraction from both East and West, the Muslims still hesitate and doubt; they hate to join in the celebration of materialistic idols and creeds, but they are nevertheless attracted by the prospect of a higher standard of living.

Some of our people are being indoctrinated with the philosophies, dogmas, and rituals of the materialistic faith, but the majority of the Muslims in Africa and Asia are still confused and disturbed. They have known for a long time that they have a faith, a revealed Law, a society, and principles which call for a state that is neither secular nor theocratic but possibly both, and that is neither autocratic nor demagogic. Muslim society is based on the freedom of the individual and the equality of everyone. Muslim society is in its essence a free, classless society. It is classless not on the basis of any economic theory but on the basis of its egalitarian laws and its refusal to recognize distinction and honor except through piety and submission to the revealed Law, whose fundamental principles are universal, humane, and democratic. Nothing that is preached by the East or West is new to the Muslims. Reason is essential in judging even their dogmas and matters of faith, just as independent reasoning is one of the four sources of their jurisprudence.

Therefore, they are often troubled when told that these modern ideologies are the fruit of modern science and a ripe Western civilization. They ask themselves if it is really necessary to part with the Creator of the universe in order to share the fruits of modern science and technology. Must they ignore their beloved prophets, their tolerant universal culture, and their nation to enjoy the benefits of this age? Are they to part with their humane society and relaxed life, their trust in the inevitability of a destiny directed and ruled by the Almighty? They refuse to believe that human destiny and history are ruled and determined by a class struggle, for a system of wages. They do not believe, either, that a classless society on a material basis will be the fulfillment of history or of human destiny. The pretension that the eternal universe is planned for such an economic theory, or for a higher standard of living, is incomprehensible to the Muslim mind. Are they to give up the solidarity and mutual welfare which they enjoy with their families, relatives, neighbors because of such reasoning and to join in the general rush for the various societies of a Godless East or West?

These are some of the questions agitating the minds and hearts of those conscious and responsible among the six hundred million Muslims of all races and nations.

I have tried, in these pages, to give a few answers to these matters.

Islam is different from Judaism; Islam, being a universal submission to God, has no concept of a particular Covenant or a specially chosen people. It also differs from the Christian view of the Kingdom of God in heaven and the separate kingdom of Caesar on earth. And it differs from other religions, such as Buddhism and Hinduism. Islam is a faith, a law, a way of life, a "nation," and a "state," with a system of jurisprudence that is continually evolving for the administration of this world and the satisfaction of human needs under the sovereignty of our Creator. Islam's Kingdom of God on earth, with its faith, its laws, piety, rituals, society, and state, is the prelude and the means to the afterlife.

The Muslims, while sharing many of the beliefs and precepts of other religions, particularly Judaism and Christianity, have a limited common ground with modern materialistic ideologies. Islam may share a belief in the importance of this world, the Kingdom on earth, but asks, "Why without God, the Creator?" And why a life whose rituals are based solely on economics? With such ideologies, Islam finds no possibility of compromise, being, as I have tried to point out in this book, a religion, a culture, a way of life, and an indivisible nation with an independent jurisprudence. Its classless community of partners has evolved from a totally different philosophy. It refuses to allow its indivisible culture and faith to be set aside in the pursuit of a planned economy or adjustment to a welfare state. Islam's institutions are unique; they do not compromise with materialist dogmas. It stands firm on individual piety and individual freedom, a close-knit family devoted to the welfare of every relative, and a classless, benevolent society.

Though this book, *The Eternal Message of Muḥammad,* may be lacking in scholarly gifts, it is a serious attempt to point out the Muslim answers to today's world. It was first published in Arabic in 1946. It was translated and later published by Muslim scholars in Indonesia and Turkey. Its second Arabic edition, to which a section on the Muslim state and constitution was added, was published in Cairo in 1954. To this English translation I have added a new section, written directly in English, on the life of the Prophet, and a number of explanatory comments and notes. Whatever may be said about the book, we have no indication that during this period any of its material has been disputed by Muslim jurists or scholars in Muslim lands.[2]

**A.R.A.**

*New York City*

[2] The Great Muslim jurists and theologians who enjoyed during their lifetime the highest offices of Sheik al-Islam in Egypt and Turkey read *al-Risālah al-Khālidah* (the original) and expressed their satisfaction. They were the Sheik of al-Azhar University, the late Mustafa al-Maraghy, and the Sheik al-Islam of Turkey, the late Ahmed Hamdi Akseki, who ordered its translation into Turkish and supervised its publication, adding a forty-page introduction. Dr. Mahmoud Hoballah, professor of Muslim law at al-Azhar and director of the Islamic Center, Washington, D.C., has read this English translation and approved of both the treatment and use of sources.

*Say [O Muslims]: We believe in Allah*
*and that which is revealed unto us and*
*that which was revealed unto Abraham, and Ishmael,*
*and Isaac, and Jacob, and the*
*tribes, and that which Moses and Jesus received,*
*and that which the Prophets*
*received from their Lord. We make no*
*distinction between any of them, and unto Him*
*we have surrendered [we are Muslims].*

KORAN, 2:136

# I

## *The Prophet Muḥammad*

*

# 1

# *The Life of the Prophet Muḥammad*

*

Lo! my worship and my prayers and my life and my death are for Allah, Lord of the Worlds. He hath no partner. This I am commanded, and I am the first of the Muslims [those who surrender (unto Him)].

*Koran, 6:163-164*

The Muslims form a nation over thirteen centuries old, and comprise at present more than six hundred million human beings in all parts of the world. The Prophet Muḥammad was the first citizen of this nation, its teacher and its guide. He lived and died in the full memory of history. The evolution of his personality, religion, and nation assumed the force of a human drama of the greatest magnitude, witnessed not only by his contemporaries but also by the rest of the world in subsequent times.

The hero of this drama did not die until his Message was delivered and a Muslim nation established in the Arabian peninsula. Says Bernard Lewis, "In an essay on Muḥammad and the origins of Islam Ernest Renan remarks that, unlike other religions which were cradled in mystery, Islam was born in the full light of history. 'Its roots are at surface level, the life of its founder is as well known to us as those of the Reformers of the sixteenth century.' "[1]

1 Bernard Lewis, *The Arabs in History* (2nd ed., reprinted; New York: Harper & Brothers, 1960), p. 36.

During the half-century following the death of the Prophet (in A.D. 632), his Message was carried forth by five of his Companions,[2] who adhered closely to the precedents which he had established for ruling his nation. Four of them[3] were intimate, reliable friends and students who had followed him from the earliest days of his call, through persecution and ultimate triumph. The fifth caliph[4] was Mu'āwiyah, son of Abu-Sufyān, the formidable leader of the opposition to Muḥammad. Mu'āwiyah's career as caliph was longer than that of his predecessors. He presided over the affairs of the Islamic community for forty years as governor of Syria, then caliph.

Yet in spite of the wealth of historical facts available to us, perhaps no prophet and religion are so little known or understood by the Western world as Muḥammad and Islam. The West, which has maintained now for several centuries a tradition of freedom of thought, a high grade of literacy, and boundless knowledge in all spheres of human learning, knows far less about Muḥammad—both as a prophet and as a leader of men who exercised a direct influence on the course of human events—than about Alexander or Caesar, whose influences have been less than those of Muḥammad and Islam.[5]

What is the cause of such indifference in a world so eager to learn and to understand? Two explanations merit consideration. The first is from the pen of a distinguished Swedish scholar, who writes:

2 The principal Companions of the Prophet, called the *Ṣaḥābah* (singular: *Ṣāḥib*) might be compared to the apostles and disciples of Jesus.

3 Abu-Bakr, 'Umar, 'Uthmān, and 'Ali—the "orthodox caliphs" (A.D. 632-661). In the Arabic, the word *orthodox* in this phrase actually means mature, well-guided, correct; the usage in this book follows that of Western scholars, who have long written of the "orthodox caliphs." The reason these four caliphs are considered thus by Muslims is that, having known the Prophet personally and lived so closely according to his principles, they are looked to as great authorities and their decisions are considered precedents.

4 From the Arabic *khalīfah,* successor.

5 Indeed, it would seem that a conspiracy of silence has replaced the old enmity in the West concerning the Message, which is diametrically opposed to so many injustices perpetrated in the name of God and an enlightened progress.

> The cause . . . may perhaps be best expressed by the proverb: Relatives understand each other least of all. A Christian sees much in Islam which reminds him of his own religion, but he sees it in an extremely distorted form. He finds ideas and statements of belief clearly related to those of his own religion, but which, nevertheless, turn off into strangely different paths. Islam is so familiar to us that we pass it by with the careless indifference with which we ignore that which we know and know only too well. And yet it is not familiar enough to us to enable us really to understand its uniqueness, and the spirit by which it has won its own place in the sphere of religion, a place which it still rightly occupies by virtue of its very existence. We find it much easier to understand religions that are completely new and strange to us—as, for example, the religions of India and China. A greater degree of insight and of spiritual freedom is required of him who would understand the Arabian Prophet and his book.[6]

A second explanation is presented by another scholar:

> History has been such that the West's relations with the Islamic world have from the first been radically different from those with any other civilization. . . . Europe has known Islam thirteen centuries, mostly as an enemy and a threat. It is no wonder that Muḥammad more than any other of the world's religious leaders has had a "poor press" in the West, and that Islam is the least appreciated there of any of the world's other faiths. Until Karl Marx and the rise of communism, the Prophet had organized and launched the only serious challenge to Western civilization that it has faced in the whole course of its history. . . . The attack was direct, both military and ideological. And it was very powerful.[7]

[6] Tor Andrae, *Mohammed: The Man and His Faith,* tr. Theophil Menzel (London: George Allen & Unwin, Ltd., 1936), p. 11 (reprinted; New York: Barnes and Noble, 1957). It will surprise Western readers to learn that the Muslim world always has been far more familiar with Christianity and Judaism than the West with Islam. Muslims have always regarded Christian and Judaic tenets and beliefs with the greatest respect and interest.

[7] Wilfred Cantwell Smith, *Islam in Modern History* (New York: The New American Library, 1957), p. 109.

The Prophet was born in Mecca. The exact date of his birth is disputed, but it is agreed to be around A.D. 570. This uncertainty is usual in Arabia, "the country of illiterate people," as the Koran called it. Even today it is difficult to establish the exact birthdates of other famous men; for instance, it is hard to date the birth of the famous 'Abd-al-'Azīz ibn-Su'ūd (or ibn-Saud), the conqueror and unifier of Arabia, a man who ruled for more than fifty years (he died in 1953), and whose personality, conduct, and biography are known in great detail.

The undisputed source for Muḥammad's life is the Koran; there are also many *siyar* (singular: *sīrah*) or biographical studies of the Prophet, written from the accounts of those who knew him personally or to whom his memory was quite vivid.

Both his parents died young, his father, 'Abd-Allah, first and his mother Āminah shortly after. It is said that he was about six years of age at the time of his mother's death. His grandfather 'Abd-al-Muṭṭalib, a prominent leader in Mecca, then took charge of him. It is related that 'Abd-al-Muṭṭalib loved the boy dearly and often kept him close beside him, even in meetings where important affairs were discussed, usually in the shade of the Ka'bah.[8] When his uncles would try to remove the child, the grandfather would prevent them, saying, "Let him be; my child will be leader of his people."

Upon the death of his grandfather, Muḥammad's guardianship passed to his uncle Abu-Ṭālib, a no less devoted patron, whose love for and protection of Muḥammad persisted long after the Prophet proclaimed his mission and the new faith. Even though Abu-Ṭālib was never converted to the new religion, he continued to show love and protection for his

[8] The Ka'bah (or Kaaba), allegedly founded by Abraham, was originally the shrine housing the chief deities of the pagan Arabs; it became the palladium of Islam, and has remained one of the principal objects for which devout Muslims make the pilgrimage to Mecca. It consists of a cubelike building, very simple in structure.

nephew, despite extreme hardships and dangers, until his death, when Muḥammad was fifty years old.

Mecca was the traditional center of Arabia in both religion and trade; it was the crossroad of commercial transit between east and west, north and south. Abu-Ṭālib's clan, the Banu-'Abd-Manāf, the most influential in all Arabia, was a part of the great Quraysh tribe,[9] and formed the important element in an oligarchy that ruled Mecca and its surrounding tribes. The Prophet's youth was that of the normal young Qurayshi —he fought the battles, joined the peace negotiations, and shared in the duties and rights of his society[10]—except that he manifested from early years a revulsion to the worship of idols. Once when he was besought to act in the name of the gods al-Lāt and al-'Uzzā, he replied with the startling answer, "Do not ask me anything for the sake of these idols. I have never hated anything more."

9 Muḥammad's immediate family on his father's side were the Banu-Hāshim or Hāshimites, so named for Muḥammad's great-grandfather Hāshim. (*Banu* means sons of, and is the plural of *ibn.*) One of Hāshim's brothers, al-Muṭṭalib, gave his name to the Banu-Muṭṭalib (Muṭṭalibites), and the son, Umayyah, of another founded the Umayyads. These three families, which will figure prominently in this chapter, were in turn subgroups within Quraysh of the clan Banu-'Abd-Manāf. To clarify relationships further, note that 'Abd-al-Muṭṭalib was the son of Hāshim (and hence a Hāshimite, not a Muṭṭalibite) and the father of Abu-Ṭālib and of Muḥammad's father, 'Abd-Allah.

10 Of these obligations, one remained extremely dear to him, even after his prophetic call, when he severed all his ties with his tribe. This was his membership in the league called Ḥilf al-Fuḍūl, which originated to protect the defenseless and guarantee the safety of strangers in Mecca. The league came about because a stranger from Yemen sold goods in Mecca to an influential member of a powerful local clan who subsequently refused either to pay the price or to return the goods, whereupon the aggrieved seller stood up in the vicinity of the Ka'bah and implored aid for himself as a stranger in the city. Several members of the Quraysh aristocracy rallied to his assistance and secured the return of his goods. Meeting next in the house of 'Abd-Allah ibn-Jud'ān, they pledged henceforth to combat oppressive acts and uphold justice. Muḥammad, then only twenty-five years old, was present at this gathering, and was so impressed with the merits of the pledge that when he commenced his mission, he legalized it in Islam. As the years went by, even after his mission had become a success, the Prophet continued to express both his high regard for the league and his willingness to abide by its provisions.

But such strong expressions of disbelief in the gods or idols of his tribe did not alienate his kinsmen and friends from him or close him out from their friendly society, for he was loved by all for his noble character and great kindness and honesty. It was only at the age of forty, when his duty to the one God compelled him to preach against idol worship, that his people began to persecute him.

Muḥammad, like the rest of the young men in Abu-Ṭālib's family, had to work and help preserve the dignity of a generation of Hāshimites who, though they were less prosperous than their predecessors, still remained proud and powerful. He acted as a shepherd, and later, while participating in business, his relations with his people gained him the name of al-Amīn (trustworthy).

At the age of twenty-five, he married a lady of forty, his first wife, Khadījah, a relative and a rich widow. They lived twenty-five years together in prosperity and happiness, and had four daughters and two sons, but of the daughters who lived and married, only Fāṭimah had descendants.[11] Muḥammad was a devoted, loving father, and was kind to children in general. In his twenty-five years of life with Khadījah, he was the ideal husband. When she died, he remained several years without a wife, and even after he married—for a number of reasons—several wives, he always remembered Khadījah. "When I was poor, she enriched me; when they called me a liar, she alone remained true." It is an undisputed fact that Khadījah was the first to believe in Muḥammad's mission—before anyone, even himself, believed in it.

When he received his first revelation while on a retreat in the countryside, he returned home frightened and shivering. Khadījah received him with the comforting words, "No, you have nothing to fear. God will never let you down; you are kind to your relatives, you are astute and patient, you give

11 Fāṭimah was the mother of Ḥasan and Ḥusain. Her husband 'Ali was a cousin and the fourth caliph. Hundreds of thousands of their descendants, known as Ashrāf, are all over the world.

to the needy, you are generous to guests, and you never fail to relieve people from distress."[12]

So was Muḥammad described by the one who knew him best before the call and the prophetic revelation. Let us now follow his role in the great drama that was destined to transform his land, his people, and the world.

Muḥammad, at the age of forty, was inclined to worship in solitude in a cave on Mount Ḥīra outside the city. It was while praying, during the sacred month of his people, that he heard a voice command him, "Read." "I cannot read," he replied. But the voice again commanded him, "Read: In the name of thy Lord Who createth . . . man from a clot. Read: And thy Lord is the Most Bounteous, Who teacheth [writing] by the pen, teacheth man that which he knew not."[13]

Trembling, Muḥammad rushed home to Khadījah and told her of his experience. She comforted him and encouraged him. After a short interlude, he again heard the voice calling to him: "Thou art the messenger of God, and I am Gabriel." Rushing back to Khadījah in a state of complete exhaustion, he asked that she cover him with a cloak. Then he heard the call: "O thou enveloped in thy cloak, arise and warn! Thy Lord magnify, thy raiment purify, pollution shun! And show not favor, seeking worldly gain! For the sake of thy Lord, be patient!"[14]

It was then Muḥammad realized what his mission to his people was to be, and that was how it began. It is this mission which forms the subject of this book—this mission which conquered the hearts of men, and continues to do so with soaring vitality over thirteen centuries later.

Muḥammad's sincerity was never doubted by those who knew him well—his wife, his attendant-secretary, and his young cousin 'Ali who lived with him; these were his first

12 A. R. 'Azzām, *Baṭal al-Abṭāl Muḥammad* (2nd ed.; Cairo: The House of Arabic Books, 1954), p. 16.

13 Koran, 96:1-5.

14 *Ibid.*, 74:1-7.

converts. And though to his grief he could not convert his uncle Abu-Ṭālib, the old man never ceased to show faith in the sincerity of his nephew: when 'Ali, his son, converted, he told him, "Go, my son; he will never call you but to what is good."

Was Muḥammad's inspiration genuine? Did he speak in entirely good faith? The Muslims, of course, had no doubt; but this was also the attitude of knowledgeable men and serious scholars. Such men were and still are convinced of Muḥammad's earnestness, faithfulness, and sincerity.

Some thirty years ago, I asked Sir Denison Ross, then dean of the London School of Oriental Studies, if he believed that Muḥammad had been sincere and faithful. He answered, "I am sure of that; he never lied or deceived; he was sincere and truthful." I asked further, "Do you believe that he was the Prophet of God?" To this he replied, "That is another matter." Modern scholars no longer question his truthfulness. According to Tor Andrae,

> Formerly, men thought that his character revealed a certain premeditation, a calculating cleverness . . . . That Muḥammad acted in good faith can hardly be disputed by anyone who knows the psychology of inspiration. That the message which he proclaimed did not come from himself nor from his own ideas and opinion, is not only a tenet of his faith, but also an experience whose reality he never questioned. Possibly he was in doubt at first as to the identity of the hidden voice—as to whether it really came from the heavenly messenger whom he had seen in the mountains of Mecca or from an ordinary jinni . . . .[15]

Muḥammad quietly preached his faith in one God for some time. He won a few converts: his best friend, Abu-Bakr, a wise, respected, and rich merchant; later, 'Uthmān and Ṭalḥah, equally important and well-to-do Meccan Qurayshis; and a number of poor citizens and slaves. Then he received

15 Andrae, *op. cit.*, p. 47.

the command to preach in public: "Thus We send thee [O Muḥammad] unto a nation, before whom other nations have passed away, that thou mayst recite unto them that which We have inspired in thee . . . . Thus have We revealed it, a decisive utterance [Koran] in Arabic . . . ." [16] With this command from God, the Prophet went forward to warn his people against idol worship and to tell them to expect a resurrection and a day of judgment.

He stood for the first time on the Hill of Ṣafa opposite the Ka'bah, where the Meccan idols were glorified, and said to the people: "Supposing I now told you that just behind the slopes of this hill there was an enemy cavalry force charging on you. Would you believe?"

"We never knew that you lied," they replied.

Then he said, "I warn you I have a Message from God, and I have come to you as a warner and as the forerunner of a dreadful punishment. I cannot protect you in this world, nor can I promise you aught in the next life, unless you declare that there is no God but the one God." [17]

They mocked him and went away. Thus began his ten-year career of active struggle and persecution in Mecca. He did not desist from preaching to his people of a punishment that would come upon the unbelieving city. He told them, in the fiery language of the early Sūrahs,[18] how God had punished the old tribes of the Arabs who would not believe in His messengers—how the flood had swallowed up the people who would not harken to Noah.

He swore unto them—by the wonderful sights of nature, by the noonday brightness, by the night when it spreads its view, by the day when it appears in glory—that a like destruction would assuredly come upon them if they did not turn away from their idols and serve God alone. He fired his Message with every resource of language and metaphor until

16 Koran, 13:30, 37.
17 'Azzām, *op. cit.*, p. 16.
18 *Sūrah* means chapter of the Koran.

it seared the ears of his people. And then he told them of the last day when a just reckoning would be taken of the deeds they had done, and he spoke of Paradise and Hell with all the glow of Eastern imagery. The people were moved and terrified; conversions increased.

It was time for the Qurayshis to take action. If the idols were destroyed, what would become of them, the keepers of the idols, and their renown throughout the land? How would they retain the allegiance of the neighboring tribes who came to worship their several divinities at the Ka'bah? That a few should follow the ravings of a madman or magician who preferred one God above the beautiful deities of Mecca was of small concern; but that some leading men of the city should join the sect, and that the magician should terrify the people in broad daylight with his denunciation of the worship which they superintended, was intolerable.

The chiefs were seriously alarmed, and resolved on a more active policy. Hitherto they had merely ridiculed the preacher of this new faith; now they would take stronger measures. Muḥammad they dared not touch directly, for he belonged to a noble family which, though reduced and impoverished, deserved well of the city and which, moreover, was now headed by a man who was revered throughout Mecca and was none other than the adoptive father and protector of Muḥammad himself. Nor was it safe to attack the other chief men among the Muslims, for blood revenge was no light risk.[19] They were thus compelled to content themselves with the invidious satisfaction of torturing the black slaves who had joined the obnoxious faction.

The struggle grew in intensity. The Meccan oligarchy was seriously disturbed. Muḥammad was in earnest: he was the Messenger of God, and was under His orders. The idols of Mecca were not gods or partners with the Almighty; they

19 Stanley Lane-Poole, *The Speeches and Table-Talk of the Prophet Mohammad* (London: Macmillan & Co., 1882), p. xxxiii.

were helpless and useless, and there was no God but Allah. This purest form of monotheism, which is the essence of Muḥammad's faith, was an impossible doctrine for the Qurayshis to accept. The polytheism of Mecca had been established from time immemorial. It was not only the religion of their ancestors but the source of their distinction in all Arabia. If it went, with it would go their honor, power, and wealth. Muḥammad was the descendant of 'Abd-Manāf, Hāshim, and 'Abd-al-Muṭṭalib, who, generation after generation, had been the leading men of Quraysh and had had its interest at heart; so why not try to settle with him, on whatever might satisfy his dream of power and ambition?

A prominent leader of the Meccan oligarchy, 'Utbah ibn-Rabī'ah, was authorized to negotiate with Muḥammad. 'Utbah called Muḥammad to the Ka'bah and there stated his proposals:

"O son of my brother, you know your place among us Qurayshis. Your ancestors are high in our pedigree, and your clan is foremost and strong. You have shocked and disturbed your people. You have broken their unity; you have ridiculed their wisdom; you have insulted their gods; you have degraded their religion; and you have even denied piety and pure faith to their ancestors."

Muḥammad then said, "I am listening."

'Utbah continued, saying, "If you want wealth, we will all contribute to make you the richest of us all. If your object is honor and power, we will make you our leader and promise to decide nothing without you. If, even, you think of royalty, we will elect you our king. If that which you experience and see"—meaning the revelation and the visitation of Gabriel—"is beyond your control and you cannot defend yourself against it, we shall help cure you by spending money for medical care. It is possible for a man to be overcome by the force of an unseen power until he finds a way to a cure."

Muḥammad's answer was frustrating to the great representative of the Meccan leaders. He said, with respect, "Abu-al-

Walīd, listen to me, please," whereupon he began to recite from the Koran the basic tenets of his new creed.[20]

The negotiation was broken; a compromise was impossible. Muḥammad wanted nothing less than complete submission to the new faith. He himself was only a Messenger, and he had to carry out his orders from God and fulfill his mission faithfully.

The situation became more serious. The Meccan oligarchy resorted to violence against the growing humble element of the new congregation. They appealed to Muḥammad's dignity and to his aristocratic blood, rebuking him for being the leader of the slaves and the unworthy in the city: "Thou art followed only by the contemptible and degraded people who do not think." [21]

But Muḥammad was not sent to the aristocrats alone; he was a Messenger to all people. He was preaching what God ordered: "O mankind! Lo! We . . . have made you nations and tribes that ye may know one another [and be friends]. Lo! the noblest of you, in the sight of Allah, is the best in conduct." [22]

The persecution of those who listened to the Apostle of God continued. At last the Meccan leaders appealed to Muḥammad's sense of tribal solidarity. They explained the danger to which Quraysh and the city were exposed by the humiliation of their idols and the dissolution of Arab religious tradition. They said, "If we were to follow the right path with thee, we should be torn out of our land [and dispersed]." [23] They meant that they would be no different from the nomads of Arabia and would not be secure in their homes.

For Muḥammad that danger did not exist. God Who commanded him would provide for the defense of the faithful

20 'Azzām, *op. cit.*, p. 16. He called 'Utbah by the name Abu-al-Walīd, Father of Walīd, who was his son; this was a customary sign of respect.

21 Koran, 11:27. This was also said to Noah by his people.

22 *Ibid.*, 49:13.

23 *Ibid.*, 28:57.

and the victory of those who abided by His Law. They should know and recognize the truth that the idols were helpless stones, and that there was no God but the almighty Allah, the Creator of all, Who had no partners. They should recognize that there would be a resurrection and a day of judgment in which nothing would avail but devotion to God.

But they hated that menace of a judgment, and did not believe in a resurrection. A prominent leader, Umayyah ibn-Khalaf, took a decayed human bone from its grave and brought it to the Prophet, asking, "You say that this will live again?"

"He Who has created it in the first instance can make it return," the Prophet replied.

The arguments and disputes went on, accompanied by an intensive persecution of the Prophet's followers. Muḥammad then advised them to migrate to the opposite side of the Red Sea, to Christian Abyssinia (Ethiopia). They were received there by the Negus (emperor), whose protection they asked. According to tradition, they appealed to him in these words:

"O King, we lived in ignorance, idolatry, and impurity; the strong oppressed the weak; we spoke untruths; we violated the duties of hospitality. Then a Prophet arose, one whom we knew from our youth, whose decent conduct, good faith, and morality is well known to all of us. He told us to worship one God, to speak the truth, to keep good faith, to assist our relations, to fulfill the duties of hospitality, and to abstain from all things impure and unrighteous; and he ordered us to say prayers, to give alms, and to fast. We believed in him, and we followed him. But our countrymen persecuted us, tortured us, and tried to cause us to forsake our religion. And now we throw ourselves upon your protection. Will you not protect us?"

The Muslim refugees recited parts of the Koran which praise Christ and the Virgin Mary. It is said that the Negus and bishops thought their belief to be derived from the same sources as those of Christianity. Meanwhile, the Meccans did not remain idle. They sent emissaries with presents to the Abyssinians and petitioned them for the surrender of their escaped slaves and the other emigrants; but they were refused.

In Mecca, the Prophet and a few of his converts, who through tribal customs and clan usages could protect themselves, remained as adamant and as devoted as ever in preaching the faith and in praying publicly at the Ka'bah against its gods.

Quraysh had already tried to negotiate with Muḥammad's kinsmen, the Banu-Hāshim, for the Prophet's death, offering payment of blood money in return, but the tribe had refused the offer. Finally, the Meccan oligarchy decided in desperation to take steps against Abu-Ṭālib. In their opinion, he was the real protector of the blasphemy, although still a revered upholder of Meccan institutions and unconverted to Muḥammad's faith. They agreed to send him an ultimatum. When he received their warning, the old man was disturbed. He called in his nephew and told him that he had been warned by his tribe. "I am afraid that the masses of Arabs will rally against me. Save yourself and me, and burden me not beyond the possible."

Muḥammad wept, and answered, "May God be my witness, if they were to place the sun in my right hand and the moon in my left, I would not renounce my Message but would rather perish instead." Then he departed, but his uncle called him back and said, "Go, my son. Say what you believe; I shall never, under any circumstance, let you down."

This stand taken by the uncle, who was never converted to the new faith and who remained a leader in Mecca with its pagan traditions and codes of honor, constitutes a remarkable episode in history. Abu-Ṭālib, though strictly a traditionalist and unwilling to part with his ancestors' religion, had found it just as important or even more important not to surrender to growing pressures or persecute his protégé, of whose sincerity and righteousness he had no doubt.

The Meccan leaders were perplexed. Abu-Ṭālib's refusal

to act meant war. The Arabs were used to feuds and wars, but they could not accept this challenge, for it would have involved fratricidal slaughter in which Muḥammad's followers would be negligible. The staunch traditionalists like themselves, including a majority of the Hāshimites, Muṭṭalibites, and others, would fight for the Prophet's cause for family reasons while sharing the Meccans' religion; and those who shared his faith (Abu-Bakr, 'Uthmān, Ṭalḥah, 'Umar, and others) would be on the other side against their kinsmen. The leaders backed down, waiting for Muḥammad to realize the dangerous situation toward which he was leading his clan, its supporters, and those who believed in him.

Muḥammad was not to seek any conciliation. He was in the hands of God. He was sure that another, higher will was directing his destiny, and that the only way out was for Quraysh to see, despite all its pride and vested interests, that its shame lay in worshiping useless idols that could not direct men to piety and righteousness in this world or save them in the next on the great day of judgment. He, Muḥammad, an Arab prophet with an Arab Koran, was sent through the mercy of God to make of the Arabs a worthy people dedicated to the cause of serving mankind and their Creator.

Quraysh and its mass supporters heaped ridicule and contempt upon the Prophet and his mission, and threw dirt on him wherever he went—but to no avail. He still preached publicly, and went to the Ka'bah to pray in his own way. Ultimately, they decided to take extreme measures against his family, the Hāshimites: they refused to have any contact with them, to marry with them, or even to trade with them. They pledged themselves to that end in a proclamation which they placed in the sacred Ka'bah.

Abu-Ṭālib wisely and quietly took stock of the situation, and decided to withdraw to a valley on the eastern outskirts of Mecca, where he and loyal Hāshimites entrenched themselves. He wanted to avoid bloodshed, and all Hāshimite supporters, except Abu-Lahab, felt the same way. The Muṭṭalib clan, cousins of the Hāshimites, followed suit, and also entrenched themselves in the *shi'b* (a short, closed valley). Deprived of everything for more than two years, the Hāshimites and their supporters endured extreme hardships. Food was scarce; there was not enough to meet their needs. Some of the merciful people of the city would now and then smuggle a camel-load of food and supplies to them.

Hardly any new converts were made during this period. Most of those converts who remained outside the *shi'b* took refuge in Abyssinia. Nevertheless, the Prophet's determination and courage never weakened. He continued to go to the Ka'bah and to pray publicly. He used every opportunity to preach to outsiders who visited Mecca for business or on pilgrimage during the sacred months. He never doubted God's ultimate victory.

In the third year of boycott and siege, many Quraysh leaders began to feel guilty about isolating their kinsmen to perish in the *shi'b*. After all, the majority of those boycotted and besieged were not even converts; they were idol worshipers, like themselves, but they were going through these trials just the same, in keeping with their code of honor, for the protection of a kinsman who had always been a truthful and honest person.

The moderates found an excuse in that the proclamation suspended in the Ka'bah under the watchful eyes of the idol gods was eaten by worms. The merciful party thus took courage; their leaders put on their arms and went to the *shi'b*, where the exiles had been suffering, and extricated them.

And so, in the eighth year of the Prophet's mission, the converts, his uncle Abu-Ṭālib, and the clan that had honored its tribal tradition in giving protection to a faithful son went back to their homes.

That was not the end of bad times and suffering. Muḥammad soon lost his uncle, the veteran Sheik of Banu-Hāshim. Abu-Ṭālib was soon followed by the faithful Khadījah, the first convert of the Prophet, his beloved wife, adviser, and comforter. Hearing of the respite from siege and boycott, many of the emigrants to Abyssinia came back, but they soon met an intensified persecution and were subjected to endless suffering.

To preach in Mecca seemed hopeless, and to provoke the Qurayshis was not the best of wisdom. The Prophet then turned his hopes away from his tribe and city to other cities and tribes. The nearest and strongest competitor of Mecca was the city of al-Ṭā'if, fifty miles southeast of Mecca. With his servant Zayd the Prophet walked up the rugged mountains to that city. He visited the tribal leaders, and quietly asked their help. He was refused and badly treated. Dismissed, and followed by vagabonds and thoughtless children who drove him on and would not allow him to rest, he became exhausted. His feet bleeding, he sat and appealed to the Almighty for His mercy. The prayer that ensued has become one of the cherished legacies of the faithful appealing to God in desperate circumstances.

He gathered strength and continued on his way back to Mecca, reaching it three days later. Zayd was concerned, and asked the Prophet whether he did not fear thrusting himself into the hands of the Qurayshis, who continued to plot against the powerless in the city. "God will protect His religion and His Prophet" was the reply. The Meccans had learned of the Prophet's reverses at al-Ṭā'if and were preparing a degrading reception for him. None of the Meccan chieftains from whom Muḥammad requested protection for safe entry into the city would extend him help; but a goodhearted pagan chief, al-Muṭ'im ibn-'Adiy, took him under his protection and brought him to his home. Thus did Muḥammad re-enter Mecca—guarded by a polytheist, scoffed at by his fellow citizens, and pitied for his lot by his helpless followers.

In that sad year of recurring calamities and gloom, when tragedy seemed about to engulf Muḥammad's mission, a gleam of hope came to sustain him. During the pilgrimage season and the sacred months, when the traditional laws forbade violence, the Prophet had by happy chance converted a few people from Yathrib, who swore allegiance to him. They returned to 'Aqabah in the spring of A.D. 621 with the good news that his faith was being accepted by many in Yathrib. They were accompanied by twelve representatives of the two principal tribes, Aws and Khazraj, who in Muslim history later became known as Anṣār (helpers). The Yathribite delegation told the Prophet that their people were willing to accept Islam, and pledged, "We will not worship save one God; we will not steal nor commit adultery nor kill our children; we will in no wise slander, nor will we disobey the Prophet in anything that is right." This pledge was later called the first Bay'at al-'Aqabah (Pledge of al-'Aqabah). The second came a year later, following the pilgrims' season, when seventy of the Yathribites came again to 'Aqabah, and secretly pledged themselves and their people to defend the Prophet as they would defend their own wives and children.

Mecca was no longer a safe place for the Muslims to reside in. The Prophet then directed those who had returned from Abyssinia and other converts to emigrate and head for Yathrib. Quietly they started to move out. In a few months, more than a hundred families left their homes and migrated to Yathrib. The Qurayshis were on their guard. The migration of the Prophet to a rival city was harmful to them, and they were determined to prevent it at all cost. They decided to kill him, but collectively—representatives of all clans would plunge their swords into him—so that the Hāshimites, faced with this joint responsibility, would be prevented from taking vengeance on a single clan.

The trusted Abu-Bakr and 'Ali stayed behind in Mecca with the Prophet. 'Ali sought to deceive the spies of the oligarchy by occupying the Prophet's bed, while the Prophet and Abu-Bakr went to hide out in a neglected cave a few miles south of Mecca, on Mount Thaur. When the Meccans discovered that the Prophet had eluded them, they immediately instigated a search, but they failed to catch him, and after concealing himself in the cave for three days Muḥammad rode off to Yathrib.[24] With his arrival, a new era dawned. Conscious of this fact, the Muslims dated their new era from this year of the "flight," commonly called the Hijrah (or Hegira). It began on June 16, A.D. 622.[25]

When the Prophet entered Yathrib in the summer of that year, many leading Anṣār and a few hundred others were already converted. There were also the Muhājirūn (the Meccan Muslim emigrants), who greeted him on the outskirts of the city. The pagans and Jews gave him a good reception as well, each for a different reason. The Arab Jews were monotheists—they constituted three tribes, living as neighbors of the Arab pagan tribes who had originally come from Yemen and had gradually gained supremacy in Yathrib. The Jews hoped that Muḥammad, as a monotheist, might become their ally against the pagan Arabs and even against the Christians in northern Arabia. As for the pagans, their reason for receiving Muḥammad was not religion but rather the competition between Mecca and Yathrib. Furthermore, the Prophet was related to them on his maternal side—his great-grandmother was a member of Khazraj, the most important tribe in Yathrib—and "the enemy of my enemy" was as good a reason as any!

Members of each group tried to direct Muḥammad's camel toward their quarters so that he would become their guest. He asked them to let the animal go freely and stop where it would be best for everybody. Where it stopped, he chose his abode. Today, it is the famous shrine where the Prophet's tomb stands, and it is visited yearly by thousands of Muslim pilgrims.

24 This city was later called Madīnat al-Rasūl (the City of the Prophet), or simply al-Madīnah (the City); it is modern Medina.

25 *Hijrah* means literally emigration; the use of the word *flight* is justified more from a historical than from an etymological standpoint. The Muslim calendar dates from the Hijrah; that is, A.D. 622 is 1 Anno Hegirae (A.H.).

On that spot he lived, directed the affairs of the new nation, and built the first *masjid* or mosque of Islam; and on that spot he died.

After thirteen years of intensive struggle to survive, the Prophet had at last found a friendly city where he could defend himself and base his future operations.

The Qurayshis in Mecca were disturbed. They were powerful as owners of interests in all parts of Arabia, as guardians of polytheism and the idol gods of the tribes, and as leaders of the Arabian pilgrimage. Their city was a center both of Arabian trade and of a banking system whose moneylenders granted usurious loans to the various tribes. Muḥammad, their rebellious kinsman, had now taken refuge in a competitor town, and had created a rival base astride their important trade routes to Syria and the north. Moreover, many of their sons and daughters had migrated with him to the enemy camp. They knew that Muḥammad would never compromise in his religion, and that peace would be impossible with him.

Muḥammad, however, was not to seek refuge for safety. He was the Messenger of God to the world, and idol worship in his tribe and homeland must come to an end. His new nation would have to divorce itself from idolatry, usury, immorality, alcoholism, and vain and sanguine pride in tribalism, and above all it would have to become *muslim,* that is, submissive to God, the almighty One, Who has no partners, and to Whom all will return to be judged for whatever they have been.

His first concern in Yathrib was to build his simple place of worship, the *masjid,* where the faithful could also meet to discuss the affairs of their world. We must remember that Islam, unlike other great religions, such as Buddhism, Hinduism, and Christianity, subscribes to a political and social order which is to be carefully established and observed in the here and now as a road to the afterworld. The Kingdom of God in Heaven is achieved through piety and through a system of social and political order, namely, a Kingdom of God on earth.

The life of the Prophet in Mecca had been primarily concerned with the fundamentals of his faith: the unity of God, resurrection, the day of judgment, worship, and the purification of the soul. This concern continued in Yathrib, where the *ummah*—congregation or nation—could be organized as an independent entity. A constitution and a system of defense were needed. The new society had to engender a social order and a state. The Prophet, guided by revelation, was able to implement the political and social structure of the new *ummah,* despite exposure to a war of annihilation.

In meeting this challenge, the Prophet, with the guidance of God and his own personal aptitude, fused the Muslim congregation of various clans into a solid nation with one loyalty, Islam, and one brotherhood transcending tribal customs. The second task was an alliance with the neighboring Jews and pagan Arabs for a common defense and for security and peace in Yathrib. This was accomplished through treaty. This was the famous Covenant of Yathrib, resembling in certain aspects that of the League of Nations or of the United Nations, which aimed at the maintenance of peace and security among the various tribes and the creation of a common system of security as a consequence of common responsibility.

The next problem was what kind of defense to erect, a mobile or static one. In nomadic Arabia, static defense was but the final resort in extreme necessity, as it meant isolation accompanied by hardships. More important, it would also mean a halt in the expansion of the new faith and in the growth of the new *ummah.* Muḥammad was essentially the Prophet of God to mankind and the chosen instrument of the propagation of Islam, and whether in Mecca or Yathrib, the faith was his fundamental objective; therefore, he decided against static defense.

In the second year of the Hijrah, the Prophet initiated mobile defense, which led in the third year to the famous

Battle of Badr, located southwest of Yathrib. His forces were some three hundred infantrymen and three cavalrymen, with no armor but swords and limited supplies. His enemy, Quraysh, had three times his infantry, a hundred cavalrymen, and a large supply caravan. The Prophet's force nevertheless defeated them. The causes of the victory lay in their superior discipline and leadership and the high morale which resulted from their great faith in God and the promise of afterlife.

The Battle of Badr was a great victory, especially because it established the Muslim community as a separate political and social as well as religious entity and confirmed the power of the Prophet, but it was not decisive. Muḥammad treated his Quraysh prisoners in a chivalrous and humane way. His prestige in the eyes of the pagan bedouins[26] around Yathrib rose considerably. During the Battle of Badr, these nomads waited like poised vultures, ready to sweep down on the defeated and carry off the loot. As the Qurayshis were well established in Arabia, they would have been afraid to exploit them in adversity; however, the Prophet's party still lacked roots firm enough to survive misfortune and the Arab nomads' greed for plunder. But God saved His followers, who never boasted of their victory—it was God's victory, they all agreed; even the angels were reinforcing them against the pagans.

The first Muslim army came back to Yathrib with Meccan prisoners who were mostly of the same tribe as the Prophet, who treated them with mercy and sent them home.

In the third year of the Hijrah, while the Prophet was as usual absorbed in his worship and in his preaching, he consolidated the position of his *ummah* and looked after the defense of his city. Neither were his enemies idle. One year later they were ready, and again marched on Yathrib with a force three times as large as the one defeated at Badr. The Prophet moved to engage them, and they met on the slopes

26 The English word comes from the Arabic *badawi* (singular: *badu*), meaning nomads, as distinguished from settled populations.

of Mount Uḥūd. The fierce battle ended with the retreat of the Muslim forces and the wounding of the Prophet; but through his endurance and his resourceful and courageous leadership, he managed to save his small army. Abu-Sufyān, who was leading the Meccans, called from the top of the hill, saying, "Uḥūd for Badr; we call it even. We will meet again next year." Both forces retired to their original bases. But that was not the end; Uḥūd, like Badr, was not decisive.

Two years later, Quraysh built up a much larger force, allied itself to many tribes, and was able to mobilize an army of ten thousand men. It was well armed and equipped, and thus far greater than any force that the Prophet could muster. The attackers laid siege on Yathrib, and for two weeks pressed to break through; but they failed. The Prophet had introduced new defense tactics—digging trenches and raising barricades, at which he himself labored with the men day and night. The Prophet's faith in God and the great zeal of his followers, particularly the Muhājirūn and Anṣār, balanced the enemy's superiority in arms and numbers. A severe wind blew, accompanied by a dust storm. The morale of the Aḥzāb[27] faltered with the evening; they argued among themselves, and ultimately broke camp and retired. The Muslims followed them a certain distance. That was the last Quraysh attempt to destroy its enemy's base in Yathrib.

A year later, that is, in the sixth year of the Hijrah, the Prophet moved in force toward his home city, Mecca. He wanted to make his lesser pilgrimage (*'umrah*) to the Ka'bah, which, although it housed pagan idols, was still regarded by Muslims as sacred, because in the view of the Prophet the Ka'bah had been built by the Patriarch Abraham for the worship of God. It was in the vicinity of the Ka'bah, near the well of Zamzam, that Abraham had settled his Egyptian wife Hagar with her son Ishmael. The Qurayshis and other northern Arab tribes were the descendants of Abraham

27 Literally, *leagues,* that is, a group banded in a general alliance against the Prophet and his men.

through his son Ishmael. The Muslims therefore believed that they had the right to perform the pilgrimage initiated by their great father Abraham, the first Arab to worship Allah, the only God. But the Meccans disagreed with them, and sought to bar their entry. Finally, a ten-year truce[28] was concluded with Quraysh whereby the Prophet agreed, among other things, to postpone his pilgrimage to the following season.

The march on Mecca and the truce that resulted therefrom constitute a turning point in Muslim history: for the first time, the right of every person to preach and practice his faith freely was recognized by a formal treaty. A year after the conclusion of the truce, the Prophet and two thousand men entered Mecca, which, according to previous agreement, was evacuated temporarily of its inhabitants. The Muslims completed their pilgrimage in an admirable manner, and impressed the Meccans to such an extent that conversions to Islam increased by leaps and bounds. Delegations were sent by Arabian tribes from the four corners of the peninsula to pledge their loyalty to Muḥammad in Yathrib.

When two years later the Qurayshis violated their treaty obligations and attacked the Khuzā'ah tribe, which was allied with the Muslims, the Prophet led a march on Mecca on Wednesday, the tenth of Ramaḍān (in the eighth year of the Hijrah—A.D. 630), with ten thousand men. On that memorable day, the Prophet asked the Meccans, "What do you think I will do to you?" They answered, "You are a generous brother and the son of a generous brother." "Go," the Prophet rejoined, "you are freed."

Lane-Poole writes,

> . . . the day of Muḥammad's greatest triumph over his enemies was also the day of his grandest victory over himself. He freely forgave Quraysh all the years of sorrow and cruel scorn with

28 Known as the Truce of al-Ḥudaybiyah (a place near Mecca). The date was A.D. 628.

which they had afflicted him, and gave an amnesty to the whole population of Mecca. Four criminals whom Justice condemned made up Muḥammad's proscription list, when as a conqueror he entered the city of his bitterest enemies. The army followed his example, and entered quietly and peaceably; no house was robbed, no woman insulted. One thing alone suffered destruction. Going to the Ka'bah, Muḥammad stood before each of the three hundred and sixty idols, and pointed to them with his staff saying, "Truth is come, and falsehood is fled away!" and at these words his attendants hewed them down and all the idols and household gods of Mecca and round about were destroyed.[29]

After the conquest of Mecca, Muḥammad had to march on another stubborn enemy, al-Ṭā'if, the important dwelling place of the much-exalted idol god Hubal. It was the city to which the Prophet had journeyed in his worst days of persecution, seeking refuge but receiving humiliation instead. Ten years had elapsed since then, and now he believed that the victory in Mecca might persuade the inhabitants of al-Ṭā'if to sue for peace. On the contrary, they mobilized the great Hawāzin confederacy of tribes against him, and rallied the city people for a decisive day with the enemy of their god. The two forces met at Ḥunayn. The Muslims were then commanding the largest force in their history to date, but they were being routed and were retreating when the Prophet rallied the old Anṣār and Muhājirūn veterans. Fighting courageously, though Muḥammad was wounded, they won the day. The Prophet was so generous and forgiving to his old enemies and persecutors that some of his followers among the Anṣār objected. But the Prophet soothed them with wise and fair exhortations, and played upon their sympathies until they wept.

Upon returning to Yathrib, Muḥammad encountered delegations sent by tribes and settled peoples of Arabia. They came to do homage to him and to profess the faith of Islam. Thus was Arabia won over to Islam.

29 Lane-Poole, *op. cit.*, p. xlvii.

But what about the rest of the world? Muḥammad always conceived of his mission as being directed to all people. Already he had sent his emissaries to Arabia's neighboring emperors, the Persian and Roman (Byzantine), who ignored his Message or humiliated the messengers. The only courteous response was from the Coptic leader of Egypt. In southern Syria (modern Jordan), certain of his emissaries were brutally murdered, which occasioned the battle at Mu'tah later.[30] For some years after their army's defeat at Mu'tah, the Muslims were in a state of war with the Byzantine emperor, Heraclius, who was said to be gathering together a large force in Syria to deal with the new Arab menace on his southern frontier and to liquidate the new Arab ruler who entertained such serious pretensions.

For this and other reasons, the Prophet decided to prepare a large army and march north. This was the last military expedition he was to plan. He had pointed out the direction. A short time after his death, his companions marched north, and four years later, they conquered both mighty empires, the East Roman and the Persian.

In the tenth year of the Hijrah, the Prophet made his last pilgrimage to Mecca, and delivered his Farewell Speech at Mina to a congregation of forty thousand Muslims. He commenced, "O people, listen to me; I may not ever meet you again here after this year." Then, in a great sermon, he expressed his fears that they might lose the way of God and return to a lawless society and to tribal feuds. He ended a great law-giving speech by asking them if they thought that he had faithfully delivered his Message. They answered with one voice, "Yes!" He then said, "God, You are my witness," and descended from his camel.

The Muslims called that sermon the Farewell Speech and that pilgrimage the Farewell Pilgrimage. Since the Prophet's first call by the angel Gabriel twenty-three years earlier, revelation after revelation had continued. He had learned them

30 See pp. 181-183.

by heart and inscribed them, and so had his friends. They formed together the glorious Book of Islam, the Koran. At the end of this sermon, and as a final word, he recited in the name of God this revelation: "This day have I [Allah] perfected your religion for you and completed My favor unto you, and have chosen for you as religion AL-ISLAM." [31] His dear friends then wept. They felt that his end was near, that the Prophet had fulfilled his mission; and it was so.

The Prophet died of fever in Yathrib, which thereafter was called al-Madīnah. His life, suffering, and triumph will remain for Muslims and non-Muslims alike a symbol of modesty, faithful devotion, and dedicated service to God, a high example of manhood.

31 Koran, 5:3.

# II

## *On the Fundamentals of the Message*

*

# 2

## *The Two Fundamentals*

*

The eternal Message is based on two fundamentals: faith (*īmān*) and right-doing (*iḥsān*). On these its structure rises; from them it branches out, and on them must its beliefs depend. According to the words of the Almighty,

> Lo! those who believe [in that which is revealed unto thee, Muḥammad], and those who are Jews, and Christians, and Sabaeans—whoever believeth in Allah and the Last Day and doeth right—surely their reward is with their Lord, and there [in the other world] shall no fear come upon them, neither shall they grieve.[1]
>
> Nay, but whosoever surrendereth his purpose to Allah while doing good, his reward is with his Lord; and there shall no fear come upon them, neither shall they grieve.[2]
>
> Who is better in religion than he who surrendereth his purpose to Allah while doing good [to men] . . . ? [3]

These and similar verses set forth the directives of Islam and the total of Muḥammad's Message: beliefs, acts of worship, and laws. In them lies the secret of the Message's simplicity, its power, universality, and rapid diffusion among the

[1] Koran, 2:62. The Sabaeans were a Judaeo-Christian sect dating back to the first century A.D.

[2] *Ibid.*, 2:112.

[3] *Ibid.*, 4:125.

learned and the common people of mankind. And in them lies the history of the Message, of which Muḥammad is the final disseminator among the many since the beginning of man's time:

> Say [O Muslims]: We believe in Allah and that which is revealed unto us and that which was revealed unto Abraham, and Ishmael, and Isaac, and Jacob, and the tribes, and that which Moses and Jesus received, and that which the Prophets received from their Lord.[4]

The Message itself is eternal because God, its Author, is eternal. Muḥammad came to expound, confirm, and renew the Message, and to develop the meaning of its two fundamentals, faith and right-doing.

[4] *Ibid.*, 2:136.

## 3

# *Belief in the One God*

*

Belief in the one God as the sole and unassisted author of creation is the fundamental principle of the monotheistic religions. It is the font of the Message of Muḥammad. It is the spring from which the Almighty flooded the heart of Muḥammad with guidance and with the truths pertaining to goodness and to peace. Belief is the deep, resounding echo of that voice which called out to Muḥammad from Heaven and from earth:

Read: In the name of thy Lord who createth . . . man from a clot. Read: And thy Lord is the Most Bounteous, Who teacheth [writing] by the pen, teacheth man that which he knew not.[1]

O thou enveloped in thy cloak, arise and warn! Thy Lord magnify, thy raiment purify, pollution shun! And show not favor, seeking worldly gain! For the sake of thy Lord, be patient! [2]

And thus have We revealed to thee [Muḥammad] Our command. Thou knewest not what the Scripture was, nor what the Faith. But We have made it a light whereby We guide whom We will of Our bondsmen. And lo! thou verily dost guide unto a right path, the path of Allah,[3] unto Whom belongeth whatsoever is in

1 Koran, 96:1-5.

2 *Ibid.*, 74:1-7.

3 It is well to note what Marmaduke Pickthall, the translator of the edition of the Koran used in this book, says: "I have retained the word Allah throughout because there is no corresponding word in English. The word *Allāh* (the

the heavens and whatsoever is in the earth. Do not all things reach Allah at last? [4]

Muḥammad went out to his relatives and to their people with the call to believe in the one God, Allah. They rejected his Message and sought to turn him away from it. They suspected him, branded him a magician, a soothsayer, a madman, and sought to bribe him with wealth, authority, and rank that he might renounce his Message, but he would not. They then resisted him, persecuted him, and harmed him, but he would only say, as he said to Abu-Ṭālib, "May God be my witness, if they were to place the sun in my right hand and the moon in my left, I would not renounce my Message but would rather perish instead." He would let himself be swayed neither from this faith, which had filled his soul with contentment and to which his God had commanded him, nor from his summons to it, whether he would rule the day and the night or not! His major concern was that people should come together through the worship of the omnipotent Creator, Who has no partner (*sharīk*) in His worship.[5]

Since the dawn of time, man has been puzzled. Intuitively he has sought security in a supernatural force. From such a force he drew inspiration and succor, welcoming its blessings and evils. He offered his prayers to this force out of fear and out of greed. He lavished upon it offerings and worship. He found through his belief in this intangible force support and

---

stress is on the last syllable) has neither feminine nor plural, and has never been applied to anything other than the unimaginable Supreme Being" (*The Meaning of the Glorious Koran* [reprinted; New York: The New American Library, 1961], p. 31, tr. n.).

[4] Koran, 42:52-53.

[5] In the Arabian peninsula prior to the advent of Muḥammad, the Arab tribes had their own idols, which they worshiped each independently. Muḥammad taught them that there were no gods but Allah, to Whom all worship belonged, commanding them to renounce all other gods, who in the Koran are called "partners" in man's worship of Allah.

refuge from the dreaded physical forces of the universe as well as consolation and comfort in the hardships and pains of everyday life.

Strong intuitive feelings impel human beings to worship force. This is clearly expressed in the revelation of the Koran in the chapter called "Cattle" *(al-An'ām)*, which narrates the story of Abraham's recognition of God:

> Thus did We show Abraham the kingdom of the heavens and the earth that he might be of those possessing certainty: When the night grew dark upon him he beheld a star. He said: This is my Lord. But when it set, he said: I love not things that set. And when he saw the moon uprising, he exclaimed: This is my Lord. But when it set, he said: Unless my Lord guide me, I surely shall become one of the folk who are astray. And when he saw the sun uprising, he cried: This is my Lord! This is greater! And when it set he exclaimed: O my people! Lo! I am free from all that ye associate [with Him]. Lo! I have turned my face toward Him Who created the heavens and the earth, as one by nature upright, and I am not of the idolaters.[6]

Thus did Abraham's mind gradually move toward finding God through perception and awe of God's manifestations of power and glory in the stars, moon, and sun. His unblemished natural powers forced him to accept the fact that these astral bodies, which rise, set, and are surrounded with impediments, are subjects, or subordinates, not masters. Therefore, he turned away from their worship and, guided by his intelligence, sought the path to a chosen, perpetual, and unlimited force, the force that created and subdued the heavens and earth. Through his exercise of intelligence, the inspiration and guidance of God came to his rescue.

Man has worshiped many forces, either through sincere belief or as a means of drawing nearer that great, all-conquering force which he perceives by his native intelligence.

[6] Koran, 6:76-80.

He has worshiped ghosts and spirits, minerals and animals, stars and planets, water and fire, lightning and thunder. He has not doubted that these possessed, represented, or constituted a manifestation of power. Man has even worshiped man whenever man has displayed supernatural powers, and then has slain him when he has fallen short of the powers he was supposed to possess.

In my experience, one of the most peculiar examples of man's worship of man occurred over thirty years ago when I sat in the company of one of the gods of the Negroes of the Nuba hills in the extreme south of Kordofan, in the Sudan. We sat on the ground in the shade of a huge tropical tree while a group of naked men and women danced and sang before al-Kujūr. This al-Kujūr, whether they believed him to be the god himself or his symbol, was customarily the object of worship, to whom invocations were raised and sacrifices offered. He was the lord over the concerns of this world, and to him belonged every sanctification. His subjects would feed him, offer him gifts, and draw near him in return for his granting them rain for their crops and flocks, for pointing out the appropriate times to hunt and to make war, and for warding off calamities and diseases.

I was never able to judge whether in their eyes he was the perfect god or, like the idols of pre-Islamic (Jāhilīyah)[7] Arabia, was worshiped in lieu of something greater.

The wife of al-Kujūr approached me and began to converse through an interpreter, pointing out bruises on her leg. According to the interpreter, she had been beaten by a commoner and was at present voicing her complaint to me, supposing that I represented the proper authorities. Taken by surprise, I asked how the beating could have occurred, since her husband, al-Kujūr, was the god depicting omnipotence! I learned from the interpreter, however, that the god's

[7] *Jāhilīyah* means times of ignorance, and refers to the period in the Arabian peninsula prior to the emergence of Muḥammad and Islam.

sanctity was personal and did not include members of his family, who were regarded as ordinary people. Thereupon, I said to my companion that notwithstanding their simple-mindedness and confused religious beliefs, these people set an excellent example of democracy!

Al-Kujūr, although possessing rights, also possessed obligations; if he were to have faltered in fulfilling them, they would have put an end to him. Here is an example: if the earth should suffer from drought and vegetation should wilt, they would ask him to send rain. If he should refuse or delay, they would attempt to appease him with offers and supplication. If the year passed and drought persisted without their being able to persuade their al-Kujūr to command rain for their mercy, they might continue to wait through a few more seasons and then do away with him; or they might stone him immediately and replace him with someone whom, through good heritage and experience, they regarded as capable of unraveling mysteries and performing certain extraordinary feats.

One of the strangest tales I was told about these people concerns a complaint they filed with their government against one of their gods for refusing to send down rain. They were not to be conciliated until they had compelled the government official to imprison the god. They then continued to wait for days. Suddenly al-Kujūr asked the governor to release him, promising to bring rain in a hurry. As soon as he was released, and while he was marching with his people to the hills, rain began to fall in torrents. In other words, they did not question his abilities, nor did they consider him handicapped; they simply suspected his intentions.

There we have an example of the human mind in its simplicity. The mind of man, even when cultured, is not usually on a much higher plane. Man has worshiped spirits, matter, animals, water, fire, certain human beings, and a variety of objects.

Muḥammad's call to belief in the unity of God (*wiḥdāniyah*)[8] was foreign to the Arabs, though it may appear obvious and simple today. There had been a great need for someone to propagate the doctrine of belief in the unity of God so that the human mind would become receptive to an understanding of the universe and creation and able to direct itself toward the omnipotent Creator, thereby attaining additional force and the inspiration of wisdom.

If we were to analyze the life of Muḥammad in Mecca and contemplate the contents of his Message, we would discover that Muḥammad devoted his heart and efforts and offered his life and the lives of his followers to the crystallization of the first fundamental, belief in the unity of God. He fought his enemies and made peace with them; he shunned and then forgave them, and he appealed to peoples of other religions (Christians and Jews) to join with him in one common belief: worship of the one God, a worship which would admit no partners.

> Say: O People of the Scripture![9] Come to an agreement between us and you: that we shall worship none but Allah, and that we shall ascribe no partner unto Him, and that none of us shall take others for lords beside Allah. And if they turn away, then say: Bear witness that we are they who have surrendered[10] [unto Him].[11]

In his call to belief in the unity of God, Muḥammad displayed no forbearance or conciliation to the polytheists and idol worshipers with whom he contended. He was, however, very tolerant with the People of the Scripture. The Koran

[8] The word *wiḥdāniyah* means the oneness of God; *tawḥīd,* a term that will appear later in this book, means the act of belief in the oneness of God.

[9] "People of the Scripture" refers to those peoples who adhere to a religion centered around a revealed book—like the Bible—and therefore, specifically, Christians and Jews.

[10] "Surrender" is the meaning of the word and the concept of Islam, the religion propagated by the Prophet; surrendering is unto Allah.

[11] Koran, 3:64.

says, "And argue not with the People of the Scripture unless it be in [a way] that is better. . . ." [12] As concerns Christians, it declares, "And thou wilt find the nearest of them in affection to those who believe [that is, to the Muslims] [to be] those who say: Lo! We are Christians," [13] and it asserts in general, "Call unto the way of thy Lord with wisdom and fair exhortation, and reason with them in the better way." [14]

Tolerance of Christians and Jews in Muḥammad's Message reached a level unknown even to this age, which has witnessed the rise of nonreligionists; and this tolerance has not been attained by a considerable number of those who adhere to other faiths and claim to be religious, for they have not opened their hearts to the exercise of tolerance or displayed the mercy of God toward others.

> Lo! those who believe [in that which is revealed unto thee, Muḥammad], and those who are Jews, and Christians, and Sabaeans—whoever believeth in Allah and the Last Day and doeth right—surely their reward is with their Lord, and there [in the other world] shall no fear come upon them, neither shall they grieve.[15]

The noblest aim of Muḥammad's Message is to secure belief in the one God Who admits of no partners. All obstacles may be overcome in the attempt to achieve this unity of belief. All peoples, all nations, and even all religions would then become equal in the words of the Almighty:

> Say [O Muslims]: We believe in Allah and that which is revealed unto us and that which was revealed unto Abraham, and Ishmael, and Isaac, and Jacob, and the tribes, and that which Moses and Jesus received, and that which the Prophets received from their Lord. We make no distinction between any of them, and unto Him we have surrendered.[16]

12 *Ibid.*, 29:46.
13 *Ibid.*, 5:82.
14 *Ibid.*, 16:125.
15 *Ibid.*, 2:62.
16 *Ibid.*, 2:136.

The Apostle of God considered the goal of his mission not to initiate new religious laws and beliefs but to perfect those begun previously and to affirm true devotion in God's worship, this being the religion of Abraham, Noah, and Adam. There is no substitute for that righteous religion based on the oneness of God on which depends the unity of His creation.

He hath ordained for you that religion which He commended unto Noah, and that which We revealed unto thee [Muḥammad], and that which We commended unto Abraham and Moses and Jesus, saying: Establish the religion, and be not divided therein. Dreadful for the idolaters is that unto which thou callest them.[17]

O ye messengers! Eat of the good things, and do right. Lo! I am Aware of what ye do. And lo! this, your religion, is one religion, and I am your Lord, so keep your duty unto Me.[18]

But when Jesus became conscious of their disbelief, he cried: Who will be my helpers in the cause of Allah? The disciples said: We will be Allah's helpers. We believe in Allah, and bear thou witness that we have surrendered [unto Him].[19]

The Prophet differed with the People of the Scripture only on the question of the perfection (*tanzīh*) of the Creator; he debated with and opposed others in matters concerning both God's oneness and His perfection. He would conclude neither truce nor peace at the expense of compromising his Message because belief in the oneness of God was the basis of his mission, its object, and the object of existence.

I created the jinn and humankind only that they might worship Me. I seek no livelihood from them, nor do I ask that they should feed Me.[20]

All that is in the heavens and the earth glorifieth Allah; and He is the Mighty, the Wise. His is the Sovereignty of the heavens and the earth; He quickeneth and He giveth death; and He is

17 *Ibid.*, 42:13.
18 *Ibid.*, 23:51-52.
19 *Ibid.*, 3:52.
20 *Ibid.*, 51:56-57.

Able to do all things. He is the First and the Last, and the Outward and the Inward; and He is Knower of all things.[21]

Aside from its consequential broadening of human intelligence, the monotheism which Muḥammad preached is the source of bounty (*khayr*) and the foundation of happiness (*sa'ādah*) and of proper upbringing (*adab*), as we shall see in the next chapters.

21 *Ibid.*, 57:1-3.

# 4

# *The Consequences of Belief in the Unity of God*

*

We have seen how belief in the one supreme God is the ultimate goal of the Islamic Message. God—may He be glorified—considers the believer in Him alone a Muslim.

If we were to read through the Koran verse by verse, we would find the call to belief in God's oneness and perfection in every chapter; there is hardly a page that does not expound on or refer to these attributes.

The wisdom of this is clear: from belief in the one God stems all that is righteous; it makes for righteousness in the Message. It is the bond that unites all the component parts of the Message and strengthens them, for its position is comparable to the relationship of the soul to the body, which falls slack, deteriorates, and vanishes once the soul departs from it. Religious laws devoid of faith are like ordinary laws that fall with those who sustain them and disappear with the circumstances that produced them.

For this reason, belief in the one supreme God constitutes the dividing line between people, and not creeds and races or adherence or lack of adherence to the Muslim religion itself. The religion of Islam establishes itself as the protector of the Christian church and honors its own commitments to Jews when peoples of these faiths seek and are granted protection. Muslims are even enjoined to do battle in order that the protected religious sects may enjoy the freedom of their beliefs. "For had it not been for Allah's repelling some men by means of others, cloisters and churches and synagogues and mosques, wherein the name of Allah is oft mentioned, would assuredly have been pulled down." [1]

Islam differentiates between believers in the one God and idolaters, who receive a different kind of treatment and are accorded no respect. However, Muslims honor agreements and ties concluded with nonbelievers, provided the latter do not attempt to hamper the extension of the truth or resort to tyrannical action. In this regard, we refer to the historical case of the Prophet's pledge to Khuzā'ah[2] and his Truce of al-Ḥudaybiyah.[3] The struggle against idol worshipers is perpetual.

On the other hand, Islam admits People of the Book into the Islamic family by sanctioning marriages with Christian and Jewish women. Such kinship is not permitted with polytheists (*mushrikūn*), who are denied this distinction. "Wed not idolatresses till they believe; for lo! a believing bondswoman is better than an idolatress, though she please you; and give not your daughters in marriage to idolaters till they believe, for lo! a believing slave is better than an idolater, though he please you." [4] Islam even goes so far as to consider it defiling to do so: "The idolaters . . . are unclean. So let them not come near the Inviolable Place of Worship [the Mosque] after this their year." [5]

This intolerance of idol worshipers and of their gods who are made partners with Allah in worship is not due to blind obstinacy or indulgence in bigotry, for if that were the case, Islam would have treated equally members of all other faiths. Islam met with a great deal of insolence and evil from People of the Scripture, but this did not prevent the Islamic Mes-

1 Koran, 22:40.
2 Khuzā'ah was then an idol-worshiping tribe.
3 See Chapter 1, footnote 28.
4 Koran, 2:221.
5 *Ibid.*, 9:28. The Mosque is the Masjid al-Haram in Mecca, in which stands the Ka'bah.

sage from differentiating between them and polytheists. This may be explained in terms of the Islamic attitude that belief in the oneness of God is the ultimate goal of human endeavor and the path to perfection. Once the servant realizes that he is the creation of the great Creator, he admits by the same token that his ties with the Creator are those of a personal relationship, as between father and son; he realizes that he is but one of the endless products of the only Creator, and that the only acknowledged tie uniting Creator and created is that of faith. Bonds of faith are unseverable, furthering the cause of progress, righteousness, and charity by one accord; the source of faith is surrender to the one Will. With this, our existence in this world becomes related in principle and united in aim.

If all men could open their souls to this belief, their tasks would become easy. And if we could depict man as possessing perfect faith in God's oneness and fulfilling his duties in accordance with this faith, it would be possible to picture that creation most capable of wickedness, man, as becoming the finest creation of God, because then he would no longer need to be coerced and guided by anything but his faith. This would enable us to conceive of this world under the government of conscience.

For this reason, belief in the one supreme God was the whole object of Muḥammad's devotion, the true reason for the success and clarity of the Message. The abolition of the concept of polytheism is accompanied by the destruction of its sources of corruption. The Message of Muḥammad claims that all were born under faith to worship God alone; then they deviated. If they were to return to this worship, they would be on the right path.

On probing into the history of the religions of mankind, we discover that association or partnership of other subjects with God for worship was often the result of innovations introduced by man, who multiplied and diversified his gods. Innovators and corrupters set themselves up as representatives of these gods, as their supporters and guardians and as their trustees and deputies, usurping for themselves the power of the gods. Then these men of unworthy aims conspired and cooperated in their endeavors to pervert the masses, and ended up by imprisoning them in a jumble of nonsense and frivolity. Priests and the like, trustees and leaders of the people, who had set themselves up as guardians of the mysteries of religion were themselves in reality the gods who directed the destiny of the captivated masses.

The first trace of association in worship (*al-shirk*) appearing in history is the transformation from idol worship to man worship, or the worship of those who were the servants of the idol. Periods of such despotism in Egypt and Mesopotamia lasted thousands of years. Not a part of the world has been free from this worship, from the dawn of history until the present. Whatever may have happened to change the forms of worship, polytheism and the despotism of the priesthood went hand in hand.

As for unity of belief, it is accompanied and attended by a sense of fair play, like man's shadow; for the God to Whose worship the prophets, including Muḥammad, summoned the faithful is free from passions and selfish aims. He requests no property and no sustenance from His creation. He needs no trustees, no deputies, and no mediators; He ordains, "Ask and it shall be granted unto you." He is closer to them than their jugular veins; He is most merciful and most capable; He is the Creator and Molder, the Bountiful and the Forgiver, the Giver and Withholder, the just Ruler and great Avenger, the Omniscient and All-Informed, the Master of His bondsmen's destinies, the Cherished and the Wise.

Such qualities and virtues have placed Godhood in a position above and beyond any limitation, and have rendered creation under Him equal in His judgment, with the most pious being the favored of God and those most just to God's bondsmen the closest to Him.

Just as tyranny and selfishness accompany *al-shirk,* so are justice and equity associated with the belief in the unity of God (*tawḥīd*). For that reason, the ultimate goal of Muḥammad's Message is belief in God alone. To Islam, He is above everything. The glorious Koran declares, "Lo! Allah forgiveth not that a partner should be ascribed unto Him. He forgiveth [all] save that to whom He will." [6]

A faith free from impurities and emanating from the heart is served eventually by all the munificence known to it. The faithful man discovers that his account with God is to be settled directly with God. Thus he places this account before God only, and commits neither major nor minor sins deliberately. Once faith finds this man, it will have found the perfect man.

If a society were composed of such men, it would be sustained by mercy and charity, for among the traditional injunctions of Islam we find, "Truly, none of you believes if he does not desire for his brother what he desires for himself," "The merciful are shown mercy by the Merciful," and "Grant mercy to those on earth, and He Who is in Heaven will grant you mercy." These, therefore, are the conditions for a happy society.

It was not peculiar that some of the Khārijites,[7] during the period of civil war between 'Ali[8] and Mu'āwiyah,[9] preached the abolition of human government; they contended that there is no rule other than the rule of God. If the rule of God

6 *Ibid.*, 4:48.

7 The Khārijites, or Khawārij, formed the earliest religio-political group in Islam. They constituted the body of men who turned against 'Ali, after having supported him against his rival Mu'āwiyah. They opposed Quraysh's monopoly over the caliphate, and were responsible for much bloodshed during the first three centuries of Islam.

8 'Ali (A.D. 656-661), as was mentioned in Chapter 1, was the son-in-law of the Prophet—he married Muḥammad's daughter Fāṭimah—and the fourth and last of the orthodox caliphs.

9 Mu'āwiyah belonged to the Umayyad branch of Quraysh. He founded the Umayyad dynasty, with Damascus as capital, and became the first caliph (A.D. 661-681) of the dynasty (661-750).

were to materialize, conscience would be its king, justice its law, and common traditions its admonisher.

Because of its truthful concepts and its recognition of human nature, the Message of Muḥammad undertook to achieve reform through faith and law. Leadership was granted to those whom the faithful selected to execute what the Message had legislated, thereby insuring the proper conduct of human affairs.

We have seen how belief in one God is necessarily accompanied by the triumph of all virtues in the believer, who no longer exists for himself but for all his brethren in God's creation. It erases from the believing soul every evil. In this cleansed soul, excellence flourishes and the will to sacrifice for the common welfare prevails.

The believer cannot be tyrannical, because he would be acting contrary to an important characteristic of God: justice. He cannot be a hardened brute, because his Lord is most merciful. He cannot be a liar, a deceiver, or a hypocrite, because his account is with the omniscient God Who "knows the stealthy looks and that which the breast conceals." He cannot be weak or cowardly, because he realizes that this would not benefit him so long as the decision rests in the hands of God.

If we should thus continue to enumerate human shortcomings, we would see how the faithful are shielded from them by faith. We would also discover that all noble traits are welcome to the believing and confident soul who enters the worship of God, and thereby His Kingdom of mercy, once it has answered the call: "But ah! thou soul at peace! Return unto thy Lord, content in His good pleasure! Enter thou among My bondsmen! Enter thou My Garden!" [10]

This soul, serene in its faith, lives in a happiness enjoyed only by believers in the unity of God. It is possible for those of us who dwell on the margin of faith and who ask God for

[10] Koran, 89:27-30.

guidance to visualize the confident soul actually in a paradise on earth, for the spiritual happiness which it would then enjoy is the sweetest that Paradise can provide.

This faith in the one God and the virtues inevitably attending it purify the soul from evil and wickedness and elevate the human mind. Atheism and partnership in worship or polytheism occupy the mind with the world of the senses and surround it with a cordon of falsehoods, falsehoods which emanate from the preachings of magicians, soothsayers, and the sects that dwell upon the worship of personified gods who are divided and whose authority is distributed and disputed. Such worship serves only to imprint on the human mind a picture of the nature of humans or the absurdities into which they have fallen. Belief in the unity of God and perfection do just the opposite. They induce the mind to think, contemplate, and act wisely. For the God Whom Islam preaches brings together authority and virtue. He is with man wherever he may be. There is no need for an intercessor to reach Him; and He cannot be reached with the senses. He must therefore be approached by the exercise of intelligence. A way to Him is to be sought through His vestiges; hence, human intelligence must ponder His creation.

That the Message of Muḥammad took pains to stress this point may be deduced from the sayings and deeds of the Prophet. The verses of the holy Koran reiterate time and again the call to contemplation and the exercise of intelligence. They scorn the imitators, the self-glorifiers, the recanters, and the unmoved with stinging and pinching words. At the same time, they praise the thinkers, the searchers, and those who put their talents to good use in search of truth in the vestiges and monuments of the universe.

It is worthy to note that the abolition of *al-shirk* in the Arabian peninsula by the Message during and following the days of the Prophet and the triumph of the virtues attending belief in the one supreme God was not as simple as commonly has been alleged. It was accompanied, rather, by violent hostilities and bitter feelings.

The Almighty declares, "And they marvel that a warner from among themselves hath come unto them, and the disbelievers say: This is a wizard, a charlatan. Maketh he the gods One God? . . . Lo! this is a thing designed. We have not heard of this in later religion. This is naught but an invention."[11]

The Message of Muḥammad triumphed over nonbelief and removed the foremost obstacle in the way of elevating the human soul. It liberated man's mind from the petrifaction encasing it. Unhampered, man's mind could then inquire and contemplate freely, with such results that the Message itself almost became jeopardized. Scholars and learned men have agreed that in his Message Muḥammad achieved unprecedented success. The annals of mankind admit no success similar to that attained by the Prophet.

That his Message at first was strange and repulsive in the eyes of his people has also been universally acknowledged. To them it was heretical and unprecedented. Therefore, it was met with obstinacy, ridicule, and rejection. The events of the twenty years the Prophet spent in propagating his Message—which he had to conceal in the beginning—amply attest to this.

If the call to belief in the oneness of God was unique, then the effect of this call on man in terms of innovations introduced in his life and into the world as a whole was of still greater uniqueness. For the Arabs who once buried their infant daughters alive and gloried in the shedding of blood and in plunder now put on the garb of humility and knelt to invoke the blessings and approval of God. The family in which the son once had the right to inherit the wives of his father became the purified family. The tribe which acknowl-

[11] *Ibid.*, 38:5-8.

edged no right other than that dictated by the blood relationship of its members now produced one (Khālid ibn-al-Walīd)[12] who returned to the Christians of Homs (Emesa) their taxes because he had failed to protect them.

Those who once enslaved people now began to revere God; and, in their championing of truth, they feared the blame of no one. Out of the most hardened brutes there would now emerge a caliph who, when confronted by a woman in a gathering of the faithful, would reply, "A woman speaks the truth, and I, 'Umar, am mistaken." This is the same 'Umar who, in a letter, strongly admonished one of the greatest of his conquering generals, whose son had brought harm upon a Christian member of a conquered people, the Egyptians: "O 'Amr,[13] would you enslave a human being born to be free!"

If one should ask why corruption has captured the world today while believers fill the earth, we would reply with the words of God, "And most of them believe not in Allah except that they attribute partners [unto Him]," [14] and with the words of the Prophet, "Truly, he does not believe, no, he does not believe, he does not believe, he whose neighbor is not safe from his injustices."

Can the People of the Book, in the East or in the West, boast of individuals who have secured their neighbors from injustice? And, by the same token, has a Muslim wished for his brother what he has wished for himself?

[12] One of the outstanding military geniuses of Islam. Khālid was launched on a brilliant military conquest for Islam which continued under the rule of the first two caliphs, Abu-Bakr (A.D. 632-634) and 'Umar ibn-al-Khaṭṭāb (634-644). It is also recorded that he who ordered the repayment of the Christian tribute was the commander-in-chief, Abu-'Ubaydah.

[13] 'Amr ibn-al-'Āṣ, who subdued the Nile Valley and the Berbers of North Africa by A.D. 642, following which he was made governor of the area by 'Umar. 'Umar's reproach is a striking example of the effect of Islam upon its followers.

[14] Koran, 12:106.

Humanity will persist in experiencing misfortunes, wars, and dissension among nations and among classes until the principles underlying belief in the unity of God fill the hearts of mankind.

# 5

# *Right-Doing: The Practice of Mercy*

*

In my opinion, right-doing (*iḥsān*), the second fundamental of the Message, consists of acts of righteousness. Almost every chapter of the Koran refers to right-doing as the concomitant of faith.

The entire Islamic law (Sharī'ah)[1] does no more than elucidate, sanction, order, or prohibit that which does or does not constitute righteous action. Islam is a way of life, unique among religions in defining the roots and derivations of right-doing. Islamic law has provided in detail the bases and modes of life which the Muslim should follow in all matters pertaining to man's relationships to God and to the creations of God, including the servant's ties with his Lord through praying, fasting, and undertaking the pilgrimage as acts of worship (*'ibādāt*).

These acts of worship, which enrich the soul and purify the body, thereby influencing the personality of the Muslim, are likewise a collection of rules which in turn help improve the relationship between the individual and society. By emphasizing discipline and proper conduct, they facilitate the achievement of social solidarity (*takāful*), which is indispensable for the righteous community and which encourages

1 The word *Sharī'ah* covers religion, law, and dogma, not pure law alone.

cooperation among human beings in every circumstance as the foundation of progress.

There is no better indication of how effective acts of worship have been than the changes wrought on Arabs and similar nomadic peoples who had previously been removed from a life of intimate relationships and cooperation with others because of their proclivities for egotism and evil. Within a few years, these harsh men who had shunned worship began to worship God in the manner prescribed by the propagator of the Message: they began to show discipline and piousness, they knelt and praised God, one of their number led them in prayer five times a day, and they fulfilled their duties with promptness and regularity. Thus did they become accustomed to order, obedience, and responsibility. They became brothers to each other, the least worthy of whom felt no malice from the rest.

The Arabs who did not acknowledge the oneness of God were actually amazed at the discipline displayed by their cousins among the believers when they met them at Badr.[2] The forces of the believers formed well-arranged lines, a phenomenon formerly unknown to the Arabs in warfare. In their ranks were to be found side by side slaves and freedmen, whites and blacks, who had been united by their belief in God and the brotherhood of man.

Along with binding the servant to the Creator, acts of worship conducted according to procedures prescribed by Islam have several other effects on the soul, on the life of man, and on his relationship with his fellow man. Because of their importance, the Prophet took great care in dealing with them.

Recognizing that of the five foundation stones[3] of Islam

2 See p. 24.

3 These are (1) belief in the one and only God and in Muḥammad as His Apostle, (2) praying five times a day, (3) fasting during the month of Ramaḍān, and (4) a pilgrimage to Mecca at least once in a lifetime by those who can afford it, (5) paying the poor tax.

three pertained specifically to acts of worship (praying, fasting, and making the pilgrimage), the jurists of Islam took special pains to weigh meticulously the merits of each act and to describe elaborately the various steps in prayer. It is regrettable that most Muslims do not know much of their religion beyond its formal attributes; for this reason, it would be worthwhile and beneficial to elaborate on other aspects of right-doing, of the acts of righteousness. The bedouin would come from the remotest parts of the Arabian desert, seat himself in the presence of the Prophet, receive the essence of the Message, and then rise and depart, knowing more about it than those who are reared today in the bosom of Islam and who grow up in the houses of religion. This was not due to the Prophet's personal merits or to the fact that Arabs of yesteryear differed from their progenies of today. The reason for this was the simplicity of the Message at that time, since it was founded on common and plain principles, readily comprehensible to the ordinary people to whom it was delivered. Men therefore acted according to its precepts, proceeded in its spirit, and wove upon its loom. They did not pay mere lip service to the Message, nor did they satisfy themselves with the outward expressions while overlooking the core and essence.

The Koran on this point indicates the ease with which the Message was propounded and disseminated. In the words of almighty God, "Of every troop of them, a party only should go forth, that they [who are left behind] may gain sound knowledge in religion, and that they may warn their folk when they return to them, so that they may beware." [4]

The Message is simple because it is rooted in faith and *right-doing.* As we have seen, right-doing comprises acts of righteousness, which in turn have established readily comprehensible principles and acts of worship. These principles are rooted in mercy (*raḥmah*) and brotherhood (*ikhā'*). Mercy is

[4] Koran, 9:122.

a characteristic of God; and in the early days of the Message, the Muslims referred to Allah by the title "the Merciful" (al-Raḥmān) to such an extent that the common folk claimed Muḥammad was worshiping a god called al-Raḥmān. Muslims initiate every act, every little move, in the name of "the most Merciful," and greet one another with the formula, "May peace and the mercy of God be upon you."

The verses of the Koran are a testimony to the fact that mercy is the characteristic closest to the Prophet's heart:

> Muḥammad is the messenger of Allah. And those with him are hard against the disbelievers and merciful among themselves.[5]
>
> . . . and lower thy wing [in tenderness] for the believers. And say: Lo! I, even I, am a plain warner.[6]
>
> And We reveal of the Koran that which is a healing and a mercy for believers . . . .[7]
>
> It was by the mercy of Allah that thou wast lenient with them [O Muḥammad] . . . .[8]
>
> There hath come unto you a messenger, [one] of yourselves, unto whom aught that ye are overburdened is grievous, full of concern for you, for the believers full of pity, merciful.[9]

The prophetic traditions alluding to mercy are plentiful: "The merciful are shown mercy by the Merciful"; "Grant mercy to those on earth, and He Who is in Heaven will grant you mercy."

This fundamental precept of legislation in Muḥammad's Message—"We have not sent thee [O Muḥammad] but as a mercy to the world"[10]—is the foundation of progress. If mercy is removed from the heart of man, he is destroyed; and if it is removed from a people, they become a plague on earth. History relates the barbarity of peoples who were de-

5 *Ibid.*, 48:29.
6 *Ibid.*, 15:88-89.
7 *Ibid.*, 17:82.
8 *Ibid.*, 3:159.
9 *Ibid.*, 9:128.
10 *Ibid.*, 21:107.

void of mercy and who left behind them monuments to their destructiveness that have lasted throughout centuries. Take, for example, the Mongol waves under Genghis Khan and his successors: today, seven centuries later, one can still find traces of their destruction in Central and Western Asia. I have myself seen some in Afghanistan, Iran, and Iraq. It is quite likely that these traces will endure many centuries more. The Mongols were followed by similar peoples, including Muslims, even Muslim Arabs, who, knowing no mercy, spread destruction on earth; and this destruction, perpetrated by Arabs themselves, can still be seen after hundreds of years in North Africa.[11]

Mercy, the foundation of all progress, was preached by Moses, Jesus, and Muḥammad; it is, moreover, the message of all the apostles and righteous men of God. No nation rose to significance without being founded on mercy.

Certain people believe, through the exchange of stories and anecdotes concerning certain periods of the Ottoman state, that it was a great state but that a display of mercy was not among its distinguished practices. This is a popular mistake which would not withstand careful scrutiny, for in the days of their glory, the Ottoman Turks inherited the mercy God had removed from the hearts of the Arabs. The Arabs had fallen behind, and the Ottomans inherited the lands of the Arabs, dominating them as they dominated large areas of Central and Eastern Europe.

Stories of Ottoman acts of mercy in Bessarabia on the Dniester River can still be heard today.[12] The proverbs of the peasants in these parts, which were formerly in the Ottoman realm, still refer to the mercy and justice of the Turks; some even identify the departure of justice with the departure of

11 For example, the eleventh and twelfth centuries saw the immigration to North Africa of hordes of Arab nomads, such as the Hilāl and Sulaym tribes, and their subsequent century-long feud with the Berber Zanāta tribe. All were Muslims.

12 The writer was there in 1929.

the Turks. My attention has been attracted throughout my travels in Poland, Romania, and the Balkan states to numerous examples and fables that still point to the respect which individuals in these Christian nations hold for the Muslim Turk as a merciful and just person.

In 1917, while in Vienna, I was told that the Poles hoped for the arrival of Ottoman soldiers to reinforce the Austrian troops in Galicia at that time. Upon inquiry, I was told that the Poles have preserved a prophecy, handed down from their venerated men, that the herald of Polish glory and the resurgence of their national state is contingent on the reappearance of Muslim troops north of the Danube. Strangely enough, although these troops appeared as allies of the subjugators[13] and partitioners of Poland, a year did not pass after the crossing of the Danube by Ottoman soldiery before Poland became once more a truly independent and unified state.

Such fables, stories, and proverbs that I heard in the Balkan states led me to seek a broader knowledge of Muslim history in the Balkans. I concluded from my readings and observations that the Muslim exercise of justice and display of mercy had made the Ottoman hold in Europe possible. Under the banner of justice and mercy, the Balkan nations emerged from the slumbers of despotic rule and discovered for themselves the meaning of equality and equity. It suffices to note that despotic enslavement had been a practice commonly accepted in Central and Southern Europe until it was abolished by the Ottomans. The Moldavians, Poles, and Magyars had concluded interstate agreements with each other to extradite every peasant who fled the estate of his boyar.[14] Also, when land was sold, the peasants living on it were incorporated in the sale.

The Ottomans came to Europe bearing in their hearts the

13 Germans and Austrians during World War I.

14 *Boyar* was the title by which the great feudal lords of these countries were known; they constituted the landed aristocracy.

sentiment of mercy ordained by the Koran. The Turks were not superior either in equipment or in numbers to the nations they dominated. They fought and conquered to the gates of Vienna with justice and mercy paving the way through mountains, seas, and valleys, as these qualities had once paved the way for their Arab predecessors through Africa and Asia.

The Turks had a powerful ruler in Sultan Selim I (1512-1521), who was known for his cruelty, having massacred many of his household members. The Turks themselves referred to him as Selim the Grim. He conceived the notion of uniting the religion and language of the state, but he met strong opposition from the jurists and their head, the supreme religious spokesman of Islam, the Shaykh (Sheik) al-Islām. Consequently, the Sultan buried his notion out of deference to the tenets of Islam, which provide for respect for the rights of Christian subjects and the display of mercy toward them. This was the effect of that mercy which God had planted in the heart of the propagator of the Message, Muḥammad, and of his followers. Mercy is a pillar of Islam and an attribute of God. If it is uprooted, the state withers and disorder rules until God designates those fit to be called the people of mercy (*ahl al-raḥmah*).

If one gazes at the world today, he is bound to notice that mercy has been removed from the hearts of men. Have not men turned more beastly than the fiercest of beasts? Have not those who consider themselves civilized surpassed Genghis Khan in cruelty? Are not air raids on city dwellers the worst form of barbarity? Are these not, moreover, signs of imminent universal destruction?

Mercy, the *sine qua non* of Muḥammad's mission, is not the preserve of man alone. Certain tenets of the religious law relate to the humane treatment of animals as well. This indicates the extent of the Prophet's concern with mercy in disseminating his Message. Islam came forth and abrogated many of the practices of the Arabs. It had been customary for an Arab to torture animals, for instance, by slicing the ears of beasts of burden and tying a camel to the tomb of its dead master that it might die with him. The religious law forbade the torturing or killing of birds for pleasure and the pitting of animals against each other, as in bull and cock fights. It prohibited the overloading of beasts and rendered obligatory the careful tending of flocks. If the law goes unheeded, Muslim judges are empowered to dispossess the owners of suffering animals.

These ordinances had a great effect on the bedouin and the uncivilized. It has been alleged that 'Adiy ibn-Ḥātim, a very devout Muslim, was often seen breaking and distributing little crumbs of bread to ants; he asserted that they were neighbors and therefore entitled to rights. It is also said that Sheik Abu-Isḥāq al-Shīrāzi was walking along a road one day accompanied by several friends. A dog came upon them, and one of the companions sought to drive him away. The professor scolded him, saying, "Do you not see that we share the road with him?"

According to a saying of the Prophet (*ḥadīth*), "If you behold three mounting an animal, stone them until one descends." Works on law (*fiqh*) abound with prescribed practices in dealing humanely with animals, revealing the extent to which Muslim law is concerned with extending mercy to the creatures of God.

Mercy, therefore, is one of the basic principles of Muḥammad's Message. Moreover, it constitutes the cornerstone of the organized state. It is deemed preferable that a person occupy himself with endeavors other than praying, fasting, and making the pilgrimage and that he even do without his mosque, synagogue, or church if mercy is removed from his heart. A religion or a state shorn of mercy turns to deceit and oppression.

# 6

# *Right-Doing: Brotherhood*

*

The second precept of right-doing is *brotherhood,* which has become a world cry, cherished by all the people of this age.

Arabian society was divided by tribal prejudices and uncurbed individualism and human society was dominated by racial bigotry and pride in lineage when the Prophet appeared with his call to brotherhood, echoing the cry of God: "O mankind! Lo! We have created you male and female, and have made you nations and tribes that ye may know one another [and be friends]. Lo! the noblest of you, in the sight of Allah, is the best in conduct."[1] His preaching of brotherhood was part and parcel of his preaching of mercy, for he had determined that through the observance of both, obstacles would be overcome, and people would achieve happiness and thus discover Paradise.

> But he hath not attempted the Ascent. Ah, what will convey unto thee what the Ascent is! [It is] to free a slave, and to feed in the day of hunger an orphan near of kin, or some poor wretch in misery, and to be of those who believe and exhort one another to perseverance and exhort one another to pity.[2]

According to a certain prophetic tradition, God attends to His worshipers in every instance and situation, and benef-

1 Koran, 49:13.
2 *Ibid.,* 90:11-17.

icence toward man is considered beneficence toward God. Although He needs not man's beneficence, God is pleased when this beneficence is practiced between men as though it were being rendered to Himself. For this reason, it is unlikely that anyone would dispute the fact that brotherhood and mercy are at the root of the principles pertaining to right-doing in the Message of Muḥammad, as they constitute its ultimate goal. The Message has not overlooked a single approach while endeavoring to interest and encourage people in the exercise of brotherhood and mercy, whereby man shuns selfishness and egotism.

Nay, but ye [for your part] honor not the orphan, nor do ye urge the feeding of the poor; and ye devour heritages with devouring greed and love wealth with abounding love. Nay, but when the earth is ground to atoms, grinding, grinding, and thy Lord shall come with angels, rank on rank, and Hell is brought near that day; on that day man will remember, but how will the remembrance [then avail him]? He will say: Ah, would that I had sent before me [some provision] for my life! None punisheth as He will punish on that day! None bindeth as He then will bind.[3]

The call to brotherhood was as foreign to the Arabs as the call to belief in the unity of God and the command to disseminate this belief. Glorifying only in chauvinistic clannishness, the Arabs at first rejected the call and would not fraternize with those whom they considered inferior to themselves, that is, slaves and the weak. The use of compulsion was inevitable, therefore, because brotherhood was essential to the success of the Message. But how was this to be accomplished when the Arabs derided the followers of Muḥammad, who consisted then mainly of slaves and the poor? These early converts had become brethren in God to the lords and the nobility, in a brotherhood so all-encompassing that the proud were heard to say, as had been said to Noah, "Thou art fol-

[3] *Ibid.*, 89:17-26.

lowed only by the contemptible and degraded people who do not think."[4]

The Koran has emphasized this noble principle, enlarging it to include the brotherhood of all humanity: "O ye messengers! Eat of the good things, and do right. Lo! I am Aware of what ye do. And lo! this, your religion [nation], is one religion [nation],[5] and I am your Lord, so keep your duty unto Me."[6]

Once the call to brotherhood was firmly established in the believer, God generously lavished upon the faithful His greatest blessing, declaring, "And remember Allah's favor unto you: how ye were enemies and He made friendship between your hearts so that ye became as brothers . . . ."[7] This call to brotherhood was not confined to the Muhājirūn and the Anṣār only, but was universal:

> Say: O People of the Scripture! Come to an agreement between us and you: that we shall worship none but Allah, and that we shall ascribe no partner unto Him, and that none of us shall take others for lords beside Allah.[8]
>
> He hath ordained for you that religion which He commended unto Noah, and that which We revealed unto thee [Muḥammad], and that which We commended unto Abraham and Moses and Jesus, saying: Establish the religion, and be not divided therein.[9]
>
> Say [O Muslims]: We believe in Allah and that which is revealed unto us and that which was revealed unto Abraham, and Ishmael, and Isaac, and Jacob, and the tribes, and that which Moses and Jesus received, and that which the Prophets received from their Lord. We make no distinction between any of them, and unto Him we have surrendered.[10]

[4] *Ibid.*, 11:27.
[5] Islam is a religion and a nation; in this context, the word *ummah* means nation.
[6] Koran, 23:51-52.
[7] *Ibid.*, 3:103.
[8] *Ibid.*, 3:64.
[9] *Ibid.*, 42:13.
[10] *Ibid.*, 2:136.

Muḥammad's Message is a call for all peoples to worship God only and to form one nation under God. The brotherhood it preaches is one of belief; it makes no distinction between nations, between races, between conquerors and conquered. It preaches a brotherhood so vast in scope as to encompass the outermost fringes of humanity. It condemns aggression and preaches the ways of God with wisdom and fair exhortation. The Message advocates that the ways of God be observed particularly in times of war against aggressors, and most particularly when the aggressor is being defeated. For in the view of the Message, the concept of human brotherhood is like a lantern that guides the faithful in the darkness of war. The faithful fight not to lay upon lands or to plunder or to conquer and humiliate peoples, but for freedom of belief. "There is no compulsion in religion. The right direction is henceforth distinct from error."[11] "And if they incline to peace, incline thou also to it, and trust in Allah."[12]

Even when Muslims war against pagans, Islam considers human brotherhood the most important principle. In the eyes of the faithful, paganism is the worst form of nonbelief; the believer's soul, intelligence, and destiny are linked with saving the unbelieving pagan from God's anger. While he acknowledges a common brotherhood with the pagan, the believer nevertheless presses him as an act of mercy until he renounces his unbelief.

Once the pagan surrenders to God, he becomes fully equal to the believer and deserving of equal rights with him. Warring on the unbeliever, therefore, is an act of mercy resulting in a more perfect brotherhood. At no time does the believer question the right of the unbeliever to mercy and brotherhood.

We may assert, therefore, that mercy and brotherhood are two fundamental precepts of Muḥammad's Message, vener-

[11] *Ibid.,* 2:256.
[12] *Ibid.,* 8:61.

ated both as means and as ends in themselves, even in the severest stages of disagreement and war, and that universal brotherhood is the ultimate aim of Islam, contrary to the allegations of non-Muslims and ill-wishers that Islam is the religion of the sword.

Right-doing, or acting righteously, requires that man strive for universal brotherhood with mercy as his banner and guide in every time and place. In this respect, the Message of Muḥammad achieved its greatest effect. But one of its greater miracles was the brotherhood it brought about among certain segments of mankind that were at greatest variance and farthest apart. From a perusal of the history of mankind prior to the advent of Islam, and a study of the circumstances engulfing those nations extending from the Himalayas in the east to the Pyrenees in the west which later acknowledged Islam, we can readily comprehend the magnitude of change wrought by this call to brotherhood and mercy in the souls of hundreds of millions of people over the centuries.

The brotherhood which Muḥammad preached remains the finest quality that dwells in the hearts of present-day Muslims, even though they may be somewhat removed from the spirit of Islam. This is as readily discernible to modern-day travelers in Muslim lands as it was to Ibn-Baṭṭūṭah[13] seven centuries ago.

I became conscious of it for the first time as a young man in 1913, while visiting Albania during the Balkan wars. I knew no one in that country. Arriving by way of the Adriatic and disembarking at Kotor, I proceeded to Cetinje, the old capital of Montenegro when the inhabitants of the Mountain were at war with the Ottoman state. I posed as a correspond-

13 Ibn-Baṭṭūṭah was a famous Muslim traveler of the fourteenth century who undertook a series of travels across all the lands that were listed in the dominions of Islam, starting from his native land, present-day Morocco, to which he returned toward the end of his life. In his *Travels,* he describes the lands he visited and their peoples, rulers, social customs, and characteristics; his descriptions, although not free from error and exaggeration, constitute one of the finest sources of information about the fourteenth-century Muslim world.

ent for a British newspaper, but actually I was trying to enlist on the side of the Turkish and Albanian defenders of Shkodër. Noticing an Islamic name on a shop in the city, I introduced myself to the owner and immediately received a warm welcome that seemed almost prearranged, notwithstanding the fact that we could converse only by signs. Before long, the owner introduced a *khojah* (*faqīh*)[14] who knew a little Arabic, and we began to understand each other. The shopkeeper looked after all my affairs until I arrived in Shkodër. Throughout my journeys from north to south, I was passed on from hand to hand as each person entrusted my care to the next. It is doubtful that so much attention would have been lavished upon me had I been among my own kinfolk. This was a tribute to the brotherhood of Islam in the trying days of the Balkan wars.

I encountered this very same spirit in North Africa from Egypt to Algiers during the First World War. I experienced it again in India in the welcome accorded me by those who delighted in the knowledge that Egypt had become an independent nation and that I was its envoy to Afghanistan.

This spirit, engendered by the call of Muḥammad's Message to brotherhood, I have also observed in Iran, Afghanistan, Turkey, Iraq, Syria, and other lands where Muslims reside. In this spirit the Afghan in the East or the Fulani[15] from West Africa takes pride; to this spirit he entrusts himself when he covers thousands of miles on his way to Mecca, for he moves on from relative to relative, from friend to friend, until he arrives in Arabia, where Muḥammad first sent out the call to this universal brotherhood.

Once, on the second day of a five-day journey by car in 1938 from Riyāḍ, the capital of the Najd, to Mecca,[16] I saw

14 The *faqīh* (Arabic) or *khojah* (Turkish) is a scholar learned in the Koran and in Muslim tradition.

15 A member of one of the Negro tribes of Nigeria.

16 A distance of about 550 miles; the roads were unpaved then. The Najd is a northern province of Saudi Arabia.

two men proceeding on foot. When I inquired as to their points of origin and their destination, I discovered that they could not understand Arabic, for they were foreigners hailing from Kandahar in Afghanistan. Since the pilgrimage season was approaching, I surmised that they were en route to Mecca, and offered them a ride. During the nights spent on the way, and despite the fact that we did not understand each other's language, the spirit of brotherhood manifested itself in every expression. These men had traveled from afar with no possessions in this world other than the brotherhood bequeathed by Muḥammad in his Message that related them with the Baluchis,[17] Persians, and Arabs whose countries they had crossed on their way to Mecca.

Undoubtedly, the manifestations of brotherhood decline in those Muslim lands where the observance of Islamic religious tenets is weak owing to the emergence of racial barriers and particularly to the triumph of materialism over the soul of man, which greatly damages the bonds of brotherhood even in the home and within the family.

The impact of Muḥammad's call to brotherhood and mercy on the history of the Muslims has been of greater consequence than any corresponding call in the history of mankind. Some authorities might disagree and cite Jewish solidarity as an example. However, this solidarity is rather the product of an exceptional set of circumstances derived from persistent persecution of the Jews and their subsequent dispersal in many lands where they had to accept the status of a minority; what unites them is a set of religious and racial ties based on blood, not the belief that calls to human brotherhood. As for the brotherhood which Muḥammad preached and which Islam planted in the heart of man, its most exalted days were days of past glory. The Ottomans carried this concept into Eastern Europe, as the Arabs before them had carried it into Western Europe and unknown parts of Africa and Asia. Peoples under

[17] The tribes of Baluchistan, now a province of West Pakistan bordering on Iran.

their banner were as equal as the teeth of a comb: no preference was shown for an Arab over a non-Arab except in regard to his piety and love of peace, and a Muslim claimed no more authority over a non-Muslim than what God had decreed.

As non-Muslim citizens, peoples belonging to other religious sects in Islamic domains were regarded as *ahl al-dhimmah,*[18] enjoying rights and obligations not unlike those of the Muslims. They were entitled to what is decreed by justice and mercy, and were obligated to observe the tenets of brotherhood.

18 Refers to those taken into the protection of Allah; *ahl al-dhimmah* is a term applicable to members of other monotheistic beliefs (Christians and Jews) to whom the Muslims granted protection in return for the payment of *jizyah* taxes. See Chapter 13 for a discussion of these topics.

# III

## On Social Reform

*

# 7

# *Purifying the Individual's Moral Character*

*

The Islamic Message introduced a social revolution unprecedented in the East or West in ancient or modern times.

One of the most important aspects of this revolution was the moral and spiritual transformation which Muḥammad exemplified in his deeds and personality and in the principles he advocated in accordance with the letter and spirit of his Message. This transformation is at the root of the precepts aimed at social amelioration, for the reformation of the individual is the basis for the reform of society.

In His description of Muḥammad, the Almighty declares, "And lo! thou art of sublime morals."[1] And Muḥammad says, "I was sent in order to complete the virtues of character," and "My Lord has made me upright and has surely done so."

Noble qualities abounded in his fine character; truthfulness, beneficence, recognition and fulfillment of duties, forbearance, meekness, fortitude, courage, profundity, humbleness, forgiveness, and loyalty were a few of the outstanding traits that endeared him to the hearts of men. His followers became so attached to him that they did not hesitate to renounce their unbelief and even forsake their fathers and sons.

Centuries have gone by, but the character of Muḥammad has remained so distinctive and forceful that not even those

[1] Koran, 68:4.

skeptical of his Message can ignore it. The words of God are a testimony to that: ". . . in truth they give not thee [Muḥammad] the lie, but evil-doers give the lie to the revelations of Allah."[2]

His exemplary conduct had the greatest influence on the spiritual and moral transformation which was accomplished both in his day and following his death. The faith he espoused and the religious tenets he preached have had similar consequences. The principles of equality, brotherhood, justice, and freedom which he defined as integral elements of faith have accomplished their task by engendering a righteous character and a noble spirit in society. Of greatest effect has been the belief in the one supreme God, to Whom belongs all power and authority, in Whose hands lies the power to reward and punish, to grant and withhold, and in Whose Kingdom and worship people become equal. This belief perfects the human spirit, liberates it, and directs it toward the common welfare and the all-powerful God Who controls the destiny of all things and judges acts by the intention that motivates them, of which He is aware. With this belief Muḥammad pointed out the path to virtue.

He who has attained a virtuous character does not deceive, for he cannot conceal his deception from God or derive any benefit therefrom. Truthfulness, therefore, has become one of the mainstays of moral character in Muḥammad's Message. Lying and deceiving draw one away from God and bring only ruin to one's undertakings. Thus, it is impossible for the truly believing Muslim to be a liar or a deceiver.

The believer possesses a brave heart, and has the courage to express his views. He fears not death because he is possessed only by God. His soul is exalted, and he is propelled forward, even to martyrdom if necessary, in order to defend the truth and to protect himself and his brethren in bondage to God against tyranny and disdain. He who is faithful to

[2] *Ibid.*, 6:33.

this belief cannot be a yielding coward. He lives to defend himself and his fellow man against the evils of life, and endeavors to repel them with his own life.

The believer holds that God is the One Who gives and withholds, granting freely to whoever pleases Him without account; he is therefore not miserly with his possessions, but is a generous giver. Thus does he please the supreme Giver; he seeks His bounty and favor by living generously with his brethren, God's bondsmen. The believer cannot then be selfish; his belief prevents him from occupying himself with possessions, for he knows he would thereby deprive the children of God from sharing in His bounty. He seeks to express his humanitarian inclinations by being charitable to others and by leading a life of contentment with himself, his relations, his neighbors, his nation—with all people.

He is well-mannered, sociable, faithful, and sincere because such traits are essential for the perfection of his faith through his submission to the supreme Being, Who has elevated him and appointed him as His representative on earth, His *khalīfah*.

The Islamic doctrine which Muḥammad preached and firmly established in the hearts of his Companions and other followers is in itself the greatest pillar of social righteousness. This doctrine has given birth and organization to a spiritual, moral, and virtuous life for the Muslim, and thus occupies the supreme position in his heart. A substance has value and importance only to the extent that it leads to righteousness, that it glorifies and solidifies this spirit.

In the Islamic society which enjoys true faith, the spirit of materialism cannot dominate a man's character and behavior in the way it has dominated much of the world in recent times.

It has been related that when Sulaymān, the Umayyad caliph (A.D. 715-717) and the son of 'Abd-al-Malik, went to al-Madīnah for a visit, he sent for Abu-Ḥazm and asked him to give a discourse. Abu-Ḥazm dutifully obliged, addressing the Amīr al-Mu'minīn (Commander of the Faithful) in these words: "Take not possessions from other than their proper place, and deposit them not except with whom they belong." The Caliph inquired, "And who is capable of so doing?" Abu-Ḥazm replied, "He whom Allah has granted control over the affairs of subjects as He has granted you." The Caliph then said, "Preach to me, O Abu-Ḥazm."

Abu-Ḥazm proceeded: "Know that this command fell to you upon the death of your predecessor, and it will depart from your hands in the same manner it came into them." The Caliph then asked, "Why do you not come to us?" Abu-Ḥazm answered, "And what would I do if I came to you, O Commander of the Faithful? If you drew me nearer, I would be distracted from my way; and if you sent me away, you would disgrace me; and you do not possess what I would ask for, nor do I possess anything that I fear you for." The Caliph then said, "Ask me, then, for what it is you want." And Abu-Ḥazm replied, "I have already asked Him Who is more capable than you; whatever He grants, I accept, and whatever He withholds pleases me."

Here we have an example of the imprint of Muḥammad's Message on the character of man, exalting and purifying it.

The annals of Muḥammad's Companions and followers—for that matter, of Muslims everywhere—abound with fine examples of Godliness, kind treatment, the shunning of turpitude, and faithful counseling of God's bondsmen.

It is said that one Yūnus ibn-'Ubayd sold tunics of different values; some were worth four hundred dirhams each, and others only two hundred each. Entrusting his nephew with the care of the shop, Yūnus departed to offer his prayers. A bedouin entered the shop and asked for a tunic priced at four hundred, but received one priced at two hundred instead. The bedouin liked it, was perfectly satisfied, bought it, and departed, carrying the tunic on his arm.

While on his way, he came upon Yūnus, who recognized

his tunic and asked the bedouin how much he had paid for it. The bedouin replied that he had paid four hundred dirhams. "But it is not worth more than two hundred," said Yūnus. "Come with me and I will exchange it for you." The bedouin replied, "This is worth five hundred in my country, and I am pleased with it." Yūnus then declared, "Do not say that, for the counsel of religion is more rewarding than the provisions of this world." Returning to the shop, he refunded two hundred dirhams to the bedouin, and scolded his nephew, saying, "Are you not ashamed? Do you have no fear of God? You would accept gold and abandon the counsel of the Muslims!" The nephew replied, "May Allah be my witness, he accepted it only because he was pleased." The uncle then said, "But have you pleased him as you would please yourself?"

It has been said about Muḥammad ibn-al-Munkadir that in his absence his servant sold a bedouin a piece of goods worth only five dirhams for ten. The master looked for the bedouin all day, and when he found him he stated, "The boy erred and sold you for ten what is worth only five." The bedouin, astonished, replied, "But I was pleased!" Muḥammad replied, "Even if you were, we would please you only with what pleases us," and returned him five dirhams.

Such is the character of the person who has been truly influenced by the Message of Muḥammad and who has abided by the Prophet's dictum, "Truly, none of you believes until he desires for his brother what he desires for himself." The true Muslim does not deceive, cheat, or swindle.

The effect of Muḥammad's Message was decisive on those who followed its guidance. It called not for extravagance, pretentiousness, or boastfulness, but for faith and good deeds both openly and silently, for according to Islam it is more appropriate that man fear God than his fellow man.

A person was once asked to testify before the Caliph 'Umar. The Caliph asked him to bring forth someone who knew of him. He produced a man who praised him generously. 'Umar thereupon inquired, "Are you his closest neighbor who knows him inwardly and outwardly?" "No," the man replied. "Were you his companion on the journey which reveals a man's character?" "No," he again replied. "Perhaps you deal with him in dinars and dirhams, which reveals the honesty and integrity of this man?" "No," was the answer. "I think you behold him in the Mosque, whispering verses of the Koran, lowering and lifting his head in prayer." "Yes," replied the man. 'Umar then snapped, "Away with you, for you know him not!" And turning to the would-be witness, he commanded, "Go and bring forth someone who knows you."

# 8

# *Solidarity*

*

Lo! this, your religion [nation], is one religion [nation], and I am your Lord, so worship Me.[1]

You will see that the faithful, in their having mercy for one another and in their love for one another and in their kindness toward one another, are like the body; when one member of it ails, the entire body ails, as one part calls out to the other with sleeplessness and fever [said the Prophet].

The difference between Islam and most other religions is that it did not content itself with merely establishing acts of worship and abandon the needs of society to a Caesar or any form of temporal governing body. Rather, Islam established ways of conduct, relationships, and rights and obligations for the individual vis-à-vis members of his family and the nation and for the nation vis-à-vis other nations. The reform of society was the main target of Islam. Even acts of worship contribute to the achieving of this reform. Within the framework of human society, the Islamic nation is a compact union having recourse to itself, possessing an inner sense of responsibility for its own members, and resisting decay, both individually and collectively.

This social solidarity (*takāful*) is apparent in all aspects of Muḥammad's Message. The history of mankind shows that

[1] Koran, 21:92 (and 23:52). See Chapter 6, footnote 5.

few societies have developed as strong a sense of solidarity or have cooperated as closely or acted as mercifully as have Islamic societies.

The individual's responsibility for the community in Islamic societies and conversely the community's responsibility for the individual are of primary magnitude, constituting a trust of life and the highest of its responsibilities. It is for that reason that Islam introduced community worship. As the Prophet has said, "This religion is sure; penetrate deeply into it with patience and moderation, for he who rides his horse too hard covers no distance at all." [2] Islam also enjoins the group not to neglect the individual, obligating it to safeguard his various interests, to respect his rights and freedom, and to harmonize different interests. In Islam, praying in groups is preferred many times over to praying individually.

The individual is thus an integral element of the Islamic society; he perfects it and is perfected by it, he gives to it and receives from it, and he protects it and is protected by it. Developing this two-way responsibility is Islam's principal way of achieving reform and social solidarity. Islam has impressed the meaning of these two types of responsibility on the individual and collective conscience in order to guarantee for Muslims the life of a unified, sound, happy, and productive body in a classless community. According to the Prophet,

> Every one of you is a shepherd, and every one of you will be questioned about those under his rule: the amīr [ruler] is a shepherd, and he will be questioned about his subjects; the man is a ruler in his family, and he will be questioned about those under his care; and the woman is a ruler in the house of her husband, and she will be questioned about those under her care. Thus, every one of you is a ruler and is responsible for those under his care.
>
> Unto me it has been revealed that you should be humble in order that you might not be proud over others.

[2] In this connection, Islam forbids a man to be a monk, and allows no priesthood.

In the words of the Koran, "Hast thou observed him who belieth religion? That is he who repelleth the orphan, and urgeth not the feeding of the needy." [3] "Those who entered . . . the faith . . . prefer [the fugitives] above themselves though poverty become their lot." [4] Islam has the individual say in his invocations, "Place not in our hearts any rancor toward those who believe." [5] When this precept is practiced to the full, the heart of the individual is dedicated to society and to his complete submergence in it.

To the group, Islam declares:

> The believers are naught else than brothers. Therefore make peace between your brethren . . . .[6]
>
> The blood of the Muslims shall be answered for; for the least worthy among them is entitled to their protection, and their hand is lifted against those who are against them [said the Prophet].
>
> Help your brother whether he is the doer of wrong or wrong is done to him. They [his Companions] said, O Messenger of Allah! We can help a man to whom wrong is done, but how could we help him when he is the doer of wrong? [The Prophet replied:] Hold him back from doing wrong.

An outstanding illustration of the decree that society be responsible for the individual's behavior can be found in this parable by the Prophet:

> A party of men went into a boat and each occupied a position in the boat. One man began to chop a hole in his spot with an ax. They said to him, "What are you doing?" He replied, "This is my position and I will do with it as I please." Now, if they should hold back his hand, he and they would be saved; but if they should leave him alone, he and they would be doomed.

This understanding between individual and society of common responsibility for common interests is the basis for resisting social ills, and every method for achieving reform

[3] Koran, 107:1-3.
[4] *Ibid.*, 59:9.
[5] *Ibid.*, 59:10.
[6] *Ibid.*, 49:10.

would remain fruitless unless preceded by such an understanding. Man's position as God's representative on earth and as trustee over its resources cannot assume a definite form until he recognizes this social responsibility. Those who seek to resist social ills are duty-bound to awaken first the conscience of the individual toward the community and then the conscience of the community toward the individual. They must also stress the implications of these two types of responsibility. This must continue until the individual assumes a filial and beneficent attitude toward the community and the latter a motherly and protective attitude toward the individual.

By recognizing these two responsibilities and by reflecting on them, we derive what is commonly referred to today as the "general consensus" or "public opinion," that alert guardian of the nation's existence—if founded on foresight and unity of purpose and aim. Public opinion is the fearful power which holds rulers and individuals in the right path, moves the nation to act justly, and causes it to tremble with anger if harmed or touched with corruption, as would the body of an individual if similarly affected. Public opinion is the sharpest weapon to be found for ridding the community of its social ills and for accomplishing what laws fail to accomplish. It is the watchful eye that insures the execution of laws and the observance of those ethical rules and righteous ordinances which the community enacts.

Islam thus takes special care to make public opinion the guardian against the individual's deviations and the community's excesses, enjoining the right and forbidding the wrong. Establishing the individual's and the community's mutual responsibility is one of the most important acts of Islam and the soundest possible foundation for a righteous social life.

In the Koran we read,

> And the believers, men and women, are protecting friends one of another; they enjoin the right and forbid the wrong.[7]

[7] *Ibid.*, 9:71.

And there may spring from you a nation who invite to goodness, and enjoin right conduct and forbid indecency. Such are they who are successful.[8]

And according to a prophetic *ḥadīth,*

When the sons of Israel fell into sin, their wise men preached abstinence, but they would not abstain. Thereupon they sat with them in their sittings, ate with them and drank with them, and the Lord struck the hearts of some with those of others and He cursed them with the tongue of David and Jesus, the son of Mary, for their defiance and transgression.

He who abides by what is right in the eyes of God or of the community ought not be shaken if shown hostility by anyone, whoever he may be. Our greatest social ills stem from the fact that a righteous public opinion has yet to be formed. Quite often individuals and groups will declare openly their hostility against the venerated tenets of religion, against the state, and against common rights, and yet others will not lift a finger to admonish because they are unaware of their rights and duties. People are disunited and selfishly inclined because they lack unified ethical and cultural training. Different streams have poured into them, diluting the moral character, thinking, and faith of the nation and making one and the same object at once both right and wrong—right to one group and wrong to another.

To evaluate both individual and social responsibilities, and thus to establish a uniform, righteous public opinion, is impossible without preaching and persuasion. If everyone would truly recognize his rights and obligations, a united and strong public opinion would emerge, correcting that which has been distorted and removing the tainted.

Preaching with wisdom and fair exhortation in order to reach the depth of man's soul, to sow the seeds of goodness and love of truth in him, and to extirpate the roots of evil

8 *Ibid.*, 3:104.

and the causes of ills from him is the indispensable beginning. The key to every decision pertaining to righteousness is to reach the soul. The glorious Koran refers to this when it says, "Lo! Allah changeth not the condition of a folk until they [first] change that which is in their hearts . . . ." [9]

Social education built on persuasion was one of the powerful weapons used by Islam for achieving social righteousness. The Prophet constantly utilized the Koran and his own example and words to penetrate the hearts and minds of men so they might learn the truth and attain righteousness, uphold reason, and dispense with pretexts laid before themselves and God.

For that reason, the period of law-making and securing commitments followed the period of calling to God's worship. The Messenger of God continued to summon people for thirteen years, until his call had filtered into their hearts and they had begun to occupy themselves in their assemblies with his Message, inquiring into its great truth. Only after the Message had spread and a supporting public opinion had been formed for it in Yathrib did Muḥammad call for the establishment of a Muslim state as the guardian of law and enjoin adherence to its tenets.

Thus did Islam attend to the ills of Arabian society at that time: first by summoning, then by legislating. Today, those who wish to attend to society's needs should follow this course. They must look upon the Message as the foundation of righteousness before they can legislate. They must abandon haste in favor of a gradual process of legislation. Only in such a manner can they prepare the atmosphere and make society ready to receive orders and accept commitments.[10]

Briefly, then, Islam first used the Message to reform society and resorted to legislation thereafter in order to protect the

[9] *Ibid.*, 13:11.

[10] The manner in which liquor was prohibited in Islam, first by preaching and then by progressive legislation, illustrates how Islam accomplishes ends by gradual steps.

objectives of the Message. Islam made faith and right-doing the principal goals of every facet of life. Rights and obligations for both the individual and the community were given substance according to the precepts of right-doing. Every obligation as well as every right recognized in Islamic society revolves on right-doing toward the individual or the community, and every act that would remove good and bring forth evil, whether it yields gain to its perpetrator or to another, is forbidden.

For this reason, we find that Islam has concerned itself with all phases of life, defining the nature of responsibility within the limits of each phase for the purpose of realizing the overall objective: a life of contentment for all peoples of the world as a prelude to a more exalted and happier life in the next world.

The Prophet of Islam absolved no one person from his responsibility toward another. The Commander of the Faithful is responsible for the believers, his deputies and trustees for those under their jurisdiction, the head of the family for his family, the wife for her home, and the individual for his neighborhood as for himself. In the last analysis, every individual in the Islamic community is responsible for the rectitude of the entire community because, as we have seen, he is charged with the task of raising himself and summoning others to God for the sake of rendering this society upright. He preaches truth and cooperation in order to achieve beneficence and piety.

The emphasis on individual and collective responsibility is part and parcel of the teaching of right-doing, the second fundamental of Islam after belief in the one God. No armor is more suitable for resisting evil and the ills of society than Islamic ethical upbringing, upon which the fortunes and status of men in Islamic society have always rested; it is the element which solidifies the community and preserves it from decay.

Muḥammad's Message emphasized and bolstered interdependence and solidarity among the newly converted Muslims until the Prophet had molded the Anṣār of Yathrib and the Muhājirūn of Mecca into an all-encompassing brotherhood which ultimately transcended brotherhood based on lineage and kinship. The Message gave rise to a closely knit and unified nation which became the font of all authority; the consensus of that nation was law, and its word was decisive. This nation came to vouch for its members, who became a responsible living force enjoying a faith and possessing a religion perfected only through loyalty to the community, and sacrificing for its cause. "Think not of those, who are slain in the way of Allah, as dead. Nay, they are living. With their Lord they have provision."[11]

In Islamic communities that have preserved Muslim traditions, I have witnessed an incomparable sense of interdependence and solidarity which no social architect could improve on as a basis for a world society.

I have seen certain Tuareg tribes of North Africa display this blissful solidarity in their lives. No one among them lives for himself only; he lives for his people. My attention was first attracted to them by a Muslim who left his own country and settled among the Tuaregs in Fezzan.[12] He enjoyed their protection, lived by their gracious bounty, and then departed in search of a living in order to repay them their favor, leaving his family in the protection of this Islamic community. But ill luck accompanied him, and he was unable to earn enough. He came to us in Misurata in Tripolitania seeking aid; it was offered to him so he could return to his family.

He returned to Misurata after an absence of about a year. It was assumed at first that he was returning from his family, but this was not the case. When asked why he had not gone

[11] Koran, 3:169.

[12] This was during World War I; I was then with the Muslim resistance force, fighting the Italians in Libya. Fezzan, Tripolitania, and Cyrenaica are the three political divisions of Libya.

back to his family after the first encounter, he replied: "Since we last met, I have traded with what came into my hands, and what I now possess is sufficient to take back to the Tuaregs." "To the Tuaregs," I inquired, "or to your children?" "To the Tuaregs first, for they nourished my children during my absence. I will now be responsible for the children of those absent among them, and I will divide what Allah has granted me between my children and those of my neighbors."

He was asked whether the entire community shared his attitude toward neighbors, and he replied, "We share together and alike blessings and misfortunes; grace is with him who displays it, and a member would be ashamed to return to the camp empty-handed, in shame not before his household members but before his neighbors, who await his return in the same manner as does his family." As a modern non-Muslim writer puts it:

> In Muslim society the family will always care for its old people, its orphans, its idiots, its ne'er-do-wells and even its delinquents. In this it offers a marked contrast to the modern West, where relatives are all too often looked upon as disagreeable acquaintances and where the misfits are frequently left to their fate or thrust into public institutions. If Islam is not a welfare state, it at least produces whole welfare families where everyone is cared for whether they deserve it or not.[13]

This communal spirit is not a peculiarity of the Tuaregs and similar desert folk, nor is it a condition of their tribal solidarity; it is rather the Islamic spirit, more evident among those who still live in seclusion from modern materialistic life. This spirit is to be observed in Islamic villages and towns which still bear faithfully the stamp of Islam, whether the town is in the East or in the West and whether the inhabitants are Arabs or non-Arabs, whites or blacks.

Muslim peoples in many localities still live the life of pleni-

[13] Lt. Gen. Sir John Bagot Glubb, *The Great Arab Conquest* (London: Hodder and Stoughton Ltd., 1963), p. 368.

tude, contentment, interdependence, and solidarity in search of beneficence. They still remain close to being that righteous society ordained by the propagator of the Message, Muḥammad, as contrasted with tens of millions of Muslims who have been seduced by modern materialistic cultures and who live for themselves and prefer to gratify their lusts rather than to be beneficent toward even their relatives, let alone their neighbors.

# 9

# *Beneficence*

*

Beneficence (*birr*) is one of the great pillars of the Message and a clear way to social righteousness.

The term appears with many meanings in the Koran, depending on the context. It may signify truthfulness, goodness, and right-doing in the broadest sense as well as obedience to God.

By beneficence is meant here acting rightly by offering comfort to the poor, to the less fortunate, and to those of our brethren in the community who have fallen on evil days in their search for a satisfactory and independent life owing to such factors as natural handicaps, orphanhood, illness, misfortune, or ignorance, among other causes.

The Message of Muḥammad surpasses all other righteous messages in defining beneficence and in expounding the duties of the individual and of the state in keeping with this virtue. In this regard, the broad concepts of the Message deserve the attention of men of clear judgment and insight.

As the holocaust of World War II raged among the fascist, communist, and democratic systems, a speedy interpretation of the injunctions of Islam and of the decrees of Muḥammad was called for, because in them might be found guidance and a solution for the problems of the world, particularly when people differed so widely over what should constitute the right solution.

We have seen how Islam fights social corruption by preaching and by drawing upon public opinion, and how it makes of solidarity and the communal spirit a religious fundamental necessary for attaining a righteous way to God. The faith of an individual cannot be perfected, nor can a nation fulfill its duties or a state its trust, unless the faithful undertake continuously to establish solidarity and the communal spirit firmly in their hearts and to make them essential rules of life.

Let us now examine the means by which Islam remedies the problem of poverty, which is the greatest ill of human society.

Islam does not consider poverty a reason for despising a man, for a poor man, even in his need, may be superior in the eyes of Islam to men of wealth and authority. This consideration gave the poor their first consolation. When Islam first examined the lot of the poor, it discovered that poverty was caused by an inability to earn, either because of some handicap or because of the absence of an opportunity to work.

As for the man who is handicapped by an incurable ailment, Islam obliges the community to support him as a duty, not as a matter of voluntary charity or willingness. "And in their wealth the beggar and the outcast have due share";[1] thus does the Almighty protect their dignity.

Concerning the man who cannot earn because he lacks an opportunity to work, Islam compels the state to find him work. Islam discourages begging and calls on Muslims to be above it, for he who gives is better in the eyes of God than he who receives. The Prophet once asked a beggar whether he had anything worth a dirham, and the beggar answered that he had. Muḥammad sold the object for him and bought him a rope and an ax, inserting the handle into the ax himself. He then told the beggar to expose himself no longer to

[1] Koran, 51:19. Here is another example of the difficulty of translating the Koran. The word *sā'il,* translated here as beggar, also means he who needs to ask; and *maḥrūm,* given here as outcast, actually means he who is denied bounty, or a sufferer from necessity and need.

the humiliation of begging but to put himself to work hauling firewood.

The rule in Islam is to work and earn. Islam has urged this by every means, even preferring it to retirement in the worship of God. It has also exacted justice for the community by obligating the state to help find work for those who lack the means and to protect those who fail.

Islam attempts to lessen the difference in living standards of its adherents, thus combating luxury in the upper social brackets and warding off misery in the lowest. In doing this it utilizes two media: conscience—the stronger of the two—and law. It makes the happy immortal life available only to those who give to deserving relatives and friends and to the poor.

Because of Islam's powerful appeal, the conscience of the Muslim would not rest were he to eat, dress, and make merry while his neighbors and relatives were unable to earn a living; Islam strongly urges him to exert himself, to be satisfied with less and curb his desires, for the sake of aiding the grieving and the needy. Islam even decrees that the master feed and clothe his servant as he would feed and clothe himself.

Al-Ma'rūr ibn-Suwayd once said about Abu-Dharr, a pious Companion of the Prophet,

> I saw Abu-Dharr and his servant both wearing the same type of garment, and when I asked the reason for this he replied that he heard the Messenger of Allah declare: "They are your brothers; Allah placed them under your care. He whose brother is under his care, let him feed him of what he himself eats and dress him with what he himself dresses. Do not give them overburdening work, and if you do so, then help them with it."

Islam does not content itself merely with awakening the conscience of men, but empowers the state to appropriate from the excess wealth of the individual when necessary in order to insure the needs of the poor and miserable.

In reality, Islam wars openly on luxury, on hoarding wealth,[2] and on usury, declaring:

They who hoard up gold and silver and spend it not in the way of Allah, unto them give tidings [O Muḥammad] of a painful doom, on the day when it will [all] be heated in the fire of Hell, and their foreheads and their flanks and their backs will be branded therewith [and it will be said unto them]: Here is that which ye hoarded for yourselves. Now taste of what ye used to hoard.[3]

Those who swallow usury cannot rise up save as he ariseth whom the devil hath prostrated by [his] touch.[4]

Allah will blot out usury, and causeth charity to prosper.[5]

When Islam imposes the poor tax (*zakāh*) on earnings and wealth and forbids usury, it seeks to raise the standard of the poverty-stricken and to lower the standard of those who are given to excess so that the life of all may become happier and more orderly. By prohibiting excessive luxury, Islam spreads material riches so as to produce the greatest benefit for all. The banning of hoarding leads to circulation of wealth, and the prohibition of usury leads to sharing. A person should not find enjoyment and prestige in wealth but in right-doing and beneficence. He should not find security in treasures but in the solidarity of the Islamic society, a society which fulfills its responsibilities by neglecting and rejecting none. A man should not find security in usury but in the joy of earning and sharing with his brethren who put their work to good use.

The Islam which has fought the ills of poverty through awakened consciences and legislation has made work the basis of its aims. It has not confined the rewards to this life

2 The orthodox view is that gold and silver maintained in vaults, though doing so is unpious, are legitimate property as long as the owner pays the annual *zakāh*, or 2½ percent of the holdings, to the needy.

3 Koran, 9:34-35.

4 *Ibid.*, 2:275.

5 *Ibid.*, 2:276.

only but has made the promise of further rewards in the afterlife. Islam has decreed further that one should exert himself in preference to religious seclusion and that the believer should strive to perfect his work.

Islam wards off poverty by preaching virtuous behavior. It curbs the forces of evil and vice through law and reason. If its methods were more widely employed to crush evil and vice and to propagate virtue and goodness, the Islamic family would cohere and every member would realize his duty and moderate his desires. This would constitute one of the most effective weapons for resisting poverty, for the greatest causes of poverty are excessive cupidity, indulgence in vices (such as intemperance in the use of liquors and other intoxicants), and neglect of the body's health and of the religious decrees which are designed to regulate both body and spirit. Were we to adopt the Islamic ways of exercising mercy and displaying charity together with its principles of brotherhood and cooperation, and were we to awaken the religious conscience of the nation in this connection, we would have dealt poverty the fatal stab, and never again would it find its way into so many homes.

The state can combat poverty effectively by fulfilling its duty to grant security to the unemployed, basing its policy on the principles of solidarity preached by Islam, as in the words of the Prophet: "Believers are in relation to one another as [parts of] a structure, one part of which strengthens the other." In the interest of the general welfare, the state can also distribute alms to those who have no other recourse and create work for people, even if it must compel certain individuals to assume the specific tasks they are capable of performing.

Islam has granted broad powers to the head of the state; as guardian of the law and the general welfare, he may make as many decisions as cases demand and shape matters in conformity with the fundamental purposes of Islam and with the Sharī'ah.

Islam has established clearly the principle of equality, the greatest of principles for resisting social evils, particularly poverty. It has planted this principle in the conscience of the Muslim and has caused it to govern his actions in his worship and in his social conduct.

The world owes a debt to the Message of Muḥammad for teaching man to turn his back on pride and not to exalt himself over his fellow man. The righteous Muslim does not even think that he is more worthy than his own servant, although he is lord over him. The Prophet himself was rebuked in the Koran for having sought to convert a group of Arab chiefs to the faith, and thereby to gain the adherence of their followers, while neglecting a poor, weak man who had come seeking the faith. In the words of the Almighty,

> He frowned and turned away because the blind man came unto him. What could inform thee but that he might grow [in grace] or take heed and so the reminder might avail him? As for him who thinketh himself independent, unto him thou payest regard. Yet it is not thy concern if he grow not [in grace]. But as for him who cometh unto thee with earnest purpose and hath fear, from him thou art distracted.[6]

Laws in existence today rarely show a greater concern for the poor and their lot than the decrees of Muḥammad's Message. Islamic law has established and defined the poor tax, its forms, and its means of distribution, as it has specified in detail those who are entitled to it, their rights, and their obligations. In general, the Message urges Muslims to condition themselves to respect others and to hold them in esteem: "O ye who believe! Let not a folk deride a folk who may be better than they [are], nor let women [deride] women who may be better than they are; neither defame one another, nor insult one another by nicknames. Bad is the name of lewdness after faith." [7]

[6] *Ibid.*, 80:1-10.
[7] *Ibid.*, 49:11.

If this understanding were imprinted on the minds of kings, princes, and rulers, of the masses, of the poor and the wealthy, of proprietors and workers, as ordained by the Message of Muḥammad, social disunity would disappear. Envy and hatred would be dissipated, as would dissensions and evils leading to strife and war; the strong would no longer dominate the weak, nor would the resurgence of the weak end in their humbling those who had dominated them.

Admittedly, there are provisions for equality in the laws and decrees existing today in Europe and America; yet such provisions have failed to prevent strife, war, and corruption. Egotism and materialism never reached in any earlier time the heights they have attained in our age of egalitarianism, sustained by modern laws; nor did parsimony and selfishness attain in the age of feudalism the levels of today; nor did the spirit of evil and concomitant rancor and envy prevail as it has during the last hundred years, in spite of the extension of so-called civil rights; nor did people organize themselves into associations, parties, and professional societies to contend with other groups on the scale prevailing in the present age, while all talk about their rights—and none about their duties.

When the Message of Muḥammad established equality as a right, it made this right an adjunct of duty and faith, implanting this trinity deep in the heart of the believer. It controls his conscience, which therefore knows no deception or hypocrisy, and warns, "Lo! the hypocrites [will be] in the lowest deep of the fire . . . ."[8]

The social order of Islam is not based on the disputations of authorities, or on a balance of power lasting only until upset; it is based, rather, on the solidarity existing among all members of Muslim communities and on their common purpose of existence: spiritual perfection for the individual and the nation. The goal of Islam's teaching is for all endeavors to be upheld by good intention, aimed at pleasing God.

[8] *Ibid.*, 4:145.

The social order preached by the Message of Muḥammad, then, employs the conscience of the individual and, collectively, of the group as well as the authority of the state as the means for guaranteeing what is right. It would denounce the entire community were the community or any of its members to lose sight of the common good. Expressions of the Islamic order acquire value only insofar as they are conducive to confirming the good intention of an undertaking.

Muslims are not much concerned with methods of government—with whether they are monarchical, republican, authoritarian, or democratic in form. What they are most concerned with is that the aim of government, social welfare, be realized in order that all members of society enjoy equality. An individual or a race is to be distinguished only for good conduct and love of peace.[9] There is no worthiness in one or all if the general welfare is not made the aim of life.

If equality along modern lines fails to curb excessiveness and materialism and cannot prevent class struggles and racial wars, then it is an illusion reflecting no truth. Islam seeks truths, not illusions: "God looks not into your faces but into your hearts."

It is apparent, then, that the principle of equality in the Islamic definition constitutes one of the greatest pillars of beneficence and one of the most powerful weapons against the ills of poverty. Islam has preached beneficence by every means from persuasion to the force of law and the power of the state:

> Allah will blot out usury, and causeth charity to prosper.[10]
>
> Ye will not attain unto piety until ye spend of that which ye love.[11]
>
> Hast thou observed him who belieth religion? That is he who repelleth the orphan, and urgeth not the feeding of the needy.[12]

9 The question of "racial characteristics" will be discussed in Chapter 27.

10 Koran, 2:276.

11 *Ibid.*, 3:92.

12 *Ibid.*, 107:1-3.

Nay, but ye [for your part] honor not the orphan, nor do ye urge the feeding of the poor . . . .[13]

The Book of Allah and the life of His Prophet, Muḥammad, reveal abundantly the virtue of acting according to the way of God and of regarding this world as a steppingstone to the next. The propagator of the Message concentrated much of its force on achieving beneficence for the poor, the downtrodden, the weak, the handicapped, and the needy; beneficence toward them was an imposed duty that could not be circumvented. When the Arabs refused to pay the poor tax after the death of the Prophet, the first caliph, Abu-Bakr, though advised to take no immediate action, declared: "May Allah be my witness, if they should withhold from me even the tether of a camel which they used to render to the Prophet, I would fight them for it!" In other words, he would direct the entire force of the state to fight a people who would deny the poor their right, even if in value it amounted to no more than a rope for tying an animal!

The Islamic call to beneficence and right-doing led to the establishment of religious endowments (*waqf*) designated for charity. With beneficence cleansing his soul, the Muslim sets aside a part of his property for the care of even cats, dogs, and other animals. Nūr-al-Dīn Maḥmūd[14] gave over part of his property in Damascus to sheltering aged animals until their death.

Muslim annals abound in examples of beneficence and mercy to the less fortunate and to strangers; and that kindness which was the pride of private homes, tribes, and nations was but an expression of the Muslim spirit of beneficence and right-doing.

13 *Ibid.*, 89:17-18.

14 Son of Zangi, who founded the Zangid dynasty (1127-1262); he succeeded his father in his Syrian possessions and undertook successful campaigns against the Frankish kings of the Levant. He was indirectly responsible for the rise of Ṣalāḥ-al-Dīn (Saladin).

According to the Message of Muḥammad, beneficence, as also the *zakāh,* is not confined to the peoples or religion of Islam, but is rather universal, incorporating all the downtrodden of mankind.

> Allah forbiddeth you not, with regard to those who warred not against you on account of religion and drove you not out from your homes, from dealing kindly and justly with them. Lo! Allah loveth the just dealers.[15]
>
> The alms are only for the poor and the needy, and those who collect them, and those whose hearts are to be reconciled, and to free the captives [slaves] and the debtors, and for the cause of Allah, and [for] the wayfarers . . . .[16]

For beneficence to be effective in this age, it must be based on the principles and methods propounded by Muḥammad in his Message, as they have been effective and enduring. We must strive to attain its objective by analyzing our age—the sources of its wealth and the lot of its peoples—in order better to insure the welfare of the community and please God. Although the religious law of Islam decrees that only a part of a Muslim's income is the poor's due, a pious Muslim does not hesitate to render much more when necessary. In this spirit did the Caliphs Abu-Bakr and 'Umar volunteer their wealth for the poor, the one the whole and the latter half of his holdings.

The spirit of Muḥammad's Message is manifest in the fact that by rendering the poor tax, the Muslim does not absolve himself from further claims to his possessions; as long as there is need for the exercise of beneficence and charity, this need must be met.

We should therefore invoke the inspiration and guidance of the Islamic religious law and propagate the beneficence on

[15] Koran, 60:8.
[16] *Ibid.,* 9:60.

which the Muslim state should rest, establish security and solidarity for society, and put an end to class warfare. "And whoso doeth good an atom's weight will see it then, and whoso doeth ill an atom's weight will see it then." [17]

[17] *Ibid.*, 99:7-8.

# 10

## *Justice and Freedom*

*

We shall discuss in this chapter the two fundamental principles which are indispensable to fortifying society and directing life along the path leading to the general welfare: freedom and justice.

Before the advent of Islam, people lived either according to tribal rule, as was the case in the land of the Arabs, or as subjects of states or princes, as was the situation along the periphery of the Arab peninsula in the dominions of the Romans, Persians, and Ethiopians. Each country had its individual conditions and system, depending on the circumstances, and the rules governing these lands were not based on universal or firm human principles to insure their existence.

In Arab lands, the rule of force prevailed; selfishness and egotism were exalted; people gloried in killing and plundering, and many prided themselves on trampling upon the rights of others and gaining control over their possessions. People rejected human, national, and racial brotherhood, denying equality to those outside the tribe, to associates (*mawāli*),[1] and to other Arabs. They mocked any justice not based on the dictates of force, and they cherished absolute

[1] The term *mawāli* (singular: *mawlā*) meant non-Arabs who sought and received protection from an Arab tribe or individual.

freedom, dying willingly that they might preserve it; it was their own freedom, and they shared it with no one.

The Persians, Romans, and later the Byzantines, the Arabs' neighbors, despised the Arabs, and would not acknowledge any right of equality for them or honor their concept of justice. The power of the Persians was centered around their king—Khosrau II (A.D. 590-628) in the time of the Prophet—to whom belonged all rights, and an entourage which possessed only those rights that Khosrau granted or withheld. The development of the resources of the land was subordinate to his efforts to become king over all people. He was surrounded by aides, princes, and armies. They bolstered his throne and shared some of his power, but they were not altogether safe from being called upon at any moment to sacrifice their lives, possessions, and sons for Khosrau. Indeed, the Persian Empire was firmly established and seemingly perpetual, as the Sassanidae[2] had ruled for four centuries. But the empire rested on militarism and arbitrary rule, not on the principles of justice, freedom, equality, and brotherhood.

Byzantium thrived in the same way for over a thousand years, and its mentality was not different from that of Ctesiphon.[3] The Caesars were emperors of the West and, according to their allegations, of the whole world. The Khosraus were their rivals in the East. Zoroastrianism appeared to have left as much of an imprint on the character of the Persian Empire as Christianity on Byzantium. The Christianity of Byzantium did no honor to its Christians, who in no way practiced the brotherhood, peace, and mercy preached by our master Jesus. So narrow was the vision of the Byzantine rulers that they did not acknowledge the right of any state to independent existence; in their eyes their order was universal.

2 The Sassanidae were the ruling dynasty of Persia which the Arabs overthrew under the leadership of the Caliph 'Umar about A.D. 637.

3 Ctesiphon was the capital of the Sassanidae before its conquest by the Arabs in June, A.D. 637, under the leadership of Sa'd ibn-abi-Waqqās, the Arab general. The Arabs call the city Mada'in.

People either had to acknowledge this or be considered ignorant of the fact that they were within the sphere of this order.

In the ninth century, an envoy of Charlemagne informed the Byzantine emperor that his master was preoccupied in a war with the Saxons, and that these Saxons were barbarians and a perpetual menace. The emperor interrupted him, asking, "Who are those barbarians of whom I have not heard and who, therefore, can be of no consequential importance to cause your master all this trouble? I give them to you and consider your master relieved of them." When the envoy returned to Charlemagne, he informed his master of what the emperor had granted him, upon which Charlemagne declared, "Had he given you a pair of boots instead of the Saxons, he would have been of more help to you on your long and arduous journey!"

Such was the world in the eyes of the Caesars, Khosraus, and the Arab tribes when Muḥammad appeared, reminding man that he is only of Adam and that Adam is of dust: "O mankind! Lo! We have created you male and female, and have made you nations and tribes that ye may know one another. Lo! the noblest of you, in the sight of Allah, is the best in conduct." [4]

And such was the world when 'Umar, Muḥammad's disciple who conquered the dominions of the Caesars and the Khosraus, rebuked his governor, whose son had acted arbitrarily toward a Christian Copt: "O 'Amr,[5] would you enslave a human being born to be free!"

The appeal of the Message of Muḥammad for justice, equality, and freedom was new to that world. Islamic law became the font of freedom and truth, defining the rights and obligations of individuals and groups. The weak lifted their heads and were mocked by their former oppressors, who repeated what their predecessors had asserted: "Thou [Mu-

[4] Koran, 49:13.

[5] 'Amr ibn-al-'Āṣ. See Chapter 4, footnote 13.

ḥammad] art followed only by the contemptible and degraded people who do not think."[6] They did not realize that God willed the destruction of the world of greed, egotism, tyranny, and oppression, and that He demanded that the standard of truth be raised and that there be an end to falsehood. The religious law of Islam comprises clear and noble principles governing human conduct, as revealed by the Ominiscient to one of the most virtuous men known in the lengthy annals of mankind, Muḥammad; these principles affirm that justice and freedom in the conscience of the believers are an integral part of their beliefs and of their innermost selves.

Islam made these principles an inseparable part of belief, thereby affirming, immortalizing, and safeguarding them against the whims of deceit, treachery, pretentiousness, and distorted and abominable preachings.

The Muslim would not be a Muslim if he doubted that the poorest and most incapacitated of his brethren shared equal rights with him; for they are all servants of God both in this world and in the next, the noblest being the best in conduct. This justice is what makes almsgiving to the needy a duty of those capable of providing for them, not a favor.

Justice and equality were apparent during the first Muslim era, when belief prevailed and ruled man's heart. With such understanding did Abu-Bakr, immediately following his election to the caliphate, proceed into the market as an ordinary person seeking to earn a living for himself and his family. When this became a topic of discussion, Muslims consulted each other over the matter, and decided to consider him a hired employee of the community. They prevented him from working and arranged a salary based on his needs, which amounted to a few dirhams, for him and his household. This did not distinguish him in his appearance and livelihood from the rest of his people.

[6] Koran, 11:27.

'Umar succeeded Abu-Bakr in the great days of Islamic belief. He strengthened Islam's authority, as he was a caliph selected from the people. It was he who defeated the Persians and Byzantines, and yet he patched his garb with his own hands and sewed soles onto his footwear. It never entered his mind or the minds of the Muslims that aside from the authority vested in the office, the caliphate should distinguish between the caliph and members of the Islamic community. He was entitled to their allegiance and obedience only as holder of the office and guardian of the law.

Justice and equality constituted a deep-rooted belief which people accepted willingly and observed by the most stringent law; they were a spiritual reality working both overtly and covertly for the establishment of a righteous and stable society.

The Sharī'ah treats believers as brethren, wherever their domicile may be; they are deserving of rights which cannot be denied. Therefore, the believer is entitled to beneficence, help, protection, inheritance, loyalty, and counsel by the decrees of faith and the Sharī'ah. He is entitled to justice, whether the ruler be present or absent, whether the law be in effect or not, for it is a right which he derives from his conscience by the judgment of his faith. Such justice eradicates communal prejudices and bigotry and places equality above every consideration, for the Muslim owns what is his in every time and place.

Islam outdistances all rules of modern justice in declaring:

> Lo! Allah enjoineth justice and kindness . . . .[7]
>
> O ye who believe! Be ye staunch in justice, witnesses for Allah, even though it be against yourselves or [your] parents or [your] kindred . . . .[8]
>
> . . . and let not hatred of any people seduce you that ye deal not justly. Deal justly, that is nearer to your duty.[9]

[7] *Ibid.*, 16:90.

[8] *Ibid.*, 4:135.

[9] *Ibid.*, 5:8.

Islam ordains, ". . . if ye judge between mankind, . . . judge justly." [10] "And if ye give your word, do justice thereunto, even though it be [against] a kinsman . . . ." [11]

Islam has made justice the foundation of the entire world order in the words, "And the sky He hath uplifted; and He hath set the measure, that ye exceed not the measure, but observe the measure strictly, nor fall short thereof." [12]

Islam has placed justice above everything, weighing in an equitable balance between the infidel and the Muslim, the enemy, associate (*mawlā*), and ally; for in Islam's sight they are all the same and equal before justice: ". . . and let not hatred of any people seduce you that ye deal not justly. Deal justly, that is nearer to your duty."

In this regard, the Islamic Sharī'ah deserves attentive consideration, for in many respects it is still ahead of modern civilization in terms of progress achieved.

The Imām Ibn-al-Qayyim[13] said, "Allah (may He be praised and glorified) sent His messengers and revealed His books[14] that people may measure with the justice on which Heaven and earth have dwelt. Where the signs of justice appear and justice unveils its face in whatever manner, then the legislation and religion of Allah will be perfected." That is, religious laws or dogma must conform with justice. According to the Imām al-Shāṭibby, "The ordinances of the Sharī'ah were decreed only for the welfare of people, wherever this welfare is to be found."

The imāms of Islam agree that justice is the ultimate aim of the Sharī'ah, for above all else, it binds decrees with the justice ordained by God.

Freedom in Islam is one of the most sacred rights; political

[10] *Ibid.*, 4:58.
[11] *Ibid.*, 6:153.
[12] *Ibid.*, 55:7-9.
[13] A medieval authority on Muslim theology. *Imām* means a leader of any kind—a jurist, an intellectual leader, etc.
[14] By *books* is meant the ones revealed by God: the Bible, the Koran.

freedom, freedom of thought, religious freedom, and civil freedom are all guaranteed by Islam and carried forward to a point in the distance that has left modern civilization behind.

History still relates examples of this in the audiences of caliphs and princes, even after the rule in Islam had become despotic. People in the days of 'Umar ibn-'Abd-al-'Azīz[15] raised questions in his very presence concerning his right and the right of his house to rule and possess the caliphate. The same has been related of the audiences of al-Ma'mūn.[16] Di'bil ibn-'Ali al-Khuzā'i, the poet, satirized a number of 'Abbāsid caliphs one after another while they were at the apogee of their reign and championed their 'Alid rivals[17] without having his freedom curtailed or suffering any mishap.

Islam's protection of freedom was responsible for the success of the Muslims in their best days, particularly in the period of Arab hegemony which followed closely on the appearance of the Message. Because they upheld freedom, the Muslims succeeded in extending their rule in the East and the West, from China to Spain. Muslims have always been enjoined to battle to safeguard the freedom of belief and the sanctity of places of worship of those who differed in religion but were allied to them or entitled to their protection as subjects of their realm.

The hearts of the Muslims were filled to overflowing with the meaning of freedom. They oppressed no man who delved into the mysteries of the universe and adopted for himself a theory or claimed a certain opinion. Freedom of learning was

15 An Umayyad caliph (A.D. 717-720) noted for his piety; not to be confused with 'Umar ibn-al-Khaṭṭāb, his maternal grandfather.

16 Al-Ma'mūn, an 'Abbāsid caliph (A.D. 813-833) at Baghdad, headed a period of brilliant cultural development, patronizing men of letters and professions. The apex of 'Abbāsid attainments was reached during his reign.

17 The 'Alids were partisans of 'Ali, son-in-law of the Prophet and fourth caliph of Islam (A.D. 656-661); they were the legitimists of Islam who sought to replace the 'Abbāsid dynasty with a dynasty from among the descendants of 'Ali.

guaranteed to the Sabaeans[18] and the Magians,[19] the Christians and the Jews, who were permitted to express their beliefs unmolested. Muslims likewise enjoyed considerable freedom in this respect and were not restrained by their Sharī'ah. From what is known, the only restrictions placed on freedom of opinion, belief, and expression in Islamic states were those aimed at eliminating disturbances, riots, and unrest endangering the safety of the state.

The princes and rulers of Islam, as a whole, did not make it their policy to investigate ideas, views, beliefs, and scholarly research except where these might have had a direct and immediate bearing on their rule. In the Middle Ages, Muslims and non-Muslims plunged into academic and religious discourses with a degree of freedom hardly countenanced by some nations today.

Justice and freedom are two common principles whose necessity and virtue have been agreed upon as indispensable to the maintenance of a sound society. Islam implanted them in the conscience of men, and defended and protected them with its authority.

18 The Sabaeans acquired *dhimmi* status under the Muslims.

19 *Magians* or *Majus* refers to the Zoroastrians who, although not enjoying the status of People of the Book, nevertheless were granted *dhimmi* status and enjoyed the protection of the Muslims.

# IV

## The Islamic State

*

# 11

## *Some Basic Principles of the Islamic State*

*

In recent years numerous independent Muslim states have emerged in Asia and Africa. Coincidental with their emergence, national organizations and parties have come into being, intent upon basing their forms of government on the principles of the Sharī'ah. Various views have been advanced as to the proper form of Islamic rule and the manner of formulating constitutions compatible with the requirements of Islam and capable of achieving its purposes.

Because of their wide geographic distribution, Islamic states comprise different peoples, cultures, traditions, customs, and forms of government. The needs of these states vary with different locations and social environments. Hence no one uniform constitution would be applicable to all, since the circumstances and interests of each country call for interpretations based on independent reasoning in order to produce the constitution most compatible with the purposes sought by the Sharī'ah. Indeed, this variety of constitutions and forms of government may be more effective in realizing the objectives of Muslim law than a single uniform constitution, provided they comply with the general principles of the Sharī'ah and the moral norms of Islam. This is because diversity in laws regulating public matters may be in itself necessary for the realization of the purposes of the Sharī'ah, which aims at the interests of Muslims living under different conditions.

The emergence and evolution of Islamic jurisprudence, together with the diversity of views advanced by scholars and jurists who sought to interpret its provisions and who were definitely affected by their local conditions and circumstances, may be a good guide to what we think is right in this regard.

Thus, the Islamic constitution sought by the Indonesians, Pakistanis, Arabs, or other Islamic peoples may be similar and compatible in essence although different in their details—the laws, decrees, and proceedings rendered necessary by the needs and the general welfare of the community.

What, then, are the ideal constitution and Islamic form of government capable of unifying Muslims without hampering legislative and social evolution, as called for by the requirements of justice and general welfare at a given place or time?

Upon perusal of the holy Book and Islamic traditions (*sunnah*), and upon examination of Islamic history during the era of the orthodox caliphs, we find that Islam is definite and conclusive on all general principles suitable for all times, places, and peoples. When these principles are implemented, therefore, one can witness the flexibility of the Sharīʿah and its disposition to independent reasoning. The Sharīʿah in effect upholds the guidance given by the Prophet in his utterance, "You know best your own earthly matters." Thus the way is open for reason and human judgment to distinguish between right and wrong and to choose the road to the general welfare.

This is perhaps the virtue of Islam which renders it an eternal way of life and law for all mankind and thus upholds the pronouncement of the Almighty, "Surely We have revealed the Koran, and surely We are its Guardian." [1] For if Islam were otherwise, it would not have been a religion easy to observe. It would have caused hardship to people at various times and places and would not have met the challenge of their changing needs.

Thus, with the clarity of Islam on general principles and

1 Koran, 15:9.

morals, the fact that it relegates many matters to settlement by interpretation and reasoning is not a source of weakness in its eternal laws but of continued life.

Let us now advance some examples. Islam does not approve of a state based on the domination and power of one person or party. Its concept is that a state must be based on the consent and cooperation of the people. Islam commands consultation in the injunctions, "We have not sent thee [Muḥammad] as a warder [a tyrant] over them";[2] ". . . consult them in appropriate matters [*amr*]";[3] and "Their [the Muslims'] affairs are [decided] by consultation among themselves." [4] It has made consultation a general principle whose application is mandatory and whose observance is to be respected by all Islamic states and communities at all times. Human experience has demonstrated the continuous character of this principle and its uses. However, Islam avoided defining a single method for consultation or specifying certain forms from which we were to select whatever might be suitable at a given time or place, for such particulars would have caused us hardship; the choice of the rules regulating consultation was left to us, with trust in our loyalty to our religion and to ourselves. The Prophet says that deeds are to be judged by their intent, and that every person will be rewarded by God according to his intentions. It has been left to us to decide, within the scope of this principle, the forms of consultation and the manner in which it should be conducted with a view to meeting our needs and securing general stability and the consent and satisfaction of the people. Therefore, we find that the principal Companions of the Prophet (Ṣaḥābah), followed by the heads of state (imāms) and jurists, exercised independent rea-

2 *Ibid.*, 4:80.
3 *Ibid.*, 3:159. There is no exact English equivalent for the Arabic word *amr;* the meaning concerns consultation on whatever Allah and the Muslims deem important.
4 *Ibid.*, 42:38.

soning on this subject. They put forth varying views regarding the *manner* in which consultation was to be conducted, and left to us a valuable legacy of varied precedents:

1. In the early days, matters were referred to the people at the mosque or to a selected group at a meeting, or a number of the principal Companions of the Prophet were invited for an exchange of views.
2. At a later date, consultation was held by referring the problem, on a special occasion, to those among the leaders of opinion and the dignitaries present.
3. Then we find that in certain cases it was confined to one or more persons selected by the head of state for their sound judgment and the public respect which they enjoyed.

The heart of the matter was the good intentions of the leaders of the people, their fear of the Almighty, and their compliance with His commands. Within this context, they made use of consultation in a manner satisfactory to themselves and in harmony with the circumstances and the needs of the time.

Muslims have long agreed that the competent consultants should be *ahl al-ḥall wal'aqd,* meaning those who loosen and bind. The criterion of their authority is that if they agree on a course of action, it will be accepted by the people, and if they repudiate it, it will be rejected by the community.

Once we determine who are the competent persons suitable to be considered as natural leaders whom people follow, we then will have found those who truly enjoy public confidence, and the nation is ideally represented by them. The problem, however, which has persisted throughout Islamic history concerns, in the first place, the question of agreement as to who should be designated as natural leaders, whose approval, for instance, would suffice to guarantee the people's election of a caliph, and, second, the manner of selecting these electors. Opinion has been divided on these questions. Some have stipulated simply that the leaders should be learned men;

others have said they would designate both scholars and other prominent figures in the community; still others have favored those scholars who are capable of independent reasoning.[5]

The truth, of course, is that the determination of natural leaders is not a simple matter. City dwellers differ from those in the country, since the social structure in rural areas is not the same as it is in centers of population and industry. In one age, they may be composed of prominent scholars, and in another, they may be the dominant figures in their tribes, regions, or countries. In our age, they may be the leaders of parties, communities, or unions. Hence the question raises genuine differences of opinion as to how to define, recognize, and select natural leaders who will fulfill their important functions of legalizing the authority of the ruler and representing the people in all matters. Consideration must be given to differences among peoples, traditions, and customs as well as among the various generations and times.

Therefore, a constitution formulated in a manner enabling these leaders or representatives of the people to express their opinion and permitting the imām to consult with them varies in accordance with the considerations already referred to. What may occur in this respect in the form or constitution of one Islamic state may be at variance with the provisions of another, but whatever the means, they ultimately must be based on the sovereignty of Muslim law—the Sharī'ah—and rest on the free consent of the people. This may serve to clarify what is subject to reasoning and what to tradition in choosing a form of government and writing a constitution consistent with Islam and its purposes.

Another example of the specific application of the Sharī'ah is provided by the question of the imāmate, that is, the selection of the head of state: the qualifications of an imām, his rights, and his duties. In this respect, we also find that the

[5] The first caliph, Abu-Bakr, was elected in a general public meeting in which the community as a whole participated.

Sharī'ah is clear as to what is established and permanent in matters relating to the imām himself and the imāmate, leaving flexible and unspecified other matters to be determined by the exercise of reasoning and considerations of public interest and general welfare.

Ever since the Muslims met at Saqīfat Bani-Sā'idah following the death of the Prophet and declared their allegiance to Abu-Bakr, the imāmate has been the subject of dispute among Muslims, giving rise to various schools of thought. Even though the great majority have adopted the views of the orthodox Muslims (*ahl al-sunnah*), the subject is not devoid of differences in many details. It may be said that the Muslims did not unanimously agree except on two points: the imperative necessity of the imāmate itself to prevent chaos, and their desire to observe the tenets of their religion.

It is not our intention at this point to deal with the theoretical aspects of this subject or to question the beliefs and views which are still held by many sects, including the Sunnites (90 percent of the Muslims), Shī'ites, and Ibadites. This dispute is merely referred to in order to point up the distinction between what is mandatory according to the Sharī'ah and what may be left to discretion. The latter is decided in a manner compatible with the public interest, the requirements of life, and the circumstances of the particular time and place.

When we consider these differences, we find that they include many matters relating to the imāmate, even the title itself. Hence the Muslims called the head of state a *khalīfah* (successor to the Prophet), an *amīr al-mu'minīn* (commander of the faithful), an *imām* (leader), and a *sulṭān* (ruler or king).[6]

This difference of opinion began immediately after the Prophet passed away. When the people met at Saqīfat Bani-

[6] In Muslim history, there are many cases of rulers who established their authority in certain regions of a caliph's domain by force and later legitimized it by securing the caliph's consent. These rulers were usually called sultans or kings.

Sā'idah, the situation was far from clear to them. The Anṣār, from al-Madīnah, said to the Meccan Muhājirūn, "One amīr from us and another from you," while the latter said, "From us the amīrs and from you the ministers." In other words, one faction upheld the principle of the singularity of the imām, and the other upheld the principle of plurality. By general consensus, Abu-Bakr was chosen as the one leader because of his outstanding character. In the words of 'Umar, "Abu-Bakr towered above all others."

We are not concerned here with discussing the basic need for the imāmate or whether this matter should be left to discretion, religious law, or other considerations, since the question was resolved by the unanimous decision (*ijmā'*) of the Companions of the Prophet at the proper time.[7] The Muslims, having established the imāmate, proceeded to lay down the imām's rights and duties in order to guarantee him the powers necessary for guarding their earthly and spiritual interests in a totally new society, born as the result of Muḥammad's teaching, guidance, and struggle. This was to be a self-supporting and mutually reliant society in which all people would enjoy complete equality as dependents of Allah, the only distinction among them being piety, and in which no one would exercise authority except by law emanating from the Sharī'ah. It was indeed a revolutionary society founded on completely new principles and established in a world used to the divine right of kings and the force of arms of emperors.

It was in this society that the imāmate emerged, the Sharī'ah prevailed, and new rules and principles of a highly sacred and progressive character were established. These rules and principles have developed into a permanent constitution for Muslims under which no ruler may grant or adopt any priv-

[7] According to Muslim jurisprudence, *ijmā'* (the agreed view of the Ṣaḥābah) can serve as one of the sources of constitutional law or other legislation. In descending order of importance, the sources of law in Islam are (1) the Koran, (2) *sunnah* or tradition, (3) *ijmā'* and (4) *qiyās,* which means analogical deduction, that is, arriving at an answer by deduction from decisions in similar or parallel cases.

ilege or power except within the framework of the Sharī'ah. It defines public and individual rights and duties, and no earthly body, not even the nation itself, can alter or modify these human rights and duties. Under these rules and principles, for instance, the imāmate is a trust, with the imām as a trustee, acting within the general principles of the constitution and in accordance with public welfare.

As a unique and unprecedented Islamic institution, the imāmate cannot produce its finest results except in a devout nation whose affairs are regulated by a clear constitution based on the Sharī'ah and changeable at the will of the nation within its specific regulations to meet the changing interests and needs of the community.

Experience through the ages has indicated that if a Muslim nation becomes corrupt and tyranny pervades all its ranks, the people will not be bound by the limits of the Sharī'ah and disorder will prevail. Under such conditions, the rights and duties of both the governor and the governed would be neglected, strife would be rampant, and the supremacy of the law would be challenged. These calamities may only be averted by the re-establishment of an Islamic order and a constitution based on popular support, giving effect to the divine will. It would clearly embody those fundamental principles which are eternal as well as those of a subordinate nature which are susceptible to change in order to meet the interests of the public. For the Sharī'ah has vested in us Muslims the right to exercise discretion and reason to achieve its purpose of securing stability, satisfaction, and the orderly Muslim life.

What, then, are the accepted principles regulating the office of the head of the Islamic state? After reviewing numerous opinions of Islamic scholars and jurists belonging to various schools of thought, and upon examination of Islamic history, I feel that the Sharī'ah, out of divine wisdom, laid down only a few basic principles pertaining to the office of the head of state. These basic principles include the installation of an imām, who should be of mature age and a man of wisdom, enjoy popular support, and be a person who draws on the assistance of good citizens and on the counsel of the natural leaders. In addition, he is expected to be a guardian over the interests of all his subjects and an upholder of the law. But if he disobeys the commands of God and disregards the interests of the people, he will be repudiated. Apart from these few principles, the Sharī'ah has left it to people to endeavor through reasoning to adopt whatever additional conditions may suit them best, in a manner compatible with the general tenets of Islam and its universal character.

On the question of national sovereignty and the principle that the nation is the source of all power within the accepted meaning of the present age, Islam has its own and independent course at variance with that of modern concepts of sovereignty.

Islam is a universal religion with its proper ideology and principles relating to dogma, law, morals, ideals, rights, and obligations; it is not bound by locality, race, nationality, or color. Thus, Islam's concept of sovereignty lies in the Sharī'ah. In other words, it lies in those eternal principles of Islam on which its mission has been predicated. Therefore, it is not the prerogative of a nation—as a whole or in part, whether in agreement with the head of state or not, whether represented by a constituent assembly or not—to tamper with the eternal charter of rights and duties ordained by God for all men, singly and collectively, in a particular land and throughout the human race at large. These principles are sovereign and eternal, because it is only by the will of God that their continuity is maintained. This is a great and a fundamental Islamic concept, of which Islamic scholars should always be conscious. It should be advocated and made known particularly in this age, because it raises the common bonds of humanity above race or nationality and establishes human rights at a higher level than national sovereignty or national interests.

At the present time, sovereignty has different meanings to non-Muslims (and their emulators among Muslims) and to Muslims. In Islam, it comprises several component forces that combine to establish its authority. These are the Sharī'ah, the nation, and the the imām, who is the guardian of the Sharī'ah and the chosen of the people. By virtue of these factors, the Islamic order is superior to others. It safeguards the general principles of morality and the foundations of public justice, human equality, and brotherhood. It predicates rights and duties upon principles of universality and eternity as commanded by the Almighty, and it thereby blocks the way to personal preferences and passions, fanaticism, and partisanship. No nation, king, head of state, or layman can repudiate human rights and duties on the pretext that the nation is free in the exercise of its full sovereignty.

Hence, the meaning of sovereignty under the Sharī'ah is different from that conceived of in the constitutions of non-Muslims as well as present Muslim constitutions that are modeled upon them, because these last rest on national sovereignty. As we have already indicated, in Islam, sovereignty does not materialize except through a combination of three elements: the Sharī'ah, the nation represented by its leaders, and the chosen imām, the head of state. In them jointly lies the power called sovereignty. In early times, it resided with kings; outside Islam, in recent times, it belongs to the people; in Islam, it is embodied in this trinity.

This concept of sovereignty under Islam guards against human passions and indulgence in obtuse opinions. It is a safeguard for human rights and duties without parallel in the ideologies of nations either prior or subsequent to the establishment of Islam.

The expression of this sovereignty may not be exercised by a single will, as, for example, in the name of the people, represented by a majority party, or in the name of a king, or in the name of a dictatorship, whether communist or otherwise. It can only be exercised through the will of God, as expressed in His sacred Law, and the will of the state, as expressed through the nation and the government combined. From these joint three wills, human rights and duties are specified and safeguarded in all lands and at all times.

When, for instance, the Koran says, "Lo! Allah enjoineth justice and kindness, and giving [to others]," [8] and "Let not hatred of a people incite you not to act equitably; be just; that is nearer to piety and observance of duty," [9] and "O ye who believe! Be ye staunch in justice, witnesses for Allah, even though it be against yourselves or [your] parents or [your] kindred . . . ," [10] then not the nation nor the imāmate nor both together can go beyond justice and equity as directed by the Sharī'ah, even if it were to be done in the name of national sovereignty and the right of a country to what is called self-determination.

It follows that the nation itself should not be the sole source of power, in the sense of being at liberty to do anything it deems fit with itself or others. Such freedom of action is restricted by the principles of public morality, of justice, and of human rights and duties as ordained by God.

But the nation is completely free to adopt its own form of government and constitution and to enact statutes within the limits of this joint sovereignty. It is sovereign over all matters, but must conduct itself within the limits of the revealed Law of a higher authority, namely, that of God, the Source of existence, Who has placed man on earth and entrusted him with the responsibility of government with a view to safeguarding justice and equity. Thus says the Koran: "O David! Lo! We have set thee as a viceroy [made thee a ruler] in the earth; therefore judge aright between mankind, and follow not desire lest it beguile thee from the way of Allah. Lo! those

[8] Koran, 16:90.

[9] *Ibid.*, 5:8.

[10] *Ibid.*, 4:135.

who wander from the way of Allah have an awful doom, forasmuch as they forgot the Day of Reckoning." [11]

Yes, the nation is the source of power. Under the Sharī'ah, kings and heads of state can only rule with the consent of the nation. It is the nation that sets up and regulates the state, elects its government, and determines what is in its interest and what is not. In all these matters, the nation is the source of power, a power which, however, must function within the orbit of Islamic principles.

Because it relates to divine directives, the sovereignty of the Sharī'ah may not be repudiated by individual or collective action or by any other force. All views or actions which form a barrier between the people on the one hand and justice and right as ordained by Islam on the other have no justification or support in the Islamic religion, even though they may have the support of the sultan or the nation. A nation may not trespass on the interests of people of other lands, or act through its laws and legislation without regarding the welfare of others. Likewise, the majority may not arbitrarily legislate against or act unjustly in relation to individual or collective rights on the assumption that it thereby expresses the general will or majority of the nation at a given time.

This concept of sovereignty imprinted on the minds of contemporary Islamic as well as non-Islamic nations, which inspires complete freedom of action in the national interest, is wrong from a theoretical Islamic point of view. Islam has established certain sacred principles of law for all mankind. It is not bound by what is known as national interest if this interest is incompatible with the interest of all people. Its pursuit of the general welfare supersedes what may appear to be the welfare of a special community. On this point, the right arising from national sovereignty, as conceived by interpreters of modern democratic constitutions, is qualified by and subject to the general rights of humanity at large, as determined by Islam.

11 *Ibid.*, 38:27.

I have touched on three subjects in the course of discussing the basic forms of an Islamic state: consultation, the office of the head of state, and the sovereignty of the nation. These involve the major principles upon the interpretations of which constitutions generally are based. They have been provided by Islam through its historic evolution and by the views of Islamic jurists and theologians. They are unambiguous and well-defined with regard to established and eternal principles, and changeable and flexible wherever change and flexibility are desirable.

The principal objective of the discussion, now that people in all Islamic lands are examining the form of Islamic rule and the constitutions proper to themselves, is to demonstrate in particular to the Muslims by some examples that their religion is practical, that it does not entail hardships, and that the forms of Islamic constitutions may vary in order to serve the public interest and to realize what is good and avoid what is harmful so long as they remain within the limits of eternal Islamic principles.

Provided that Muslims act in good faith with due respect for the Sharī'ah and set up constitutional regimes compatible with their conditions, they will be establishing Islamic forms of government more suitable and beneficial to them than those systems in which they only imitate what are called communist democracies or capitalist democracies. In this way, the Muslim people would set an example for others, as they are called upon to do by the holy Koran when it says, "Thus we have made you a middle nation" [12]—that is, opposed to all extremes—and they would succeed in solving problems that have proved to be insoluble to others. They would also meet the spiritual and physical needs of man, thereby affording civilization and human life the two indispensable ingredients for peace, stability, and prosperity. A human being is no animal whose only concern is fulfillment of natural appetites;

12 *Ibid.*, 2:143.

neither is he an angel whose total endeavors are directed toward the spirit. Adopting moderate courses has been a characteristic of the Islamic Message. It has taken into consideration the continuous needs of the spirit and the body. To regulate these needs, it enunciated eternal rules which may not be repudiated, and left subordinate matters subject to change in a manner consistent with the changing interest of this world.

The eternal Islamic Message is concerned with the public interest of humanity at large, which cannot be superseded by any interest claimed by a particular class or nation for itself. It has established public authority to define and regulate the particular rights and duties of citizens, provided that its power is derived from the three combined elements of sovereignty already defined and from its consistent loyalty to general human rights, which are also an integral part of the duties of any Islamic government. It has enjoined all nations to refrain from acting on the supposition of their supremacy and assuming that the interests of any one nation take precedence over those of another. In this regard, the Koran says,

> And be not like unto her who unraveleth the thread, after she hath made it strong, to thin filaments, making your oaths a deceit between you because of a nation being more numerous [stronger] than another nation.[13]
>
> Thus We have made you a middle nation, that ye may be witness over the people, and that the Prophet may be a witness over you.[14]

[13] *Ibid.*, 16:92.
[14] *Ibid.*, 2:143.

# V

## On International Relations

*

# 12

# *The First Islamic State and Its Foreign Relations*

*

The summons to Islam began secretly. When publicized, it aroused a great deal of controversy, resulting in the persecution of Muslims. The Prophet then suggested that his embattled followers migrate to Abyssinia, which they did, thus inaugurating the earliest international relations of the Muslims.

Muḥammad remained in Mecca, an outcast, preaching the way of God with wisdom and fair exhortation, and the Hāshimites and Muṭṭalibites took refuge in a valley in Mecca, where they remained until the boycott instituted against them by the Meccan leaders was lifted.

There followed a period of calm during which the people from the valley and the emigrants in Abyssinia, men, women, and children, returned to Mecca on the assumption that they would receive shelter. But matters became worse once more, and the Prophet ordered them to migrate for the second time to Abyssinia, where, even in exile, they met with new dangers. For Quraysh again sent emissaries, headed by 'Amr ibn-al-'Āṣ,[1] bearing gifts to the Negus (emperor) and to the Abyssinians in order to persuade them to extradite the emigrants. The Muslims defended themselves by resorting to reason and clung to the right of protection for refugees, thus establishing

1 See Chapter 4, footnote 13.

their first relationship as a separate entity between the nation of Muḥammad and Abyssinia.

Soon after Muḥammad arrived in Yathrib, where he found the emigrants who had preceded him and the Helpers who had offered him their support, he concluded his first agreement as leader of the Islamic state, between Muslims on the one hand and Jews and polytheists on the other.[2] The Pact of Yathrib is one of the most valuable international agreements ever concluded by a state. It deserves analysis and evaluation, for it may serve as a lantern for Muslims, casting light on the fundamentals governing relationships between themselves and members of differing religious communities. With this covenant, the Muslims became a nation and the Islamic state was born.

The Pact amounted to an agreement for peaceful coexistence, a defensive alliance for cooperation against aggression that sought to protect a group of small states, each enjoying under the provisions of the Pact control over its own people and freedom to preach its own religion. The signatories guaranteed to aid one another and to protect each other's beliefs against anyone who wished to bring harm upon their lands and peoples. Thus, they guaranteed freedom of belief and freedom of preaching to members of the Pact, despite the diversity of their beliefs.

With this covenant, the foundations of the Muslim state were laid. All Muslims became subjects of this state, despite differences in race and tribe. From tribal leaders down to associates (*mawāli*), all formed a single nation distinct from all others. Through the Pact, this nation bound itself with nations adhering to alien creeds, and there emerged a "league of nations," formed to aid the oppressed, to give proper coun-

[2] For this treaty's provisions *in extenso,* see the author's second Arabic edition of this book, *al-Risālah al-Khālidah* (2nd ed.; Cario: The House of Arabic Books, 1954), pp. 92-97. Also, see the excellent work by Dr. Muḥammad Ḥamīdullāh (professor of International Law at the University of Othmania, Hyderabad, India), *Corpus des Traités et Lettres diplomatiques d'Islam à l'Époque du Prophète et des Khalifes orthodoxes* (Paris: G.-P. Maisonneuve, 1935).

sel for peace, and to respect the sanctity of the Muslim nation and of those who were party to the Pact and accepted the security it provided. The purpose was to safeguard the beliefs and sentiments of the signatories and their freedom to propagate their religion irrespective of differences. It was a covenant between Islamic peoples and Jews and even pagans, for in Yathrib at that time dwelt many idol worshipers who joined the Pact and thereby became another link in the chain. If there had been Christians in Yathrib then, they would not have been excluded. With the conclusion of this agreement, Islam anticipated the modern era of the League of Nations and the United Nations by more than thirteen centuries.

Before the alliance was established, there was a period of mutual defense against persecution and oppression lasting some fourteen years. Unrestrained by the benevolent preaching of the Muslims or by their conciliatory and merciful attitude, and notwithstanding blood kinship and the fact that the Muslims had peaceably abandoned their homes, Quraysh and its allies employed all the tools of malice and tyranny to strike at the Muslims' possessions and honor, tearing them apart and scattering them far and wide. For years the Muslims refused to retaliate, and called for the judgment of reason, for sanity as opposed to error; they did not favor returning force for force or resorting to compulsion.

But when the Muslims were rapidly approaching the peak of persecution and destruction, they received God's permission to join battle. War was sanctioned for self-defense, their nation, and their freedom of belief. The decision of God came down in these verses:

> Permission to fight is given to those against whom war is made, because they have been wronged; and Allah is indeed Able to give them victory; those who have been driven from their homes unjustly only because they said: Our Lord is Allah—For had it not been for Allah's repelling some men by means of others, cloisters and churches and synagogues and mosques, wherein the name of Allah is oft mentioned, would assuredly have been

pulled down. Verily Allah helpeth one who helpeth Him. Lo! Allah is Strong, Almighty—[We will give victory to] those who, if We give them power in the land, establish worship and pay the poor tax and enjoin kindness and forbid iniquity.[3]

By means of this Pact, the Prophet paved the way for a world order and laid a new basis for international relations, for the alliance was concluded on the basis of freedom, independence, and mutual security for all the signatories.

Then God sent down His sanction of war for noble and limited purposes. Certain of these decrees, such as those concerned with the repulsion of aggression and the prevention of tyranny, are negative; others, pertaining to maintaining the general welfare and righteousness, are positive—in the words of Allah, "those who, if We give them power in the land, establish worship and pay the poor tax and enjoin kindness and forbid iniquity."[4]

The duties following on victory are revealed. The aims of war are circumscribed. Contrary to the aims of all the imperialist states, they do not include territorial expansion or the incapacitation and paralysis of other nations; they do not envision the destruction of their capacity to compete in life by their exclusion from markets and fields of trade, or the monopolizing of sources of wealth, the treasures of the world, and the raw materials essential for industry, or any other action designed to enhance the power of one nation. Nor do these aims advocate the supremacy and self-magnification of any nation in this world so that it becomes more populous and "racially" superior to others. Instead, the aims of war have a defined and limited purpose: to establish freedom of worship of God, give the poor their due, enjoin kindness, and forbid iniquity.

When Europeans and Americans attempted to define the bases for legitimate war after having been consumed by

[3] Koran, 22:39-41.
[4] *Ibid.*, 22:41.

the fires of World War I, when they sought to limit the objectives of war and curb their own lusts, and concluded pacts to that effect, like the covenant of the League of Nations and the Kellogg-Briand Pact, we considered these events good omens, and said to ourselves that the principles of Muḥammad had begun to find a place in the universal discourse. We are still hoping that World War II will bring in its aftermath an end to perdition. We pray that mankind will find guidance in the rules for international relations incorporated in Islamic principles, and that people will discover a solution for the woes that beset them. For the pact of Muḥammad with the Jews and polytheists of Yathrib was the first pact of the body politic for the purpose of safeguarding peace on the basis of welfare and freedom for all.

Thirteen centuries ago, the Islamic Sharī'ah produced a system comprising pacts, alliances, mutual guarantees, and arbitration. The Islamic law considered war against aggressors a form of reprimand and discipline, not a means for torturing and crushing them. As the Koran says,

> And if they incline to peace, incline thou also to it, and trust in Allah.[5]
>
> So judge between them by that which Allah hath revealed . . . .[6]
>
> And if one party of them doeth wrong to the other, fight ye that which doeth wrong till it return unto the ordinance of Allah; then, if it return, make peace between them justly, and act equitably. Lo! Allah loveth the equitable.[7]

[5] *Ibid.*, 8:61.
[6] *Ibid.*, 5:49.
[7] *Ibid.*, 49:9.

# 13

## *Pledges, Pacts, and Treaties*

*

Muḥammad's Message bases international relations on the concept that the peoples of the world are (1) Muslims or non-Muslim citizens (*dhimmi* status), (2) non-Muslims in treaty relations with Islam (*mu'āhid* status), or (3) non-Muslims having no treaty relations with Muslims. In implementing Muslim law concerning these three general classifications, later Islamic thinkers arrived at the corresponding but larger categories of (1) *dār al-Islām* (Muslim lands), (2) *dār al-ṣulh* (abode of peace), and (3) *dār al-ḥarb* (abode of war or enmity).

As for the believers, their brotherhood is complete under Muslim law. Non-Muslims in treaty relations with Muslims are dealt with according to the terms of their pact or treaty, which, no matter what its form, represents a bond of amity. Non-Muslims having no treaty relations with Islam are broadly considered under two aspects: a land which actively persecutes Muslims and denies them the right to practice and preach their faith is Islam's perpetual enemy, whether a war is being waged or not; but a nation which treats Muslims peacefully, allowing them freedom of religion, is treated to peace in turn, and Islam may not war against it.

It is a fundamental Islamic principle that hostility may not be resorted to without reason. Islam confines the aims of war to guaranteeing freedom in worship and preaching and to guarding other fundamental human rights. The history of the Message of Muḥammad is explicit in this respect. If a situation should call for disputation and active hostility with others—and Muslim law requires that all peaceful means of settlement be exhausted first—it is not necessary, as some tend to think, that these others be given a choice of one of three alternatives: Islam, *jizyah* taxes,[1] or the sword.

The tendency for some critics to consider these three alternatives as exclusive possibilities under Muslim law, since they were prevalent in the first stage of Islamic conquests, is contrary to the record of history. The truth of the matter is that these alternatives were preceded by many pacts and treaties made by the Prophet himself and later by his successors which did not require by law any of the three choices. The right of the Muslims and their imāms to conclude whatever agreements they deemed essential for their welfare has not been disputed. The Truce of al-Ḥudaybiyah, for instance, did not demand such conditions. To the contrary, it contained terms so tolerant of the other signatories that at the time 'Umar considered them a debasement of the Islamic religion and a humiliation for Muslims in the struggle with the polytheists, and resigned himself to these peace conditions only in obedience to and respect for the Prophet.

On delving into the various pledges, agreements, and treaties made by the Prophet himself, we discover in them one persistent aim: the freedom to preach and worship peacefully. Insuring the freedom of the faith was considered by the Prophet a requisite for the triumph of the Message. Thus, it is clear that all conditions, including the *jizyah,* that might constitute an obstacle to the understanding and peaceful diffusion of the Message become obstructive, unwarranted, and invalid. It is not true, therefore, to maintain that the leaders or followers of Islam must base the establishment of peace upon a choice between Islam or *jizyah* and tribute.

1 See Chapter 6, footnote 18. The term *jizyah* usually means poll taxes paid by an individual subject; a tribute, which is the sum paid on behalf of a whole community, is also often called *jizyah.*

If we glance over the world of Islam today, individuals or groups; if we consider the relationships of Muslims with their neighbors and with each other and investigate the treaties, pledges, and agreements with which they have bound themselves; and if we then realize that such agreements enjoy the respect of all Muslims, in accordance with the words of the Prophet, we will be able to visualize the whole of mankind within a framework of common security.

We have seen how the relations of Islam are based on the classifications of believers, non-Muslims in treaty relations with Muslims, and non-Muslims having no established relations with Muslims. As for the believers, peace among them is eternal, according to the revealed Law, and can be disturbed only by acts of apostasy. In the case of aggression by one Muslim group on another, all Muslims must oppose the wrongdoers until the latter awaken to the ordinance of God and accept arbitration. Through arbitration, equity and justice, not suppression and force, will prevail, for equity and justice constitute the scales on which the conditions of reconciliation are weighed.

> And if two parties of believers fall to fighting, then make peace among them. And if one party of them doeth wrong[2] to the other, fight ye that which doeth wrong till it return unto the ordinance of Allah; then, if it return, make peace between them justly, and act equitably. Lo! Allah loveth the equitable.
>
> The believers are naught else than brothers. Therefore make peace between your brethren . . . .[3]

Muslims throughout the world have to surrender to this law as an article of faith. They are not separated by national boundaries, clannish loyalty, denominations, interests, fear,

[2] "Doeth wrong": *wrong* translates the Arabic *baghat,* which combines the meanings *do wrong* and *commit aggression.*

[3] Koran, 49:9-10.

servitude, or any other circumstance. The Muslims are one community bound by fraternal relations.

The Muslim is a citizen of whatever Muslim country he finds himself in. He is entitled to all the rights of a resident citizen and is responsible for all the obligations prescribed in Muslim law wherever he may be. For example, should he find himself in Egypt as a transient from the Maghrib[4] on his way to make the pilgrimage, and Egypt were at war, he would be expected to fight alongside the Egyptians under the same obligation he would owe his own country were it under attack. Also, were he destitute or in difficult circumstances, he would be entitled to share in the poor tax (*zakāh*) of the country through which he is passing. The Muslim community is duty-bound to guarantee his security, as he is entitled to the same rights, whatever his origin or nationality. The Islamic brotherhood between the black and the white, the slave and the free is complete; no Muslim, regardless of sectarian affiliation, entertains any doubt about this.

On this basis, the six hundred million Muslims of the world are brothers, and according to the ordinances of the Sharī'ah, they cannot war on each other under pretext of service to God, homeland, or state. If perchance they should fall into such a situation, Muslims not involved in the dispute must intervene to put an end to fighting and re-establish peace according to the Koranic ordinance mentioned above.

From this it can be seen that the ramifications of Muslim law are international and that its precepts are founded on universal human truths. Such precepts can apply to all humanity, regardless of religious or national affiliation.

In the Muslim concept of world order, a commitment made by the Muslim state and even by the individual Muslim can commit the entire Muslim community (*ummah*). Within Islam the individual possesses an authority in certain cases which approximates the authority of the community, as in

[4] Maghrib refers to the Western lands of Islam, that is, North Africa west of Egypt to the Atlantic; at present it refers to Morocco in particular.

situations involving the maintenance of the law and public morals. The Islamic order permits the individual to offer protection and assurance to an enemy and to make a pledge to an individual or a group of people, and his assurance and pledge will be respected according to the words of the Prophet: "Muslims are one, and the humblest among them is entitled to pledge them."

This respect was accorded even to a pledge given by a slave. Abu-'Ubaydah once wrote to the Caliph 'Umar that a slave had given a pledge of security to the inhabitants of a town in Iraq, and asked him for his opinion in the matter. 'Umar answered, "Allah has magnified the fulfillment of promises, and you are not faithful until you fulfill promises. Therefore, fulfill your promises to them and leave them alone." In like manner, the Muslims confirmed a woman's pledge of security. In the words of the Prophet, "We have protected whom you protected, O Mother of Hānī!" Early Muslim jurists differed over the merits of a pledge given by a slave or a woman in the name of all Muslims, and some made the honoring of such a pledge contingent on the acquiescence of the head of state; however, the majority upheld unconditionally the sanctity of a pledge given by a free Muslim male.

Let us now deal with relations between Muslims and non-Muslims. Those who have treaty relations with the Muslims may enjoy either a pledge of protection, which in modern terms means citizenship, or one of the many kinds of pledges of security; both types of commitment insure the parties to the pledge a share in mutual benefits.

The *dhimmi* pledge or pledge of protection grants security to individuals or whole communities living in the realm of Islam. The Muslims pledge guardianship and protection in the name of God, of His Prophet, and of the Muslims in exchange for the yearly *jizyah,* the individual poll tax or community tribute. Although for a time in Islam's history the term *dhimmi* caused embarrassment, because it came to imply second-class citizenship, originally it signified superior merit, for the title came from *dhimmat Allah* (God's custody). It constituted the greatest possible affirmation of the protected one's right to enjoy complete religious, administrative, and political freedom, a right which was guaranteed him in return for loyalty and the payment of what amounted to a reasonable tax to help in the defense of the state.

The *dhimmi* subject is the neighbor of the Muslim, who befriends and associates with him. None of his rights are impaired: juridically he is entitled to exactly the same justice as is received by the Muslim in Muslim courts. It is unlawful to oppress, persecute, or insult him or deprive him of his rights. He has his religion and the Muslim has his. It is the duty of the Muslim to help and protect him when necessary and to safeguard his religious and personal freedom and the freedom of his people. In return the *dhimmi* subject is expected to refrain from undertakings which might prejudice the beliefs and security of Muslims.

The early Muslim conquerors were extremely conscious of their obligations to the *ahl al-dhimmah,* the protected of God. Khālid ibn-al-Walīd returned the *jizyah* to the Christians of Homs (Emesa) following his failure to defend that city,[5] feeling that he did not possess the power to repel the attacks of the Byzantine Emperor Heraclius on the city. In his words, "We accepted [the *jizyah*] as a token of your good will and in return for defending you, but [in this] we have failed [you]." [6] More than five centuries later, during his wars with

[5] See Chapter 4, footnote 12.

[6] "After the Arab recapture of Alexandria [from the Byzantines in A.D. 646], a number of Coptic [Egyptian Christian] villages complained to 'Amr ibn-al-'Āṣ [the governor] that they had not joined in the rebellion but that, on the contrary, the Byzantine army from Alexandria had plundered them and had requisitioned food from them without repayment. The original treaty signed with 'Amr after the first surrender of Egypt had, they pointed out, imposed tribute upon them, but the Arabs [Muslims] had in return undertaken to protect them. They had not, however, been protected during Manuel's in-

the Crusaders, Ṣalāḥ-al-Dīn (Saladin) returned the *jizyah* to the Christians of Syria when he was compelled to withdraw. The *jizyah* was not a right of conquest given the victor over the vanquished; it was rather a benefit in exchange for a benefit, a compensation for a fulfilled task.

Once agreement is reached and the *jizyah* is paid, the protected, be he an individual or a community, is guaranteed equal justice with the Muslims. Moreover, the payment of this tax absolves him from any obligation for military service or for payment of the poor tax (*zakāh*), though he enjoys the right to share in the distribution of the *zakāh* since all the poor and needy, both Muslim and non-Muslim, are designated as its recipients. If, however, the non-Muslim citizen or protected person enlists in the ranks of the Muslims, he receives an equal share in the spoils of war and is also exempted from paying the tribute.

Unlike the treaty commitments of many secular states, the *dhimmi* commitment in Muslim law is based on the principle of human brotherhood and the sanctity of faith. No distinctions of race, citizenship, religion, economic status, or personal capabilities can obliterate the human rights of a *dhimmi* subject. Just as a Muslim shares rights and obligations with every other Muslim everywhere, regardless of nationality, so does the *dhimmi* subject. Accordingly, he enjoys in any Islamic state a security and equal justice disturbed only if and when he should violate the terms of the pledge. The prescriptions of the Sharī'ah are universal and require submission from all Muslims.

---

vasion, and, in consequence, they had suffered heavy losses. 'Amr immediately admitted the justice of their complaint and ordered compensation to be paid for the losses. It is just to record that the Arabs, at this period, were extremely conscientious about the mutual obligations of their surrender treaties with the conquered peoples. They demanded the full payment of tribute and poll tax, but they also recognized the obligation which rested on them to protect the people who thereby came under their guardianship" (Lt. Gen. Sir John Bagot Glubb, *The Great Arab Conquest* [London: Hodder and Stoughton, Ltd., 1963], pp. 284-285).

The *dhimmi* commitment is but one of the many kinds of relationships Muslims may establish with other peoples. They may conclude pacts of security, nonaggression pacts, concordats of friendship, trade agreements, alliances to secure peace, treaties of recognition, diplomatic relations, and so forth.

The brotherhood taught by the Message of Muḥammad has the power to guarantee durable peace not only among its peoples and countries but all over the world. The Koran says:

> O mankind! Be careful of your duty to your Lord Who created you from a single soul and from it created its mate and from them twain hath spread abroad a multitude of men and women. Be careful of your duty toward Allah in Whom ye claim [your rights] of one another . . . .[7]

It has been shown that war has no purpose acceptable to God other than the peace that is based on justice, equity, and human brotherhood; and that victory entitles the victor to one right only: prevention of aggression and injustice. Any agreement concluded at the end of a war would contradict the Islamic spirit if it were based on tyranny and oppression or the usurpation and annihilation of what constitutes the rights of men as brethren in one human family. Allah says, "And be not like unto her who unraveleth the thread, after she hath made it strong, to thin filaments, making your oaths a deceit between you because of a nation being more numerous [or greater] than [another] nation." [8]

Islam's view is that the purpose of peace agreements is not to perpetuate a state of conquest by keeping the defeated in constant deprivation and humiliation, but rather to establish the form of justice which God decrees equally for enemies and friends alike: ". . . and let not hatred of any people

[7] Koran, 4:1.
[8] *Ibid.*, 16:92.

seduce you that ye deal not justly. Deal justly, that is nearer to your duty." [9] Had the nations of the earth in former and in modern times, Muslim and non-Muslim, followed the guidance of the Koran in this context, the reaches of war would have been circumscribed and the reasons for rebellion removed.

When the leaders of modern nations assert that the purpose of war is to establish justice and equity and to prevent tyranny, they are confirming the tenets of Muḥammad's Message, although their assertions lack the force of faith based on piety; for, as we have seen again and again, war is sanctioned by the Islamic Sharī'ah only in order to repel tyranny and aggression, and is terminated when tyranny and aggression are thwarted and the justice and right enjoined by Allah prevail. In like manner, conditions of peace are not dictated by the agents of fear and greed because Allah, Who champions the right and strengthens the believers in it, assures true victory only where it serves His ends: beneficence and justice.

Had the European nations acted justly and equitably, the war of 1870 would not have engendered the causes of the war of 1914, nor would the latter have given rise to the war of 1939. Many lived to witness the great disillusionment. Guile and deceit will add but calamities to their perpetrators.

The aim here is not to single out any one nation or group of nations for blame, or to claim that Muslims have been any more truthful in their sayings and views than members of other nations or religions, but to point out that few have observed the spirit of Muḥammad's Message or abided by the truthfulness of its principles.

From the viewpoint of the Message of Muḥammad, all agreements are sacred in that they are conducted within the sight of God, in Whose name they are guaranteed. They enjoy a religious sanctity which does not permit deception or hypocrisy. Upon his succession to the caliphate, 'Uthmān wrote in a message to his officials and governors:

[9] *Ibid.*, 5:9.

Truly, Allah has created creation in right; He accepts but right. Take right and give right. And dwell upon your trust. Do not be the first to violate it and become accomplices of your successors. . . . Fulfill your vows and do not oppress the orphan or the ally [those in treaty relations]. Allah is the opponent of him who oppresses them.

Neither we Muslims nor others seem to partake of this most important aspect of Muḥammad's ethics: that the sanctity of a pledge is above all other considerations, even, in certain cases, above the sanctity of religion. Indeed, the Sharī'ah has placed the sanctity of pledges above that of Muslim brotherhood. For example, non-Muslims are entitled to blood money (*diyah*) if they are in treaty relations with the Muslims, while there is no *diyah* to the relatives of a Muslim who belong to a people with no treaty relations with the Muslims.

The Sharī'ah has also forbidden a Muslim to aid another Muslim against a non-Muslim who enjoys the protection of a pledge even for a religious cause. The Almighty declares: "But if they seek help from you in the matter of religion then it is your duty to help [them] except against a folk between whom and you there is a treaty." [10]

The propagator of the Message himself set the highest example of respect for pledges when he was negotiating with Suhayl ibn-'Amr at al-Ḥudaybiyah. While he was wording the terms embodied in the truce agreement, the son of Suhayl, Abu-Jandal ibn-Suhayl, appeared before Muḥammad weighted down with chains; he had fled the ranks of the Prophet's enemies whom his father was representing and in whose name Suhayl was negotiating with the Prophet. When Suhayl saw his son he stood up, seized him by the collar, and said, "O Muḥammad, the matter between you and myself has [already] been settled." In other words, they had agreed on terms before Abu-Jandal had come to the Prophet. Mu-

[10] *Ibid.*, 8:72.

ḥammad replied, "You speak the truth." Abu-Jandal then shouted, "O Muslims, am I to be returned to the idolaters to be divested of my religion?" But this was of no avail to him; the Prophet returned him according to the terms he had approved, although they had not yet been written down or sealed. There was no hesitation or reconsideration, as he had given his consent. Suhayl's son, a Muslim, was returned to the unbelievers over the objection of the Prophet's own followers.

Another principle stressed in the Message of Muḥammad and extremely important in our times is that a pledge may never be betrayed. Islam forbids the betrayal of a pledge, secretly or openly, as it forbids the betrayal of any trust, materially or spiritually.

What is the value of a pledge or a treaty when made to be broken or treacherously interpreted to justify the narrow interests of one party to the detriment of the other, particularly when one party has the military power to back up its arbitrary position?

Furthermore, fulfillment of a pledge may be withheld only when the common welfare of the Muslims is betrayed by the other party whose deception and ill will are beyond doubt. It is permissible then to cast off the pledge: "And if thou fearest treachery from any folk, then throw back to them [their treaty] fairly. Lo! Allah loveth not the treacherous." [11] But Muslims may not employ artifice in so doing, nor are they to surprise the other party with its denunciation, without previous warning and a period of delay. This constituted both ethics and law within the provisions of the Sharī'ah long before such principles were recognized by modern international law. The Prophet and the orthodox caliphs[12] advised their governors and military commanders to give warning before engaging in war. The jurists of Islam have agreed that the enemy must be forewarned, served with the reasons the

[11] *Ibid.*, 8:58.

[12] See Chapter 1, footnote 3.

pledge is to be discarded, and informed that the purpose is not to lay hands on his wealth, deprive him of life, or to capture him, for he might respond to what is requested and thus avoid war. To fight without previous warning deserves the wrath of God; but if all reason is lost and war becomes inevitable, then, and only then, Allah directs: "So do not falter and cry out for peace when ye [will be] the uppermost . . . ."[13]

13 Koran, 47:35.

## 14

## *Legitimate War*

*

Only when persecuted, oppressed, and prevented from migrating to Yathrib, where they could enjoy the protection provided for in the pact concluded between them and their neighbors of other religions, did the Muslims seek and receive permission to fight.

Let us now consider the causes, concomitants, and purposes of war from the Islamic viewpoint; these will help us understand a situation in which we may find a remedy for the illness of the modern world and which may open the mind to guidance and contemplation.

In sanctioning war, Islam defined its aims and purposes: to suppress tyranny, insure the right of a man to his home and freedom within his nation, prevent persecution in religion, and guarantee freedom of belief to all people.

This freedom for all people is manifest in the Koran's citation of all places of worship for the various religions—monasteries and churches for the Christians, synagogues for the Jews, and mosques for the Muslims. Islam permitted war to safeguard all these religious freedoms, as well as its own, against the attacks of aggressors. Thus says Allah: "And fight them until persecution is no more, and religion is for Allah. But if they desist, then let there be no hostility except against wrongdoers." [1]

1 Koran, 2:193. The word *wrongdoers* (*ẓalimīn*) also means *aggressors*.

With this honored verse, the Message of Muḥammad stands exalted over all other ideologies, for it limits the aims of war to repelling tyranny and dictates the cessation of war as soon as the aggressor ceases his indulgence in persecution of people because of their faith. Thus, war is not renewed or perpetuated except against a tyrant who insists on acts of tyranny, compelling people to abandon their religion. Persecution, forced conversion, and the deprivation of religious freedom are more distasteful to God than the taking of life:

> They question thee [O Muḥammad] with regard to warfare in the sacred month. Say: Warfare therein is a great [transgression], but to turn [men] from the way of Allah, and to disbelieve in Him and in the Inviolable Place of Worship, and to expel his people thence, is a greater with Allah; for persecution is worse than killing. And they will not cease from fighting against you till they have made you renegades from your religion, if they can.[2]

If we were to analyze the verses of the Koran which pertain to warfare, and revert to the circumstance of their revelation and follow the events of the Prophet's life, his wars and expeditions, war by war and expedition by expedition, there would be not the slightest doubt that the war sanctioned by Islam is the war of self-defense. Space does not permit a thorough investigation and enumeration of events, but in the books of the traditions (*sunnah*), in the Koran, and in the biographies of Muḥammad, there is sufficient explanation and detail to satisfy the inquirer concerning the objectives of legitimate war in Islam and the manner in which Islam commits itself to a war of defense. Warring on polytheists, wherever they may be, taking strong measures against them, inflicting punishment on them from behind their lines, and taking them captive are measures allowed to Muslims once

2 *Ibid.*, 2:217.

war begins; they are the result and not the cause of a declaration of war.

In the decrees of the Almighty, it is said,

> O Prophet! Strive against the disbelievers and the hypocrites! Be harsh with them. Their ultimate abode is Hell, a hapless journey's end.[3]
>
> . . . fight the heads of disbelief—lo! they have no binding oaths [pacts or pledges]—in order that they may desist. Will ye not fight a folk who broke their solemn pledges, and purposed to drive out the Messenger and did attack you first? What! Fear ye them? Now Allah hath more right that ye should fear Him, if ye are believers. Fight them! Allah will chastise them at your hands, and He will lay them low and give you victory over them, and He will heal the breasts of folk who are believers. And He will remove the anger of their hearts. Allah relenteth toward whom He will. Allah is Knower, Wise.[4]
>
> And fight them until persecution is no more, and religion is for Allah.[5]
>
> And slay them wherever ye find them, and drive them out of the places whence they drove you out . . . .[6]
>
> O Prophet! Exhort the believers to fight. If there be of you twenty steadfast, they shall overcome two hundred, and if there be of you a hundred steadfast, they shall overcome a thousand of those who disbelieve, because they [the disbelievers] are a folk without intelligence.[7]
>
> And wage war on all the idolaters as they are waging war on all of you. And know that Allah is with those who keep their duty [unto Him].[8]

These verses reveal to the reader that a state of war is assumed; they urge persistence and patience in war and encourage its pursuit until a satisfactory conclusion is attained.

3 *Ibid.*, 9:73.
4 *Ibid.*, 9:12-15.
5 *Ibid.*, 2:193.
6 *Ibid.*, 2:191.
7 *Ibid.*, 8:65.
8 *Ibid.*, 9:36.

They imply security and peace for the believers, the achievement of permanence and stability for religion, the prevention of persecution and apostasy by pressing the polytheists and defeating them, and the hope that the assailants will refrain in the end from aggression.

One of the attainments of the Sharī'ah is its practical application to everyday life; it faces human and religious facts and tackles problems with practical solutions. As long as benevolent preaching does not repel tyranny and aggression, the enemies of Islam refuse to exercise neighborliness and accept a pledge based on justice and freedom, and men of evil possess dangerous power, war will inevitably occur. Islam did not stand before these facts with crossed arms, but faced them instead with the resolution and determination that attended the Prophet when he preached the Message. Throughout his life, he enjoined that believers be prepared: "Make ready for them all thou canst of [armed] force and of horses tethered, that thereby ye may dismay the enemy of Allah and your enemy . . . ." [9] It made of the same tools used for invoking terror tools that could prevent war and preserve peace.

Once Muslims were left no alternative but war, and their right to that became clear, war was sanctioned, and peace became its supreme objective; in the words of the Almighty, "But if they desist, then let there be no hostility except against wrongdoers." [10] "And if they incline to peace, incline thou also to it, and trust in Allah." [11]

Once the sanctioned defensive war has been decided on and its causes have been ascertained, then war becomes the duty of the entire populace. By God's ordinance, sanctioned war (*jihād*)[12] becomes the obligation of every Muslim, man and woman. This obligation is to be met from the innermost con-

9 *Ibid.*, 8:60.
10 *Ibid.*, 2:193.
11 *Ibid.*, 8:61.
12 The author regards *jihād* as a purely defensive struggle, based on the assumption that once a state of war is declared, it continues until brought to a victorious end.

science in accordance with the decisions of the Islamic command, as personified by him who holds the reins of the nation's affairs.

At this juncture, the lofty aspirations desired by Islam will manifest themselves, forbidding retreat and flight, demanding patience, fortitude, sacrifice, courage, and a generous expenditure of lives and possessions and even departure from home and country during enemy occupation. "O ye who believe! When ye meet those who disbelieve in battle, turn not your backs to them. Whoso on that day turneth his back to them, unless maneuvering for battle or intent to join a company, he truly hath incurred wrath from Allah, and his habitation will be Hell, a hapless journey's end." [13]

Islam would not commit people to so severe a duty that to flee from it would incur the curse, anger, and tortures of God unless the battle were truly declared in defense of the most sacred of beliefs. Such an obligation demands that the believer be so persevering that the infidel will not be able to put him to flight, even if the odds be ten to one against him! This fortitude would be impossible if the warrior were not thoroughly convinced that he fights for a right that allows no room for doubt—the right to defend himself and his belief against his assailant. It would not be possible in a war of aggression to compel people to be patient while fighting at a ratio of one against ten, for they cannot exercise patience when they know they are the aggressors, the ones who have lit the fuse of war; they cannot exercise patience when there is no incentive to self-sacrifice.

The verses which incite to battle, the display of courage to the point of martyrdom, and the tactics of pressing the enemy, taking him by surprise, bearing down on him, lying in wait for him, blocking all his means of access and exit; and those verses which call for the sacrifice of possessions and lives and flight from the homeland for the sake of achieving victory for God—all these noble exhortations clearly urge only

[13] Koran, 8:15-16.

a sanctioned defensive war in accordance with the legislation of Islam.

It is therefore evident from the collection of verses pertaining to war in the noble Book, from the works of the Prophet himself as revealed in his traditions (*sunnah*), and from his biographies and the annals of his wars that Islam does not sanction any war of aggression, nor does it unleash war to acquire worldly gains, for with God there are many treasures. As for other purposes motivating people to battle—the striving of one race or one people to dominate another; the exaltation of one monarch or one social class over another; the territorial expansion of a dominion for military and strategic or economic aims, to acquire raw materials and commercial markets or to civilize those who lag behind in culture—in all these cases, there is no Islamic sanction for war. The aims of Islam are humanitarian and universal: its blessings should extend to all people; and the outlook of Islam is a lofty one: it regards the whole of mankind as one family to be secured against injustice. Almighty God is not the God of Muslims alone, but of the entire universe.

O mankind! Lo! We have created you male and female, and have made you nations and tribes that ye may know one another. Lo! the noblest of you, in the sight of Allah, is the best in conduct.[14]

O ye who believe! . . . say not unto one who offereth you peace [the salutation "Peace be upon you"]: "Thou art not a believer," seeking the chance profits of this life [so that ye may despoil him].[15]

Allah forbiddeth you not, with regard to those who warred not against you on account of religion and drove you not out from your homes, from dealing kindly and justly with them. Lo! Allah loveth the just dealers. Allah only forbiddeth you, with regard to those who war against you on account of religion and have driven you out from your homes and helped to drive you out, from mak-

14 *Ibid.*, 49:13.
15 *Ibid.*, 4:94.

ing friends of them. Whosoever maketh friends of them—[all] such are wrongdoers.[16]

So, if they hold aloof from you and wage not war against you and offer you peace, Allah alloweth you no way against them.[17]

Islam is constantly prepared to conclude various types of agreements with its neighbors and other nations guaranteeing the perpetuation of peace; and this would cost these nations no more than the display of a genuine desire for peace and a sincere intention to be faithful to their pledge. With such a true interest in perpetuating peace, Islam does not hasten war or make surprise attacks, but rather sets up the reason, presents it to its opponent, warns him, and lays before him the ways out of his predicament. If he is still defiant, insists on his enmity, and accepts nothing short of battle, then war will take place, and with it will come the enthusiasm, the courage and patience and fortitude, the sacrifice of self and property, exile, and all that is stipulated in the noble verses cited.

Certain people, particularly the opponents of Islam, have taken these injunctions as a pretext for smearing the Message of Muḥammad as a sanguinary ideology that uses war as a tool for overpowering peoples and depriving them of their possessions and lives; but the Message of Muḥammad is clear. It began with the abnegation of war, but when its people were oppressed and its survival became impossible without the repulsion of force by force, it sanctioned war, and upon doing so, it commanded its pursuit with the thoroughness conducive to victory. When such a victory was Islam's, it declared, "There is no compulsion in religion. The right direction is henceforth distinct from error." [18]

Islam is a successful ideology because it faces truth with truth, with frankness, and with fidelity. But as long as evil

16 *Ibid.*, 60:8-9.

17 *Ibid.*, 4:90.

18 *Ibid.*, 2:256.

men wish only evil, it would be self-defeating for people to tolerate injustice and allow themselves to be weakened in the land.

> Lo! as for those whom the angels take [in death] while they wrong themselves, [the angels] will ask: In what were ye engaged? They will say: We were oppressed in the land. [The angels] will say: Was not Allah's earth spacious that ye could have migrated therein? As for such, their habitation will be Hell, an evil journey's end; except the feeble among men, and the women, and the children, who are unable to devise a plan and are not shown a way. As for such, it may be that Allah will pardon them.[19]

The Message of Muḥammad discourages its followers from committing aggression, since almighty Allah declares, "Lo! Allah loveth not aggressors." [20] But it also decrees that they should temporarily forfeit their homelands and suffer martyrdom rather than accept a life of humiliation and deprivation.

19 *Ibid.*, 4:97-99.
20 *Ibid.*, 2:190.

15

# *War in Aid of the Oppressed*

*

The Message of Muḥammad considers warfare admissible and a virtue when undertaken to repel aggression against the weak, be it against an individual or a group, in the interest of erecting the edifice of justice desired by God on earth.

The Prophet devoted himself to the repulsion of tyranny, as did his successors, inasmuch as he commanded the authority of the Islamic polity to defeat aggressors and avert tyranny. While confirming Ḥilf al-Fuḍūl,[1] a pledge made in pre-Islamic days, Muḥammad declared, "Were I, a Muslim, called upon to uphold its tenets, truly would I respond, for Islam but adds strength to it." Islam the religion and Islam the state legally obligated the believers to war on oppression and in aid of the oppressed, whether individuals or communities, Muslims or non-Muslims, because while still a youth and before he was called to his mission Muḥammad had pledged support to Ḥilf al-Fuḍūl.

A war in defense of the oppressed may be waged by one powerful party against another, even though it may not have ties with the aggrieved. It follows, therefore, that an Islamic state may ally itself with one or more states to defend a victim.

Adherence of an Islamic state to the Charter of the United Nations is not considered objectionable from the point of

[1] See Chapter 1, footnote 10.

view of the Sharī'ah. When the intent of a United Nations action under the Charter is deemed honorable, respectful of the general welfare and justice, and aimed at guarding against oppression and repulsing aggression, then Muslims regard the Charter as meritorious, for its decree is that of Ḥilf al-Fuḍūl, to which Islam added emphasis and authority.

On the other hand, if pacts are concluded for the purpose of perpetuating tyranny, suppressing the defeated, and exterminating the weak, they become instruments of crime and aggression in the eyes of Islam and hostile to its tenets, which preach piety and beneficence. The Koran instructs, ". . . but help ye one another unto righteousness and pious duty. Help not one another unto sin and transgression . . . .[2]

In Islam's view, deeds are judged by their underlying intention—the intention can render a deed upright or corrupt. A deed acquires sanctity only if it leads to welfare and justice, this being the order decreed for all creation. "And the sky He hath uplifted; and He hath set the measure . . . ."[3] "O ye who believe! Be ye staunch in justice, witnesses for Allah, even though it be against yourselves or [your] parents or [your] kindred . . . ."[4]

The Koran, *sunnah,* and *ijmā'* concur in regarding justice as the ultimate aim of the Sharī'ah. Therefore, to fight in support of the oppressed is a deed deserving of God's reward. In this context, when the Islamic state declares war, it is within the bounds of the Sharī'ah provided the goal of the war is to establish justice and suppress tyranny.

This may be considered generally the only condition under which war is sanctioned, however immune to attack the Muslims may be, and notwithstanding the fact that such a war may not be a defensive one.

With this understanding, an Islamic state may join an organization like the United Nations if it can contribute

[2] Koran, 5:2.
[3] *Ibid.,* 55:7.
[4] *Ibid.,* 4:135.

thereby to the advancement of justice among peoples of the world. It may also propose a pact or commit itself to a pledge designed to repel tyranny and mete out justice to the weak.

Naturally, the Islamic state is not entitled to commit itself to or participate in a battle it is called to join unless it is convinced that it would be fighting in defense of a people oppressed and seeking justice, which justice could be secured only with the participation of the Muslim state.

Another pledge of early Islamic days which enjoined battle on behalf of the oppressed is to be found in the Truce of al-Ḥudaybiyah,[5] concluded between the Prophet and Quraysh. The fourth condition of the truce permitted third parties to choose sides as they wished. Accordingly, the Banu-Bakr allied themselves with Quraysh, and the Khuzā'ah tribe[6] with the Prophet. In the times of Jāhilīyah, the Khuzā'ah had been the allies of 'Abd-al-Muṭṭalib, and they sought to renew their pledge as given to the Prophet's grandfather.

The Prophet reaffirmed the terms of the alliance and renewed the pledge, adding two conditions: first, not to aid the Khuzā'ah if they turned oppressors, and second, to aid the Khuzā'ah if they became oppressed. Two copies of the pact were then drawn up, and each party was handed one.

At that time, the Khuzā'ah had not been converted to Islam; they were still polytheistic in their beliefs. The only relationship that existed between them and the Prophet was that tie they had had with his grandfather in pre-Islamic days, a tie that had not made any distinction between good and bad acts. The conditions added by the Prophet, therefore, point to the following.

First of all, he would not confirm the alliance on the basis of an undefined cooperation which might lead to action condemned by law, inasmuch as he was God's Messenger for the establishment of justice; rather, he expressly stated the condi-

[5] See Chapter 1, footnote 28.
[6] See Chapter 4, footnote 2.

tion that he would not support his allies the Khuzā'ah if they should turn oppressors.

Second, he would not withhold his support of an oppressed person, even though he might be a polytheist.

Third, he vowed to aid any oppressed person, including a polytheist or a member of a differing religion.

Fourth, the *sine qua non* of the legitimate war is *defense,* whether self-defense or voluntary defense of a victim of aggression deserving aid. In the absence of a pact, a Muslim state may choose neutrality; when it has a pact, as with the Khuzā'ah, it must honor the treaty and go to the support of the oppressed ally.

Prior to the advent of Islam, other religions made efforts to curb the excesses of war and to circumscribe its evils and calamities, but all genuine attempts succumbed before the incorrigibility of human nature.

Christianity came forward with a complete abnegation of war in the words of Jesus (may peace be with him) in the Gospel of Saint Matthew: "But I say unto you, That ye resist not evil: but whosoever shall smite thee on thy right cheek, turn to him the other also. . . . And whosoever shall compel thee to go a mile, go with him twain." [7] Those who adhere to the view that war should be abolished entirely also advert to the words of Jesus to Saint Peter: "Put up again thy sword into its place: for all they that take the sword shall perish with the sword." [8] It would appear from these Bible verses that Christianity forbids not only war but the bearing of arms as well, and in the early centuries the adherents of the Western Church resisted the idea of war, even war for self-defense, with all their power.

But Christians came to different conclusions in later times. The followers of the Eastern Church, in Byzantium, made no distinction between the person of the emperor, lord of this

[7] Matt. 5:39, 41 (the Christian Bible, King James version).
[8] Matt. 26:52.

world, and religious leadership. He had both spiritual and temporal powers. The Byzantines pursued a course contrary to that accepted by members of the Western Church. They did not stop at sanctioning the war forbidden by Christ, nor did they pursue a middle course confining war to self-defense or to the defense of the oppressed, as the Islamic Sharī'ah advocated: they consented to the emperor's sole possession of the right to declare war, and in gathering authority and power into his own hands he was bound by nothing but state interest.

The emergence of Christianity was a benefit and a blessing to humanity in the early centuries, for it taught the followers of Christ to resist the causes of evil and averted much bloodshed, plunder, spoliation, aggression, and tyranny that would otherwise have occurred. Although Christianity maintained its struggle for a long time, its adherents soon forgot the religion and mission of Christ and made of their lusts, ambitions, and interests the pretexts for oppressive wars which scarred humanity with their consuming fires in the East and in the West from the late Middle Ages until our present time.

Yet there were Christians who sacrified their lives to uphold their beliefs concerning the prevention of war and of the formation of armies. Still others made gigantic efforts to reconcile the decrees of the Gospels with the necessities of the state. These men made distinctions between legitimate war and forbidden war, and promoted discussions concerning the nature of the just war. To them, the just war was one declared by the ruler, and it conformed with sound intentions and truthfulness; he was to be free of selfish motives and savagery. In the eyes of those righteous Christians, war was a means for carrying out a just judgment rendered by the legitimate authorities; it was not instigated by egotism, and it was circumscribed by justice and clothed in mercy.

An investigation of the Christian views arising from the debates and discussions that have endured for over a thousand years points to the fact that righteous Christians did reach agreement on principles akin to the Islamic dicta for a sanctioned war—that is, a just war in aid of the oppressed.

Islamic principles could constitute the sound bases for the establishment of world justice, the exercise of mercy, and the display of human brotherhood through the curtailment of evil desires, the protection of human lives, and a durable peace built on a sacred foundation. Men of vision and intelligence cannot fail to draw upon the Islamic Sharī'ah in laying the foundation for international relations and world peace, for in the light of the noble and practical principles advocated by Muḥammad, it is possible to reinforce the pact of the United Nations and to avoid the utilization of war as a means of fulfilling human aims and ambitions. "And there may spring from you a nation who invite to goodness, and enjoin right conduct and forbid indecency." [9]

Pacts among nations may be guided by the spirit found in the verse of the Koran that reads,

> And if two parties of believers fall to fighting, then make peace between them. And if one party of them doeth wrong to the other, fight ye that which doeth wrong till it return unto the ordinance of Allah; then, if it return, make peace between them justly, and act equitably. Lo! Allah loveth the equitable.[10]

Undoubtedly, this order prescribed for the believers can form an order for all peoples. It is possible for Islamic states to enter into pacts to that effect, to fight to win respect for this order, and to turn back those who violate it.

The war waged in support of the oppressed advances no worldly aims, no national ambitions, and no revenge through envy and hatred; its purpose, rather, is to establish truth and avert falsehood. On the surface, it may appear to lead to a situation whereby a third party will intervene on the side of one party against another; yet this intervention can only be

[9] Koran, 3:104.
[10] *Ibid.*, 49:9.

undertaken for the purpose of defense, to repel attacks on the weak. Were we to consider human solidarity as the cause of progress and human justice as the foundation of that solidarity, then the act of taking a stand against the aggressor, that is, against the destruction of justice and hence of peace and progress, is an act constituting a defense of enlightenment. Under such circumstances, this act may be regarded even as the defense of the aggressor himself in that it prevents him from bringing evil upon himself.

It may be argued that such a stand constitutes an interference in the affairs of others bordering on aggression on the part of the Islamic state; it could be said that this state should concern itself only with its own affairs and should avoid the self-elected role of the policeman. But there is no escaping the fact that interference is unavoidable when the rights of the oppressed are at stake.

Thirteen centuries had elapsed from the date of Ḥilf al-Fuḍūl and the pledge of the Khuzā'ah before the European states attempted to bind themselves in the covenant of the League of Nations to a pledge similar to that desired by Islam—namely, to aid the oppressed—and thereby to affirm the principle of collective security through collective intervention in order to uphold the right and destroy falsehood.

In the last analysis, the criterion for judging an act is its underlying intention, as only the intention can render this act upright or corrupt. The purity of intention of an Islamic state that intervenes in a situation leading to war cannot be questioned, provided the act is motivated by good conscience attended by faith in a noble purpose which aims at the fulfillment of the will of God and the realization of the truth.[11]

[11] The author wishes to emphasize here that not a word of this chapter, or of the rest of this book, was intended to excuse or apologize for Muslims, their states, or their leaders; they hardly differ from their contemporaries all over the world, whether good or bad. The sole purpose of this writing is to transmit an understanding of Islam—its faith, jurisprudence, and way of life—as taught by the Koran and preached and practiced by Muḥammad, the Apostle of God.

# 16

## *The Rules and Etiquette of War*

*

When the Message of Muḥammad made its debut, war was the general rule, and it was firmly rooted in the mind of man and in his communal life. Islam began its history not by outlawing war but by restricting it to the deterrence of aggression and the defense of the oppressed. It thereby circumscribed the purpose of war, decreeing that war should cease when the enemy inclined to peace and that obligations based on pacts commanded priority over the rights of Muslims in certain legal cases. It surrounded warfare with limitations, rules, reasons, aims, and pledges and with common law, applicable also during battle, designed to render its occurrence less frequent and to minimize its horrors.

Recognizing the inherent and manifest evils of war, the Message of Muḥammad circumscribed warfare with common rules of right conduct (*adab*), defining its aims and limiting it to the repulsion of aggression, the protection of freedom of belief, and the termination of battle with just and durable agreements. Islam also applied special rules of conduct to war effective during combat that were to be observed by the warring parties.

Whenever developments between Muslims and other peoples seem likely to lead to war, it becomes a matter of duty for Muslims to warn their enemy of their intentions and to allow him time to answer and negotiate if he should so desire.

Some jurists have maintained that this interval that follows what is called today the "final ultimatum" must be of sufficient duration to enable the enemy to alert all sections of his country. Such conduct conforms to modern international law.

Certain states nowadays prefer surprise attacks on their enemies without any previous warning. Preliminary precautions prior to attack are such that the aggression-bent state can surprise its enemies completely by pretending all along to favor peace; often the true motives and pretenses for waging war may not be revealed prior to combat. Champions of modern civilization have become skilled in deception to a degree unprecedented in the history of nations. They have even concluded agreements deliberately designed to lull the other party into a sense of false security, for to catch the other party off balance assures more successful results.

This is a new form of conduct in war, or, more appropriately, a misuse of the old forms of war. There is nothing more distasteful to Islam than this, and the tenets of Muslim law reject it in spirit and in practice. Those who resort to such conduct are considered criminals deserving the wrath of God.

Along with providing that the opponent should be warned of impending war when negotiations have been terminated, the Islamic Sharī'ah also does not sanction surprise attack techniques as utilized by modern states. It respects the sanctity and security of person and abode of the opponent's citizenry in Muslim territory during the course of war. Under the provisions of the Sharī'ah, those foreign subjects (*musta'min*) [1] are entitled to rights that cannot be violated by reason of war between the Muslims and their country of origin, even though they reside in a land judicially controlled by the enemy of their native country. They cannot be mo-

[1] The words *mustajīr* and *musta'min* do not exactly mean "protected." They actually together mean one who asks to be allowed to have protection, friendship, settlement for work, et cetera—in other words, anybody whom the Muslims accept in their land as a dweller or settler for business or farming or any other trade or profession.

lested; nor can their possessions be confiscated or their lives jeopardized. They are entitled to security of life and property until arrangements have been made for them to return to their original homeland and enter the protection of their people. Then and only then should they be exposed to conditions applicable in war between combatants. The Koran says, "And if anyone of the idolaters seeketh thy protection [O Muḥammad], then protect him so that he may hear the word of Allah, and afterward convey him to his place of safety." [2]

Muslims have taken considerable precautions to respect the rights of the *musta'min*. As a matter of fact, Muslim jurists are of the opinion that the head of a Muslim state should set no time limit for the enjoyment of security by citizens of a nation at war with that state in order to eliminate the possibility of having to settle affairs under adverse conditions. The just treatment meted out to citizens of nations at war with the Muslim state reached the point where they could enjoy complete freedom while war raged between both nations, provided these citizens observed the laws of the host country, were honest in their conduct, and did not conspire to harm citizens of the host country.

Islam has established this relationship with those who enjoy the sanctity of protection during conditions of war on the basis of equity and justice. In the last analysis, are not wars but the result of the loss of equity and justice?

One of the finest episodes illustrating the respect due a man who seeks neighborliness is told of Wāṣil ibn-'Aṭa', leader of the Mu'tazilah.[3] Wāṣil and some of his friends fell into the hands of the Khārijites (Khawārij),[4] a Muslim group that observed the tenets of religion rigidly and were regarded as most prejudiced in their views. Anticipating trouble, even

[2] Koran, 9:6.

[3] The Mu'tazilah, an early theological school of Islam, were the first to champion "rationalism"; they declared the dogma of the creation of the Koran, and al-Ma'mūn legalized the dogma in A.D. 827.

[4] See Chapter 4, footnote 7.

death, Wāṣil asked his friends for permission to handle them. The Khārijites inquired about his faith and that of his friends. In reply, Wāṣil declared that they were polytheists seeking protection, and would like to hear the words of God and to learn of His promises. The Khārijites then undertook to teach them their doctrines; later they said, "Depart as friends, for you are brethren." To this Wāṣil replied, "This is not for you to bestow, for Allah (may He be honored and glorified) has said in the Koran, 'And if anyone of the idolaters seeketh thy protection [O Muḥammad], then protect him so that he may hear the word of Allah, and afterward convey him to his place of safety.' [5] Therefore, escort us to our place of safety." When confronted in such a manner, the Khārijites granted them their request, and escorted them until they reached safety.

This episode shows how protection accorded those who sought safety of abode was, in the view of certain champions of the Message of Muḥammad, a greater duty than the protection required of Muslims for each other.

One sees in the basic rules in the Message of Muḥammad regarding the conduct of war that noble principle forbidding the extension of warfare to or the harming of noncombatants. The rules decree against the killing of the aged, the young, women, the handicapped, those who have withdrawn from life to worship or meditate, those who have refrained from participating in battle, the mass of workers, farmers, and tradesmen—in other words, those who today are called civilians. It is not lawful to kill civilians. The Sharī'ah has provided precautionary measures to insulate civilians from the horrors and evils of war and to confine injury to the fighting forces. Jurists have advocated even the temporary cessation of hostilities should those whose death is not permitted be exposed to death between the ranks of the fighting forces. If we

[5] Koran, 9:6.

consider the extent of involvement of civilians during World War II—people indiscriminately bombed and blasted by explosives from their lands and abodes—we will perceive the merits of the Islamic injunctions governing conduct in war.

Is respect for human lives not to be found in this age? Is it not possible in modern warfare to apply the sword only to the bearer of the sword? Are the extremes of conduct in warfare today any different from the methods used by the Mongols in the days of Genghis Khan and his successors in their barbaric massacre of noncombatants and destruction of cities and towns, which have remained classic examples of brutality and savagery?

What is wrought today by the air and artillery bombardment of civilians is more barbaric than the methods employed by that Mongolian tyrant of seven and a half centuries ago. The destruction of all sanctified places today through unrestricted air raids defies comparison. The Islamic Sharī'ah condemns and shuns such methods, regardless of whether the Islamic state is strong or weak, triumphant or defeated. Even if Muslim jurists sanction retaliation in kind against indiscriminate destruction and killing once the enemy has begun, they certainly do not fail to agree that the Islamic state ought not to take the initiative. Those who admit retaliation in kind recall the words of the Almighty, "And one who attacketh you, attack him in like manner as he attacked you," [6] and "The reward of an evil deed is an evil the like thereof. But whosoever pardoneth and amendeth, his wage is the affair of Allah." [7] It is clear in the words and spirit of these and other verses that the purpose of retaliation in kind is to warn the enemy and persuade him to refrain from committing such crimes. The truth "But whosoever pardoneth and amendeth, his wage is the affair of Allah" is also an assurance of the Lawgiver's wish not to sanction retaliation for hostile acts, even

[6] *Ibid.*, 2:194.
[7] *Ibid.*, 42:40.

though they are contrary to the precepts of mercy and proper conduct.[8]

Would that the rules of conduct for war sanctioned in the Message of Muḥammad might govern the conduct of states which today resort to slaying civilians, destroying establishments, and burning people, their possessions, and the products of their land in order to compel them to submit and lay down their arms!

Where lies the precedent for the actions of certain modern civilized states which utilize strafing from airplanes, bombs, and machineguns in fighting bedouins who possess no more of the weapons of war than rifles handed down to them from the last century—states which turn machineguns on tents and on camels and sheep roaming in their grazing grounds?

Truly it is time for men to remember their God and the beliefs preached by Moses, Jesus, and Muḥammad, and to create rules of conduct for war which will minimize destructiveness. And where can we find such rules of conduct in warfare set forth better than in the Message of Muḥammad, which decrees that war should not aim at distortion and destruction but at making the word of God supreme?—for the word of God stands only for truth, justice, and equity, and encompasses all peoples.

This principle, engendered by humanitarianism and based on mercy, forbade the Muslims in their wars to force their enemy into submission by starving the warring nation or by preventing sinews of life like medicine and clothing from reaching the nonbelligerents.

Modern warfare has become so ruthless that armies in retreat resort to a scorched-earth policy, even if it means death for their compatriots as well as their enemies. Such a practice

[8] I firmly believe that modern technology and science have made the annihilation of life on our planet possible in war. It is quite clear that Islam forbids such devastation, and any Muslim jurist, guided by the letter and spirit of the Koran, would rather suffer than engage in retaliation in such circumstances, for it would annihilate the enemy's population.

is not sanctioned under any circumstance by the Sharī'ah. Attacks on the possessions of inhabitants left behind by advancing or retreating Islamic armies would be inconceivable. Muslims are strictly forbidden by their religion to burn plants, cut down trees, and deprive resident civilians of their means of livelihood in land that lies in the path of advancing and withdrawing armies.

Muslim jurists agree that it is permissible to kill in battle adult male polytheist fighters. They also agree, regardless of other differences, that it is unlawful to kill women and children if they do not participate in war. One can deduce from this that it is unlawful to cause harm to civilians, that is, those who do not actually participate in war, or to destroy buildings and vegetation.

Rabāḥ ibn-Rabī'ah[9] has related that, while out on a raid in the company of the Prophet, they came upon a slain woman. Standing over her body, Muḥammad declared, "She should not have been killed!" And immediately he dispatched one of his companions with instructions to Khālid ibn-al-Walīd[10] not to kill a single child, woman, or laborer. Further, the Prophet is not known to have ever killed an animal.

Mālik[11] relates that the Caliph Abu-Bakr once said, "You will encounter those who claim they have devoted themselves to God. Leave them alone to do what they have chosen to do; and do not kill a woman, a boy, or an elderly person."

Zayd ibn-Wahb[12] received a message from 'Umar ibn-al-Khaṭṭāb which stated, "Do not indulge in excesses, or deceive, or kill a child; and be fearful of God when you are dealing with peasants." 'Umar also said, "Kill not the aged, a woman,

9 A Companion of the Prophet.

10 See Chapter 4, footnote 12.

11 A leading jurist of Islam (*c.* A.D. 715-795) who formulated the school of jurisprudence named after him (Mālikite), and whose compendium is one of the oldest bodies of the Muslim law on tort.

12 One of the Arab generals in the Muslim conquests of Syria and Iraq under the Caliph 'Umar.

or a child; and avoid doing so even when armies meet and when raids are conducted."

The Imām Ibn-Rushd [13] said that Abu-Bakr warned against cutting down trees and destroying establishments. It was not possible for Abu-Bakr to differ with the Prophet of God, although he knew that Muḥammad had cut down the palm trees of the Banu-Naḍīr. The jurists explain this as a special case by asserting that Abu-Bakr knew of the incident which concerned only this tribe, referred to in the Koranic chapter "al-Ḥashr" ("The Exile").

In connection with this incident, Muslims agree on the prohibition of exemplary punishment. The Koran does not relate the episode of the Banu-Naḍīr in detail but only refers to it in the course of narration and preaching. Likewise, the incident of the Banu-Qurayẓah was referred to only casually in the course of preaching, in this verse in the chapter "al-Aḥzāb" ("The Clans" or "The Confederates"):

> And He brought those of the People of the Scripture who supported them down from their strongholds, and cast panic into their hearts. Some ye slew, and ye made captive some. And He caused you to inherit their land and their houses and their wealth, and land ye have not trodden. Allah is Able to do all things.[14]

[13] Also known as Averroës (A.D. 1126-1198), a philosopher and commentator of Aristotelian philosophy whose ideas influenced the development of Scholastic philosophy in thirteenth-century Europe.

[14] Koran, 33:26-27. The incident of the Banu-Qurayẓah is beset by known and unknown causes. What is known of the case is that they betrayed their pledge and took advantage of difficult circumstances when the Confederates (the Aḥzāb) besieged al-Madīnah. Muslim eyes went astray and their hearts lumped in their throats from fear. The Banu-Qurayẓah then reneged on their pledge and stabbed the Muslims in the back. Another reason is that they fell under the jurisdiction of the chief of the Aws, Sa'd ibn-Ma'ādh, since they were his associates, who meted out judgment to them accordingly. They surrendered on a condition, and the condition was theirs to observe. It is also said that the death sentences which they received were in accordance with Jewish law (since they were a Jewish tribe), and that Sa'd judged them by their own laws. The episode as a whole has an air of mystery about it which leads us to believe there were additional causes unknown to us.

There is not a single decree in the Koran allowing the slaying or enslaving of a prisoner, and it has never been said that the Prophet enslaved a captive. The Koran clearly grants the head of the Muslim state one of two choices (no third!)—grace or ransom: ". . . when ye have routed them, then [make] fast [their] bonds; and afterward [give them] either grace or ransom till the war lay down its burdens." [15] Ibn-Rushd relates[16] that the consensus of the Companions of the Prophet was that the slaying of a captive was unlawful.

According to the common precepts of the law, it is unlawful to slay civilians or soldiers after they have surrendered. Should the head of any Muslim state deviate from this precept, as the Prophet did with the Banu-Qurayẓah, it is for special circumstances and reasons requiring an exceptional judgment.

The sanction that certain Muslim jurists give the slaying of polytheists and idolaters does not accord, in my view, with the decrees and spirit of the Koran regarding the application of force or with the deeds of the Prophet and the Muslims in their conquests during the forty years from the Hijrah until the last days of the orthodox caliphs (A.D. 661). Those jurists who sanction death because of unbelief are not upright thinkers in a religion which requires the Muslims to pay compensation (*al-diyah*) to a polytheist whose people enjoy treaty relations with Muslims and are therefore entitled to equal justice: "And if he cometh of a folk between whom and you there is a covenant, then the blood money [compensation] must be paid unto his folk and [also] a believing slave must be set free." [17]

If death for nonbelief were permissible, as certain jurists claim, the Prophet would have put to death the unbelievers of Mecca when he conquered it as well as the Hawāzin following the Battle of Ḥunayn, and he would not have allied himself

[15] Koran, 47:4.

[16] Citing al-Ḥasan ibn-Muḥammad al-Tamīmi, a Companion of the Prophet.

[17] Koran, 4:92.

with the Khuzā'ah while they were still unbelievers. And the Muslims in their conquests from India to France would have become a plague on earth sparing no unbeliever from death. Many episodes have been related about the Prophet's pardons and acts of mercy toward powerful enemies and slayers of his most cherished friends and relatives. The biographies of his life reveal his merciful treatment of 'Ikramah ibn-abu-Jahl and of Ṣafwān ibn-Umayyah, two enemies whose fathers were also his enemies; his forgiveness of Waḥshi, the slayer of his uncle Ḥamzah, although he was but an Abyssinian slave of no significance; and his pardoning of Abu-Sufyān ibn-al-Ḥārith after the latter had insulted and expressed his enmity against Muḥammad's preachings. Such examples are clear testimony of the justice that does not permit the slaying of civilians or prisoners or those who incline toward peace.

The Prophet was informed after one of the battles that youngsters had been caught between the ranks and killed. He was seized by deep sorrow, and some said to him, "Why do you grieve? Are they not the children of polytheists?" The Prophet became very annoyed and replied, "They are more worthy than you, for they are innocent; are you not sons of polytheists? Beware of killing children! Beware of killing children!"

Bukhārī related that a funeral procession once passed by. The Prophet stood up out of reverence, and his companions followed suit, though saying to him, "It is the funeral of a Jew." To this he replied, "Is it not that of a soul! If you behold a funeral, then stand."

This respect for the human being is general, and allows for no exceptions. The slaying of noncombatants or prisoners for unbelief alone cannot be permitted.

I am totally convinced of what I have said concerning the decrees prohibiting the starving or slaying of civilians and captives, the destruction of property and land, and the use of exemplary punishment. I emphasize that the modern methods of war and their attendant destruction—the aimless artillery bombardment without previous warning of children and women, the aged and the sick, planters and laborers, on land, at sea, or from the air—are not sanctioned by the Islamic Sharī'ah.

Tradition (*sunnah*) and common law (*'urf*) provide ample rules for proper conduct in war, such as respect for the enemy's emissaries and their safe conduct and kindness to captives who, insofar as they are entitled to such benevolence, become equal in this respect with the orphans and poor of Islam: "And feed with food the needy wretch, the orphan, and the prisoner, for love of Him [saying]: We feed you, for the sake of Allah only. We wish for no reward nor thanks from you." [18]

18 Koran, 76:8-9.

# 17

# *Lasting Peace*

*

There is a sophisticated but perhaps exaggerated theory among some Muslim jurists and Orientalist scholars regarding *dār al-ḥarb* and *dār al-Islām,* that a state of war is in fact perpetual in the former until Islam is established politically, while in the latter permanent and uninterrupted peace prevails. But it is not exaggerated to say that the provisions of the Message of Muḥammad call only for a lasting, universal peace. We have explained the circumstances which gave rise to the permission to fight and the purpose as well as the range of sanctioned war. We have also shown that the war sanctioned by the Sharī'ah is an exception to the general rule calling for peace among all men.

Ample testimony for this can be found in the Koran, *sunnah,* and the history of the Muslims.

The Prophet said, "Do not desire to meet the enemy [in battle], and ask God to preserve the peace." He discouraged hopes for war, even with the worst of enemies, and besought God to perpetuate the blessings of peace.

Bukhārī related that a man approached the Prophet and said, "There is the man who fights for gain, the man who fights for fame, and the man who fights for status, but who fights for the way of God?" The Prophet replied, "He who fights for the word of God to become supreme"—not for worldly gains or ambition—"fights for the way of God."

In the days of nascent Islam, when the early believers had to defend themselves in Yathrib against the attack of the Aḥzāb (the Confederation), the Prophet would help move dirt while they dug trenches, reciting:

> O Allah, were it not for You we would not have found
> the path, nor believed, nor prayed.
> Send down Your calm and strengthen our stand once we
> meet them [in battle].
> It is they who covet this [war] upon us, for they desire
> the hostility[1] which we refused.

Had it not been for such aggression, which had to be met, peace, which constitutes the rule, would have prevailed.

Further evidence, in letter and in spirit, can be seen in the following verses of the Koran:

> O ye who believe! Come, all of you, into peaceful submission [unto Him]; and follow not the footsteps of the devil. Lo! he is an open enemy for you.[2]
>
> And if they incline to peace, incline thou also to it, and trust in Allah. Lo! He is the Hearer, the Knower. And if they would deceive thee, then lo! Allah is sufficient for thee.[3]
>
> . . . and say not unto one who offereth you peace: "Thou art not a believer," seeking the chance profits of this life [so that ye may dispoil him].[4]
>
> Allah forbiddeth you not, with regard to those who warred not against you on account of religion and drove you not out from your homes, from dealing kindly and justly with them. Lo! Allah loveth the just dealers. Allah only forbiddeth you, with regard to those who war against you on account of religion and have driven you out from your homes and helped to drive you out, from making friends of them. Whosoever maketh friends of them —[all] such are wrongdoers.[5]

1 "Hostility" translates the Arabic *fetnah,* which actually means forced conversion or apostasy.

2 Koran, 2:208.

3 *Ibid.,* 8:61-62.

4 *Ibid.,* 4:94.

5 *Ibid.,* 60:8-9.

So, if they hold aloof from you and wage not war against you and offer you peace, Allah alloweth you no way against them.[6]

Then witness the spirit of peace and love that radiates from these noble verses:

Unto this, then, summon [O Muḥammad]. And be thou upright as thou art commanded, and follow not their lusts, but say: I believe in whatever Scripture Allah hath sent down, and I am commanded to be just among you. Allah is our Lord and your Lord. Unto us our works and unto you your works; no argument between us and you. Allah will bring us together, and unto Him is the journeying.[7]

And say unto those who have received the Scripture and those who read not: Have ye [too] surrendered [to God]? If they surrender, then truly they are rightly guided, and if they turn away, then it is thy duty only to convey the Message [unto them].[8]

Tell those who believe to forgive those who hope not for the days of Allah, in order that He may requite folk what they used to earn.[9]

And argue not with the People of the Scripture unless it be in [a way] that is better, save with such of them as do wrong . . . .[10]

For each We have appointed a divine law and a traced-out way. Had Allah willed He could have made you one community. But that He may try you by that which He hath given you [He hath made you as ye are]. So vie one with another in good works. Unto Allah ye will all return.[11]

And if thy Lord willed, all who are in the earth would have believed together. Wouldst thou [Muḥammad] compel men until they are believers? [12]

6 *Ibid.,* 4:90.

7 *Ibid.,* 42:15.

8 *Ibid.,* 3:20. "Those who read not" are the polytheists of Arabia.

9 *Ibid.,* 45:14.

10 *Ibid.,* 29:46. "Do wrong" translates the Arabic *ẓalam,* which combines the meanings *wrong* and *aggression,* as does the verb *baghat.*

11 *Ibid.,* 5:48.

12 *Ibid.,* 10:100.

And We have not sent thee [O Muḥammad] save as a bringer of good tidings and a warner unto all mankind . . . .[13]

Certain critics contend that the chapters of the Koran revealed at Mecca abound with the spirit of love and forgiveness while those revealed at al-Madīnah bear down heavily on infidels and hypocrites and incite to battle and war. Such an assertion is untenable; the Book of Allah is indivisible, and most of the verses relating to war encourage patience, self-sacrifice, and strength during a war that is *already in progress,* a war to be concluded when an assuring peace is in sight. This conduct, therefore, is a consequence and not a cause of war. But let us look at some of the verses revealed at al-Madīnah:

There is no compulsion in religion. The right direction is henceforth distinct from error.[14]

Say: Obey Allah and obey the Messenger. But if ye turn away, then [it is] for him [to do] only that wherewith ye have been charged, and for you [to do] only that wherewith ye have been charged. If ye obey him, ye will go aright. But the Messenger hath no other charge than to convey [the Message] plainly.[15]

And the Almighty said to His Messenger: "Thou wilt not cease to discover treachery from all save a few of them. But bear with them and pardon them. Lo! Allah loveth the kindly." [16]

Following all the Prophet's preaching, at both al-Madīnah and Mecca, Islam relied solely on reason and resorted to the sword for defense only. This is amply borne out in the long history of the diffusion of the Message in the world. According to Sir Thomas Arnold,[17] the spiritual conquests of Islam

13 *Ibid.,* 34:28.

14 *Ibid.,* 2:256.

15 *Ibid.,* 24:54.

16 *Ibid.,* 5:14.

17 See Sir Thomas Arnold, *The Preaching of Islam: A History of the Propagation of the Muslim Faith* (2nd ed.; London: Constable & Co., 1913).

were not affected by the decline of the Islamic state or the decrease in its political strength. Sir Thomas maintains that in the days of its political defeats Islam achieved its greatest spiritual victories.

In the annals of Islam there are two important events which testify to this. First, when the Mongols and Seljuk Turks trod on the necks of the Muslims, Islam conquered their hearts, for although they were the conquerors, they adopted the religion of the conquered. In this transformation Islam was assisted by neither sword nor authority. Second, if we turn once more to the Truce of al-Ḥudaybiyah, which distressed some Muslims because the terms called for the sheathing of the sword for ten years, we discover that it was in this period that Islam achieved its greatest spiritual victory. The peaceful conquests for the faith ensuing from the Truce of al-Ḥudaybiyah paved the way for the conquest of the Meccans' hearts and the conversion of all Arabia.

The military triumphs of the Muslims were not the product of an organized standing army.[18] The idea of an organized army was not considered until the Muslims had common boundaries and frontiers established with their enemies. Only at that time[19] did an organized standing army come to be regarded as essential to the safety of Muslim lands. This was more than half a century after the death of Muḥammad.

To the Muslims, then, war is accidental; peace is the rule. And for that reason, Islam's international relations are based on the concept of lasting, universal peace, disturbed only by aggression.

18 The great conquests (A.D. 634-644) were made by tribes fighting as separate units of volunteers, which destroyed the two greatest empires of the world in that era.

19 *C.* A.D. 685-705.

# VI

## *On the Dissemination of the Message*

*

## 18

# *Dissemination of the Message Among the Pagans*

*

The minds of many, Muslims and non-Muslims alike, have been firmly impressed with the belief that the Message of Muḥammad appeared and spread under the shadow of the sword. They believe that the Arab tribes which bore the Book of Allah in their hearts carried the sword of truth in their hands as they pushed on to the West and to the East and utilized that sword to force people to bow to the Koran. Nothing is farther from the truth or more revealing of superficial and distorted inquiry. It is only proper that we regard this matter with more care in order to distinguish truth from error as we follow the course of the dissemination of the Message during different periods of time.[1]

Perhaps the reason this false notion spread was that the emergence of the Message outside the Arabian peninsula coincided with the rise of the Islamic state; this has led some to confuse the conquests of the polity with religious conversions, and explains why they cannot distinguish between the adherence of peoples to the faith and their acceptance of the message of *tawḥīd* (belief in the oneness of God) on the one hand and, on the other, their submission to the political authority of the rising Islamic state.[2]

1 See the discussion at the beginning of Chapter 13.

2 " 'Islam' signifies resignation or submission to God, and 'Musulman' means 'subject.' Allah is the One God, and it is therefore logical that all His serv-

There is a tendency to ignore the fact that Mecca and other places were conquered by an army consisting of thousands of the oppressed who had accepted the guidance of the new faith prior to the period of conquest. These had been persecuted publicly for becoming Muslims and forced to forsake their homeland as they crossed the sea twice, seeking refuge in Abyssinia, and fled subsequently to Yathrib, imploring the protection of every person of ability and means.

When Muḥammad called the people, the first to respond were members of his household; and there were those who believed and those who rejected his Message. He preached secretly. Among those who accepted the faith were some of the nobles of his people and the strong men of the Jāhilīyah, and also the forsaken and the slaves. But neither group could protect the Prophet, and the Qurayshis forced him to accept voluntary exile for his followers in a hillside retreat, where they remained for nearly three years, isolated and neglected by the members of Mecca's various tribes, the partisans of the Thaqīf tribe and others. When the confinement ended, Muḥammad began to take his Message to the tribes. Soon he returned from al-Ṭā'if, rejected by that city, and he was able to re-enter Mecca only under the protection of al-Muṭ'im ibn-'Adiy, a Qurayshi and an unbeliever, who guarded him courageously, motivated by manly virtue.

He continued to preach both secretly and openly and to expose himself and his followers to all sorts of harm until, during the season of pilgrimage, he met members of the first

---

ants should regard it as their duty to enforce obedience to Allah upon the unbelievers. What they [the Arabs] proposed was not, as many have thought, their conversion, but their subjection. And this subjection they enforced wherever they went. After the conquest they asked nothing better than to appropriate the science and art of the infidels as part of their booty; they would cultivate them to the glory of Allah. They would even adopt the institutions of the unbelievers in so far as these were useful to them" (Henri Pirenne, *Mohammed and Charlemagne,* tr. Bernard Miall [reprinted; New York: Meridian Books, 1961], pp. 150-151).

*bay'ah,*[3] young men of Yathrib (later al-Madīnah), who prevailed upon him to migrate to their city. And so he fled from the jaws of death to the bosom of friendly Yathrib. Yet even in exile his enemies would not let him rest. When they reached after him with evil hands, he went to meet them and encountered their forces at Badr, where Allah granted them permission to wage battle in these verses:

> Permission to fight is given to those against whom war is made, because they have been wronged; and Allah is indeed Able to give them victory; those who have been driven from their homes unjustly only because they said: Our Lord is Allah—For had it not been for Allah's repelling some men by means of others, cloisters and churches and synagogues and mosques, wherein the name of Allah is oft mentioned, would assuredly have been pulled down. Verily Allah helpeth one who helpeth Him. Lo! Allah is Strong, Almighty—[We will give victory to] those who, if We give them power in the land, establish worship and pay the poor tax and enjoin kindness and forbid iniquity.[4]

In its forthright and simple enumeration of the reasons for sanctioning battle, this quotation lucidly portrays the situation in a manner which should erase all doubt from the minds of those who maintain that the sword was the companion of the Book.

For fifteen years prior to the Battle of Badr, the Prophet continued to summon with wisdom and fair exhortation and to tolerate oppression; but when there was no recourse left to him other than force to defend himself and his followers, Allah granted permission, and the Battle of Badr took place. Here the weak humiliated the mighty; and in the hollows of al-Qalīb[5] one can find the remains of the virile men of Qu-

[3] The term is used to refer to the pledge of allegiance given by the early Muslims first to Muḥammad and then to the first four caliphs as a way of confirming the election to the caliphate.

[4] Koran, 22:39-41.

[5] Al-Qalīb is the name of a dry well near Badr. When the battle was over, the Prophet's forces deposited the bodies of the dead Qurayshis in the well as a means—albeit makeshift—of granting the dead a burial.

raysh who for years had inflicted torture on those who had accepted the religion of Allah out of faith and reflection.

The Prophet returned to al-Madīnah, still exercising patience and continuing to summon; but Quraysh and its partisans would not be tolerant, carrying their attack on him to al-Madīnah itself. Three years later, at al-Ḥudaybiyah, the Prophet seized the opportunity for peace and accepted conditions that he would have rejected had his Message been based on the sword, since these conditions were not pleasing to his Companions, who considered them deplorable, especially when they had not engaged the enemy or encountered defeat. Muḥammad realized that his Message could not be disseminated by the sword if it were to be welcomed: he knew his mission would conquer only through peace. The Truce of al-Ḥudaybiyah was a triumph; because of it Islam spread, and its call was heard and responded to all over Arabia. The Koranic revelation pertaining to victory[6] may have been revealed after al-Ḥudaybiyah. The provisions of the chapter were realized, and in the days of the truce, men entered the religion of Islam in waves; for Islam was the religion of Allah, resting on fair exhortation and sanctioning battle only to protect its freedom—and for no other reason.

The history of the Message in the Arabian peninsula is the history of the patience of the Muslims. Every inquiry into the details of Islamic history reveals this truth and confirms the actions of the Prophet. The decrees of the Almighty call for patience:

> There is no compulsion in religion. The right direction is henceforth distinct from error.[7]
>
> Wouldst thou [Muḥammad] compel men until they are believers? [8]

6 Chapter 48, "al-Fatḥ."
7 Koran, 2:256.
8 *Ibid.*, 10:100.

He whom Allah guideth, he indeed is led aright, and he whom He sendeth astray, for him thou wilt not find a guiding friend.[9]

If the intention of the Prophet was to tolerate evil in Mecca and al-Madīnah and to accept truce terms unsatisfactory to his Companions, some might ask, why did he go out of the peninsula and lead armies into battle against the Byzantines in Syria? Was this not in the interest of converting by the sword?

Those who do not understand how war came about between the Prophet and the Byzantines and their Arab subjects are referred to *The History of Transjordan and Its Tribes,* by Colonel Frederick Beck, who consulted reliable Muslim and other writings. According to Beck, incidentally, the first Muslim to be martyred for his faith was Farwah ibn-'Umar al-Judhāmi, in the region that is today Jordan, in A.D. 627-628 (6 A.H.). Farwah was the Byzantine prefect over 'Ammān[10] who adopted Islam and sent the Prophet gifts.[11] When the Byzantines learned of this, they sought to persuade him to renounce Islam, but he refused. They imprisoned him, and then crucified him at 'Ufrā[12] in Palestine.

In July of the year A.D. 629, the Prophet dispatched a detachment numbering fifteen men to the borders of Jordan to summon people to the true religion and to learn more about the Byzantines and their movements. They were attacked at a place known as Ṭallah, located between al-Karak and Ṭufaylah, and all but one were killed. At the same time, the Prophet sent an emissary, al-Ḥārith ibn-'Umayr, to the ruling prince of the Ghassān[13] in Syria, calling upon him to accept

9 *Ibid.,* 18:17.

10 In his *Ta'rīkh al-Rasūl* (ed. de Goeje [Leyden, 1881-1882], vol. I), 'Abd-al-Malik ibn-Hishām, the first biographer of the Prophet, maintains that Farwah was prefect also over Ma'ān, which then included most of today's Jordan.

11 A gray mule, a stallion, a donkey, linen shirts, and silken robes.

12 A watering place.

13 A Byzantine Christian Arab tribe of south Arabian origin that held dynastic sway over lands north of Arabia under Byzantine tutelage and enjoyed a

Islam, but the emissary was seized and killed. Again, about the same time, the emissaries of the Prophet arrived from the north of the peninsula bearing news of military preparations in the Byzantine camps and of the presence of the Emperor Heraclius among tribes allied to him.[14]

Such provocations led the Prophet to send an expedition to the frontier of Jordan to punish the killers of his emissaries and to investigate the strength of his enemies, the extent of their preparations, and the reasons for their massing troops on the borders of the peninsula. In September, 629, the Prophet assembled a force of three thousand at Jawf near al-Madīnah under the comand of Zayd ibn-Ḥārithah, who was to march his warriors toward Syria. The force proceeded until it approached the outskirts of Balqā', where it was met by the Byzantine and allied Arab hordes of Heraclius; battle was then joined at the village of Mu'tah near al-Karak.

The Muslims displayed great bravery in this battle, although they were relatively few in number compared to the size of the enemy's force. When the leader, Zayd, met martyrdom, Ja'far ibn-abu-Ṭālib took over, as decreed by the Prophet. His right arm bearing the standard was cut off, whereupon he grabbed it with his left; when the left arm was in turn cut off, he gathered the standard with the stubs of his upper arms and held on until he was killed, having incurred, it is said, no less than fifty wounds. When this news reached the Prophet, he declared, "May Allah grant him in their stead a pair of wings so that he may fly wherever he pleases in Paradise," and thereafter he was referred to as "Ja'far the Flier."

When Ja'far was killed, the standard passed on to 'Abd-Allah ibn-Rawāḥah, who fought until he was killed, whereupon

---

high standard of culture. They were the first outside the peninsula to accept Islam, which they came to regard as the religion of the Arabs.

14 Heraclius's army included tribes from Bahrā', Judhām, 'Ali, and Balqā'.

Khālid ibn-al-Walīd took over and withdrew with the army to al-Madīnah.

Such were the circumstances surrounding the outbreak of war between the Prophet and the Byzantines. It is clear that the Byzantines provoked the hostilities by crucifying Farwah for refusing to apostatize; their actions also indicate the persecution they undertook and the jealousy that dominated their thoughts and conduct. There is no reason to doubt that the Byzantines, motivated by pride and fear of peaceful preaching, resorted to force, harsh methods, and treachery. There was no alternative left to the Prophet, therefore, but to defend the freedom of the faith.

In the narrative of Beck we also read the story of the Christian family known as 'Azīzāt, who lived in Mu'tah in southern Jordan. When they learned that the Islamic army was approaching, two brothers of this family went out to greet it and then opened the gates of the village to it, offering food and drink to the soldiers. One of the brothers subsequently became a Muslim; the other remained a Christian. In gratitude for their assistance, the Prophet decreed that no poll tax or land tax should be levied on their descendants, and his decree was respected for thirteen centuries. It was not until 1911, following the revolt of the inhabitants of al-Karak, that the Turkish government began to collect taxes from them. The 'Azīzāt family live today in Mādiya, where they constitute a powerful clan.

The fact that the Prophet decreed that no poll or land taxes be levied on certain Christians and their descendants, a decree respected by Muslims for hundreds of years, is a testimony to an unusual forbearance, a state of will which would not permit the employment of the sword as a means of propagating and guiding the faith.

As for the conquest of Mecca by force, a quick perusal of the struggle of Muḥammad with his people, Quraysh, is sufficient to show that right was on his side. Adjudication by the sword between the two parties was inescapable, even if we were to assume that Muḥammad was not a Prophet but simply a kind and brave person who stuck by his opinions and that for these opinions he and his followers were thrown out of their homes.

As quoted in the Koran, the Qurayshis declared, "If we were to follow the right path with thee [Muḥammad], we should be torn out of our land." [15] Indeed, the Qurayshis had assumed for themselves religious overlordship and trusteeship of the Ka'bah; by this means they were able to supervise the pilgrimage and protect the gods and idols of the Arab tribes, and consequently to gain political and economic influence throughout the peninsula. The Qurayshis realized, however, that they were weak and that their control was owing not to their numbers but to the order that prevailed in the Jāhilīyah, against which the Prophet was preaching his new faith. The verse above expresses clearly the loyalty of Quraysh to this order; and had the tribe accepted the guidance of Muḥammad, it would indeed have become insignificant, as its members asserted. They could hardly tolerate the Message or his Message. For this reason, force was ordained from the start.

When the Khuzā'ah and Bakr tribes resorted to war against each other after the Truce of al-Ḥudaybiyah had been concluded, Quraysh did not hesitate to run to the support of Banu-Bakr; it cavalierly disregarded the truce, and reverted once more to the judgment of the sword. The Prophet responded to the challenge. He let the sword be the judge in a struggle that lasted for twenty years and was decided finally in favor of the Muslims on the day Mecca was conquered. According to the testimony of history, the Prophet ordered the leaders of his army not to fight unless they were resisted. And his treatment of the Qurayshis on the day of conquest is positive proof that the sword was not instrumental in spreading the Message.

It was not because of any religious prejudice or desire to

[15] Koran, 28:57.

compel others to join Islam that fighting took place in Mecca, the city which Allah did not permit to be used thereafter for fighting and in which the Prophet was allowed only one hour's fighting on one day, as he said. His purpose rather was to end religious persecution in order that people might have the right to choose their belief without intimidation or compulsion.

Accordingly, when Ṣafwān ibn-Umayyah, the Quraysh chief, surrendered and asked the Prophet to grant him the choice between leaving Mecca and joining Islam within two months after the conquest, the Prophet replied, "You have four times the choice." Ṣafwān and his father, Umayyah ibn-Khalaf, were among those who had brought the most harm upon the Muslims, torturing the helpless and mocking their Prophet; Umayyah had once scoffed, crumbling deteriorated bones in his hands, and declared, "Muḥammad claims these will live again!" Then was revealed the verse, "And he hath coined for Us a similitude, and hath forgotten the fact of his creation, saying: Who will revive these bones when they have rotted away? Say [to them]: He will revive them Who produced them at the first, for He is Knower of every creation. . . ." [16] Yet notwithstanding his long, evil record, Ṣafwān asked for and was granted a choice in religion after the conquest and his complete defeat! Is this the type of conduct one would expect from someone who is accused of disseminating his religion by the sword? [17]

Less than a dozen people were killed in the battle of Mecca, despite the magnitude of the fighting armies (the army of Islam alone was estimated at ten thousand), which clearly shows that the order underlying the Jāhilīyah had crumbled in the face of Muḥammad's Message prior to the day of conquest. The band of Quraysh was unable to arouse the ma-

[16] *Ibid.*, 36:77-78.

[17] It is often said that Muḥammad's victory over himself that day was greater than his victory over his enemies; in view of all that he had experienced from his cruel Meccan enemies in twenty years, his example was inspiring.

jority of the people to combat Muḥammad, for his beliefs had penetrated their hearts; how otherwise could one explain the speed with which Mecca surrendered when there was no real battle? The tribes went over to Islam *en masse* in the span of a day and night—they who previously had said, "If we were to follow the right path with thee, we should be torn out of our land." [18]

It is evident that the days of the Truce of al-Ḥudaybiyah did not pass by fruitlessly, for in the shadow of peace the Message found its way into souls prepared to receive the truth. The leaders of Quraysh felt the earth tremble under their feet, and they broke their pledge, but it was too late because the hearts of the people were already conquered. How else, again, can one account for Abu-Sufyān's surrender on the night of the conquest through the mediation of ʿAbbās with his nephew Muḥammad, if Mecca still truly believed in the Jāhilīyah order? Was not Abu-Sufyān the one who carried the banner of hate for a generation to counter this Message? Were not the tribes of Hawāzin and Thaqīf, his allies, still defiant, harassing the army of Islam and almost killing the Prophet following the Battle of Ḥunayn? Moreover, why did not Abu-Sufyān and other chieftains rush to the aid of their allies with their followers and carry on with the war, since Arabs by nature are persevering and grudge-bearing generation after generation? The reason is obvious: Mecca's heart had gone over to Islam and accepted the Message before the Prophet's army forced its entry.

Even the conquest of Mecca, which certain authorities consider a military event resulting in the conversion of its inhabitants, was but the means of restraining the hand of force raised against its people that they might openly declare their faith and accept the Message, to which great numbers of them had already inclined secretly.

Then following the Muslim conquest of Mecca, we find delegates from all the corners of this vast and extensive

[18] Koran, 28:57.

land—from Yemen, Najrān, Kindah, Baḥrain, the farthest northern limits of the peninsula, from Najd, Tihāmah, and every direction—journeying to al-Madīnah to pledge themselves to Islam, motivated by reason and belief.

What role could the sword serve in turning pagans away from their religion when a journey of months separated them from the Prophet, not to mention the fact that they were capable of resisting when one considers their numbers and equipment? The only service the sword rendered to nascent Islam was to protect the Prophet from falling victim to his opponents among the Arabs, Jews, and Byzantines while in al-Madīnah; it enabled him to disseminate his Message and reach with it the minds and hearts of men. The Prophet's appreciation of the importance of peace in the dissemination of the Message is what induced him, as we have seen, to sign the Truce of al-Ḥudaybiyah.

Muslims following after the Prophet merely obeyed God and His Messenger when they offered people the choice between Islam and the payment of a poll tax (*jizyah*). The Muslims were taxed, we should remember, and not only to support the state; it seems only reasonable that non-Muslim citizens should have contributed as well in return for the protection and benefits they enjoyed equally. In conquered lands, people safeguarded their possessions and their religious beliefs by paying the poll tax, which those who were capable of paying gave to the Muslim conqueror in return for his guaranteeing them all their civil and religious liberties. If the sword were the instrument of the Message, people would have had no choice, and no person in any conquered land would have been able to buy his religion with such a pittance of a payment. And if a religion is not worth a dinar to its adherent, then Islam is more entitled to his devotion than is his religion.

Is it feasible that a people would sell their religion, traditions, and patriotism for a dinar levied only on those who are capable of paying? (Women, children, the handicapped, monks, and priests were exempted.) Undoubtedly those who went over to Islam must have done so because they found Islam more pleasing to them than their former belief.

It is indeed strange that the dinar, which used to shield everything dear to conquered nations from the sword of Islam and which Islam thought little of, should have become more treasured by certain Muslim officials than the acceptance of Islam by other peoples! Such officials would discourage others from joining their religion out of fear that they might be deprived of poll-tax income! The governor of Egypt wrote to the ascetic Caliph 'Umar ibn-'Abd-al-'Azīz, informing him that the Egyptians were accepting Islam in large numbers and that consequently the poll tax revenue was decreasing. The governor asked for permission to continue levying the poll tax on them, and the Caliph replied with the moving words, "May Allah curse your view! Allah sent Muḥammad not as a tax collector but as a Messenger!"

This episode gives us an insight into the mentality that prevailed during the first century of Islam. At that time, religious tolerance was unquestionably at its highest and freedom of belief at its greatest; the governor could not have written such a letter to the caliph of the Muslims had he been living in an atmosphere of intolerance. It would appear that the governor, motivated by a sense of state interest, wrote about something which he did not regard as exceptional or loathsome; if the situation had been otherwise, he would not have escaped the unbridled wrath of the multitudes on one side or the revenge of the caliph on the other. The caliph did not reward his governor by removing him from office; he merely disapproved of the view of a man who sought to prevent people from becoming Muslims in order to collect the poll tax.

Is there anything to match the conduct of a conquering nation that gave people the choice to preserve their religion and laws in return for a token tax (so it would appear when compared to taxes in our age) and that granted them citizenship and equality with the conquerors?

No, the sword was not the implement of the Message of Muḥammad; it was rather the protector of the Message. For the motto of the Message was, "He whom Allah guideth, he indeed is led aright, and he whom He sendeth astray, for him thou wilt not find a guiding friend." [19]

19 *Ibid.*, 18:17.

## 19

# *Dissemination of the Message Among Christian Nations*

*

Some misinformed individuals pursue the belief that after Muḥammad had united the scattered ends of Arabdom and defeated paganism in the heart of the Arabian peninsula, certain hordes representing the most brutal bedouins began to spread oppression to the north and east through robbing, looting, and destroying the civilizations of Byzantium and Persia, thereby removing the forces which used to safeguard the ancient civilizations against the assaults of barbarians from the north, east, and south. Such individuals are prone to believe that the emergence of the Arabs was like the emergence of the Huns and Vandals, peoples who surged from the east driven by hunger, encouraged by greed, and strengthened by pride in their heritage, or like the drives of other uncivilized hordes, such as the Mongols and Tartars, who utilized brute force in depriving people of their possessions.

To believe such allegations concerning the Arabs, the bearers of the Islamic Message, is very far from the truth which history teaches us. Although the bearers of the Message represented the nomads of the peninsula, who were once given to looting and bloodshed, the Message which they carried and the Sharī'ah to which they adhered claimed greater possession over their souls than the pride and greed that moved them in earlier times; for that reason the legacy which they left behind differed from the legacy of like nomadic peoples who continued to be guided in their conquests by destructive aims.[1]

The Arabs set up an empire stretching from France to India and China, and the peoples put on the garb of Arabism and became guided by its precepts. Their consequent loyalty to their pledges, respect for laws, and pursuit of justice became exemplary among nations and the subject of admiration among historians and seekers of truth. The bedouins' adherence to the Message explains why they did not compel anyone to change his religion and why they dealt with human beings, individually and collectively, strictly through laws before which they had humbled themselves, drawing upon the decrees and the spirit of the Sharī'ah, whose Message they carried. Converted nomadic peoples such as the Turks and Berbers who joined Islam were also exemplary in their submission to the law, fulfillment of pledges, and tolerance, through what they absorbed of Muslim ethics. They sincerely respected the tenets of the faith and became tolerant of other religions. Judging from our knowledge of history, few ideologies have been attended by such justice, tolerance, openheartedness, and forbearance in times of strength and weakness alike as the Message of Muḥammad, whether it was disseminated by Arabs or Turks.

The Message triumphed over defiant souls and instilled

[1] Christopher Dawson, in *The Origins of Europe,* regards religious enthusiasm as the essential cause of Muslim victories, and Henri Pirenne, in *Mohammed and Charlemagne,* explains the Muslim success as follows: "The Arab conquest, which brought confusion upon both Europe and Asia, was without precedent. The swiftness of its victory is comparable only with that by which the Mongol Empires of Attila, Jenghiz Khan and Tamerlane were established. But these Empires were as ephemeral as the conquest of Islam was lasting. This religion still has its faithful today in almost every country where it was imposed by the first Caliphs. The lightning-like rapidity of its diffusion was a veritable miracle as compared with the slow progress of Christianity . . . . the Arabs were exalted by a new faith. . . . they were not even fanatical, and they did not expect to make converts of their subjects" (Henri Pirenne, *Mohammed and Charlemagne,* tr. Bernard Miall [reprinted; New York: Meridian Books, 1961], pp. 149-150).

strong ethical standards in nations noted for harshness; the word of Allah remained supreme and His ordinances were observed. As He declares to Arab and non-Arab bearers of the Message, "And say unto those who have received the Scripture and those who read not: Have ye [too] surrendered [become Muslims]? If they surrender, then truly they are rightly guided, and if they turn away, then it is thy duty only to convey the Message [unto them]." [2]

Christianity had been the triumphant religion in the Byzantine Empire. The part which stretched from the Taurus Mountains to the Atlas range in Africa today encompasses Syria, Egypt, Tripolitania, Tunisia, and Algeria, some of the first areas to be liberated by the Arabs during the days of the orthodox caliphs, the days when zeal for the new religion was at the height of its fervor.

The Christians in the conquered areas formed many nations and spoke many languages; some were Arabs and others were not. By what system of rule did the conquerors bind the conquered? We will leave the answer to Sir Thomas Arnold, a man of knowledge and an outstanding authority on the subject. In *The Preaching of Islam,* Sir Thomas maintains that the Christian church became stronger and that it progressed under the protection of the Muslims, whose rule did not hamper the course of its development.

> Indeed, so far from the development of the Christian Church being hampered by the establishment of Muḥammadan rule, the history of the Nestorians exhibits a remarkable outburst of religious life and energy from the time of their becoming subjects to the Muslims . . . under the rule of the caliphs, the security they enjoyed at home enabled them vigorously to push forward their missionary enterprises abroad. Missionaries were sent into China and India. . . . If the other Christian sects failed to exhibit the same vigorous life, it was not the fault of the Muḥammadans. All were tolerated alike by the supreme government, and furthermore were prevented from persecuting one another.

2 Koran, 3:20.

Sir Thomas enumerates cases of ill will among Christian sects and recounts how Muslim governors interceded to establish justice and to aid the oppressed without prejudice and with complete tolerance.[3]

Sir Thomas writes about the tolerance and beneficence extended by Muslims to Christian subjects in the first era of Islam. The examples and events he cites do not permit us to believe what many others assume to be thoroughly doubtful, namely, that Christian nations were forced by the edge of the sword to accept Islam. Such an accusation is false and unjustified, and we must look for other reasons to explain the Islamization of Christians.

According to Sir Thomas, under an order based on security and guaranteeing freedom of life, property, and religious beliefs, the Christians, particularly in the cities, enjoyed great wealth and success during the early period of Islam, and some exercised great influence in the courts of the caliphs. He cites many testimonies to that effect and refers in particular to the case of two brothers, Salmāwah and Ibrāhīm, who held the rank of vizier, including the position of minister of the treasury of the Muslims. When Ibrāhīm became ill, the Caliph al-Muʿtaṣim visited him in his home; when he died, the Caliph was seized with deep sorrow and ordered his body to be brought to the court, from whence the funeral procession started. Among other Christian viziers mentioned is Naṣr ibn-Harūn, who headed the vizierate for the Buwayḥid ruler ʿAḍūd al-Dawlah;[4] the latter is said to have built a large number of churches and houses of worship.

Sir Thomas enumerates examples of religious toleration concerning churches which the caliphs ordered constructed, and to which they made donations, in the northern part of

3 Sir Thomas Arnold, *The Preaching of Islam: A History of the Propagation of the Muslim Faith* (2nd ed.; London: Constable & Co., Ltd., 1913), pp. 60 ff. The quotation above is from p. 68.

4 Literally, "the supporting arm of the state"; he held political sway from 949 to 983 as the actual ruler of Baghdad and its territorial holdings with the caliph serving mainly as his instrument.

the peninsula, in Iraq and in Syria; some of these churches built in the first Islamic era remain standing today. Among them can be listed the Church of Abu-Sarajah in old Cairo and others in Fusṭāṭ (in Cairo). Nothing is more illustrative of Muslim tolerance than the fact that in the early period of Islam (the Umayyad period) the governor of Iraq and Fars, Khālid al-Qasri, a Muslim, built a church for his Christian mother to worship in; this was at a time when the Message was encountering violence, a time of perpetual war between Muslims and Christian Byzantines. Those interested in more details should turn to Sir Thomas's work and to the Islamic and non-Islamic sources he cites.

During the early periods of conquest, Muslim and Christian Arabs shared a common brotherhood, and exercised such forbearance that the Christian Arab would fight alongside his Muslim cousin as a champion of Arabism and in response to the justice instituted by the Muslim. And the annals of the Muslims abound with cases of Christian individuals and groups in Iraq, Syria, and Egypt who, while remaining loyal to their Christian beliefs, expended their efforts and blood in assisting their cousins to erect an Arabian empire.

In the Battle of al-Jisr (the Bridge), when the army of al-Muthanna was shaken and besieged between the Euphrates and the Persian army, the Christians of Banu-Ṭay, the best supporters of their Muslim Arab brothers, carried on a strong attack and protected the pass for the Muslims. When al-Muthanna returned and sought the help of the people to erase the shame of defeat sustained at the bridge, the Christian Banu-Numayr were the bravest to rush to his aid. In the Battle of Buwayb, Christian Arabs fought side by side with Muslim Arabs; true glory on that day went to a Christian of Banu-Taghlib, who, during the most heated phase of the battle, sought out the commander of the Persian army and cut off his head; having gained the booty (*ghanīmah*), which consisted, among other things, of the fallen commander's horse, he returned running through the ranks of the Muslims, boasting of his lineage as a Christian of the Taghlib, while the Muslims showered praise on him for his assistance.[5]

Taghlib remained Christian; it was the one tribe that refused to pay *jizyah* and insisted on paying the *ṣadaqah*[6] instead in emulation of their Muslim brethren. The Caliph 'Umar ordered that their wish be granted, saying, "Do not humble Arabs. Take the *ṣadaqah* from Banu-Taghlib."

In his book, Sir Thomas cites a number of reasons Christians abandoned their religion in different times and places, and supports his arguments with facts presented in a scholarly manner. Such evidence is a source of pride to Muslims of every generation and every nation, for it bears testimony to the forbearance, magnanimity, and sense of justice characterizing the relationships of Muslims with those who differ with them in beliefs. Historians say that Christians apostatized to Islam, among other reasons, because of admiration for the new religion and its advocates; because of disappointment with divergences in their own religion, despair of reform, ill treatment by their coreligionists, or neglect by priests and spiritual fathers; because of ambition for wordly things; and because of guidance from Allah. When historians of other faiths cite such diversified causes in analyzing the Islamization of Christians, it proves that the sword was not the instrument of Muslim belief.

To be sure, there have been cases in Islamic history when Christians were not free from persecution; these were related to events in the caliphates of the 'Abbāsid al-Mutawakkil, the Fāṭimid al-Ḥākim, and certain Mamlūks. Al-Mutawakkil was hard on the Muslims themselves: he was cruel to the Shī'ah (the 'Alid) and Mu'tazilah sects; in the case of al-Ḥākim, the target of his cruelty was Muslim groups other than the Shī'ah.

[5] The Battle of al-Jisr was fought and lost by the Arabs against the Persian Empire on the Euphrates north of the town of al-Ḥīra in the autumn of A.D. 634; the Battle of Buwayb was won south of al-Ḥīra, also on the Euphrates (between Kūfah and Najaf), in the autumn of A.D. 635.

[6] A form of taxation levied only on Muslims, who were required to pay it as an imperative act of piety; the tax was for the needy.

If Christians were harmed because of bigotry, they had only to remember the fate of Muslim groups under such caliphs. Nevertheless, persecution constituted the exception, not the rule; sporadic, isolated events in a history of over a thousand years hardly distract from the fact that the Muslim display of forbearance and honorable conduct is not always paralleled in the annals of other peoples and religions.

Most of the cases of persecution experienced by Christians in distant times were prompted by envy of their wealth and influence, by a belief that they had abused their sources of power, or by fear. In incidents centuries apart, the Christians themselves wronged their coreligionists residing within Islamic boundaries while they engaged in acts of spying and treachery. Therefore, certain rulers mistreated them and instigated the masses against these few unsavory persons. The annals of Egypt, Syria, and the Ottoman and Andalusian states refer to isolated events which, when scrutinized, can be traced back to politics, not to religious motives of compelling others to adopt the religion of the Muslims. A point that authorities agree on, and one which is a source of Muslim pride, is that throughout their history they did not avail themselves of arbitrary and harsh laws like those prevalent in Spain under Ferdinand and Isabella, in France under Louis XIV when Protestantism was a target, and in England against the Jews preventing their entry for four centuries.

Sir Thomas maintains that the survival of Christian churches and faiths in isolation in the Islamic East during those long centuries is absolute proof of the widely exercised forbearance of the Islamic states.

The sword, therefore, was not the Islamic approach to closed minds, while in some other lands it became the means of saving Jewish and Muslim souls and the souls of dissident Christian sects. How can the Muslims do otherwise when they know that their Prophet allied himself with Christian tribes, was loyal to them, guaranteed their freedom of possession and belief, and insured the security of their monks and priests?

According to the noble Koran, "And thou wilt find the nearest of them in affection to those who believe [to be] those who say: Lo! We are Christians. That is because there are among them priests and monks, and because they are not proud." [7]

[7] Koran, 5:82. "Not proud" in the Arabic text signifies humbleness or modesty.

# 20

## *The Crusaders Adopt Islam*

*

In response to the summons of first the Arabs and later the Turks, Christian nations around the Mediterranean joined Islam willingly. Perhaps more revealing and astonishing was the conversion to Islam of large segments of Crusaders.[1] Brought together from every nationality and generation, they came to the East with hearts filled with hatred and blood dripping from their hands, and slashed in their progress even the throats of Christians who did not respond to their preaching, differed in opinion, or belonged to Christian sects other than theirs. Yet before long, these cruel hordes were adopting the ethical standards of their enemies; their hearts were opened and their bigotry was curtailed. They learned forbearance from those they hated, and those who came to them from the West as reinforcements were startled by the ethical conduct which they found among their coreligionists, transcending malice and hatred. In sum, many of the leaders and many of the rank and file among the Crusaders who invaded lands to cut the throats of Muslims embraced the Message which they had set out to destroy. This is one of the most unique effects of tolerance.

One of those who turned Muslim during the first Crusade

[1] Jane Soames Nickerson writes, "Mohammedanism has been called the greatest of all Christian heresies" (*A Short History of North Africa* [New York: The Devin-Adair Company, 1961], p. 56).

was Renaud, the leader of the German and Lombard groups, who became Muslims with him. Many turned Muslim during the Second Crusade: Sir Thomas tells of a monk of the order of Saint Denis, formerly a private chaplain of King Louis VII, who was accompanied in this Crusade by a large group. Here is what the monk relates in bitter terms:

While endeavouring to make their way overland through Asia Minor to Jerusalem, the Crusaders sustained a disastrous defeat at the hands of the Turks in the mountain-passes of Phrygia (A.D. 1148), and with difficulty reached the seaport of Attalia. Here, all who could afford to satisfy the exorbitant demands of the Greek merchants, took ship for Antioch; while the sick and wounded and the mass of the pilgrims were left behind at the mercy of their treacherous allies, the Greeks, who received five hundred marks from Louis on condition that they provided an escort for the pilgrims and took care of the sick until they were strong enough to be sent on after the others. But no sooner had the army left, than the Greeks informed the Turks of the helpless condition of the pilgrims, and quietly looked on while famine, disease and the arrows of the enemy carried havoc and destruction through the camp of these unfortunates. Driven to desperation, a party of three or four thousand attempted to escape, but were surrounded and cut to pieces by the Turks, who now pressed on to the camp to follow up their victory. The situation of the survivors would have been utterly hopeless, had not the sight of their misery melted the hearts of the Muḥammadans to pity. They tended the sick and relieved the poor and starving with open-handed liberality. Some even bought up the French money which the Greeks had got out of the pilgrims by force or cunning, and lavishly distributed it among the needy. So great was the contrast between the kind treatment the pilgrims received from the unbelievers and the cruelty of their fellow-Christians, the Greeks, who imposed forced labour upon them, beat them and robbed them of what little they had left, that many of them voluntarily embraced the faith of their deliverers. As the old chronicler says:

"Avoiding their co-religionists who had been so cruel to them they went in safety among the infidels who had compassion upon them, and, as we heard, more than three thousand joined themselves to the Turks when they retired. Oh, kindness more cruel than all treachery! They gave them bread but robbed them of their faith, though it is certain that contented with the services they performed, they compelled no one among them to renounce his religion." [2]

This is the testimony of the monk. According to Sir Thomas,

> The increasing intercourse between Christians and Muslims, the growing appreciation on the part of the Crusaders of the virtues of their opponents which so strikingly distinguishes the later from the earlier chroniclers of the Crusades, the numerous imitations of Oriental manners and ways of life by the Franks settled in the Holy Land, did not fail to exercise a corresponding influence on religious opinions. One of the most remarkable features of this influence is the tolerant attitude of many of the Christian Knights towards the faith of Islam—an attitude of mind that was most vehemently denounced by the Church. When Usama b. Munqidh, a Syrian Amīr of the twelfth century, visited Jerusalem, during a period of truce, the Knights Templar, who had occupied the Masjid al-Aqsā, assigned to him a small chapel adjoining it, for him to say his prayers in, and they strongly resented the interference with the devotions of their guest on the part of the newly-arrived Crusader.[3]

Sir Thomas then asserts that the Message of Muḥammad attracted to its fold a considerable number of Crusaders even in the early period, the twelfth century, which has captured the attention of those who delve into their records.[4]

The impact of the Crusaders' admiration for Ṣalāḥ-al-Dīn's (Saladin's) courage and virtues was such that many of their leaders and followers abandoned their religion and relatives

[2] Sir Thomas Arnold, *The Preaching of Islam: A History of the Propagation of the Muslim Faith* (2nd ed.; London: Constable & Co., 1913), p. 88. The last paragraph is quoted from *De Ludovici vii. Itinere,* in Jacques-Paul Migne, ed., *Patrologia Cursus Completus: Series Latina* (Paris, 1844-1864), CXCV, 1243.

[3] Arnold, *op. cit.,* pp. 89-90.

[4] *Ibid.,* p. 90.

and entered the religion of Islam. This was the conduct of the English leader before the victory of Saladin in the decisive Battle of Ḥiṭṭīn (1187). Certain Christian historians have asserted that six of the princes of the King of Jerusalem, Guy de Lusignan, were seized by the devil the night of the battle, went over to Islam, and joined the ranks of the enemy without being compelled to do so by anyone. The matter reached a point where Raymond, the ruling prince of Tripoli, came to an understanding with Saladin whereby he agreed to call upon his people to join Islam.

When the Crusaders took to a third war to avenge the fall of Jerusalem in the siege of Acre, they were exposed to hardships and hunger, and many of them fled to the ranks of the Muslims. Among these were those who believed, those who returned to their people, and those who persisted in their Christianity but chose to remain and fight in the ranks of the Muslims. Sir John Mandeville, a contemporary of the Crusaders, asserted in this connection that certain Christians apostatized from their religion and became Arabs either out of poverty and ignorance or through distress. Certainly one cannot expect a Crusader like Sir John to explain what the Muslims call guidance except in terms of ignorance and distress. What concerns us in this matter is that the poor, the distressed, and the lost whom Mandeville mentioned joined the Islam they had come to wipe out by their own choice because they were attracted to it and not because of compulsion and persecution. In truth, certain Christian historians, both contemporary with the Islamic conquest and the recovery of the holy places and those of a much later period following the downfall of the Frankish state in all Syria, cite the joy of native Christians over their liberation from the rule of the Crusaders. Sir Thomas maintains that they settled down to Islamic rule and reconciled themselves to it with an eye to the future, in the same way that Muslim rulers continued in their old custom of forbearance and openheartedness toward members of other religions.

If what we have mentioned serves as a testimony to the dissemination of the Message by the exercise of reason among Islam's greatest warring opponents during the most uncertain days of the Islamic state—the days of Crusader and Tartar raids—we also have another testimony from the Christian patriarch at Khurāsān, during the most glorious days of the Arabian Umayyad state, with which we shall terminate this chapter. The Christian patriarch, Yusāb III, the Jacobite, sent a missive to a fellow patriarch in which he declared:

Where are thy sons, O father bereft of sons? Where is that great people of Merv [in Persia], who though they beheld neither sword, nor fire or tortures, captivated only by love for a moiety of their goods, have turned aside, like fools, from the true path and rushed headlong into the pit of faithlessness—into everlasting destruction, and have utterly been brought to nought, while two priests only (priests at least in name), have, like brands snatched from the burning, escaped the devouring flames of infidelity. Alas, alas! Out of so many thousands who bore the name of Christians, not even one single victim was consecrated unto God by the shedding of his blood for the true faith. Where, too, are the sanctuaries of Kirmān [in Persia] and all Persia? It is not the coming of Satan or the mandates of the kings of the earth or the orders of governors of provinces that have laid them waste and in ruins—but the feeble breath of one contemptible little demon, who was not decreed worthy of the honour of demons by those demons who sent him on his errand, nor was endowed by Satan the seducer with the power of diabolical deceit, that he might display it in your land; but merely by the nod of his command he has thrown down all the churches of your Persia. . . . And the Arabs, to whom God at this time has given the empire of the world, behold, they are among you, as ye know well; and yet they attack not the Christian faith, but, on the contrary, they favour our religion, do honour to our priests and the saints of the Lord, and confer benefits on churches and monasteries. Why then have your people of Merv abandoned their faith for the sake of those Arabs? And that, too, when the Arabs, as the people of Merv themselves declare, have not compelled them to leave their own religion but suffered them to keep it safe and undefiled if they gave up only a moiety of their goods . . . .[5]

Is there a clearer explanation for the Message's acceptance by Christians than its appeal to the heart and reason? We have reviewed for you testimonies from both the first and the seventh Islamic centuries, from both the East and the West, from warriors and from pacifists. Everything has changed—nations, centuries, and circumstances—except the truth that has attended the Message since its emergence and the precepts embodied in the Koran in Allah's words, "There is no compulsion in religion. The right direction is henceforth distinct from error." [6]

It is our right, we, the descendants of just, equitable, and merciful peoples in the East, as Muslims and as Christians, to strive for a rebirth in which we shall serve as examples and spokesmen for freedom of belief and of opinion in a world that has become intolerant of those who differ in their views. Our forefathers were the protectors of this freedom and its supreme example. Let us inherit this tolerance, and let us bear its standard.

[5] Quoted in *ibid.*, pp. 81-82.
[6] Koran, 2:256.

# 21

## *Bringing Islam to the Europeans*

*

The dissemination of the Message of Muḥammad in Eastern and Western Europe has been accompanied by a history worthy of good remembrance and entitled to the pride of the Muslims.[1] On the other hand, unfortunately, there have undeniably been situations betraying the ill will of many Europeans who, in order to strengthen their religious views, resorted to the harshest of methods and the most repulsive deeds.

1 "There was no propaganda, nor was any such pressure applied as was exerted by the Christians after the triumph of the church. 'If God had so desired' says the Koran 'He would have made all humanity a single people,' and it expressly condemns the use of violence in dealing with error. It requires only obedience to Allah, the outward obedience of inferior, degraded and despicable beings, who are tolerated, but who live in abjection. It was this that the infidel found so intolerable and demoralizing. His faith was not attacked; it was simply ignored; and this was the most effective means of detaching him from it and leading him to Allah, who would not only restore his human dignity, but would open to him the gates of the Musulman state. It was because his religion compelled the conscientious Musulman to treat the infidel as a subject that the infidel came to him, and in coming to him broke with his country and his people. The German became Romanized as soon as he entered 'Romania.' The Roman, on the contrary, became Arabized as soon as he was conquered by Islam. . . . When it was converted to Christianity the Empire, so to speak, underwent a change of soul; when it was converted to Islam both its soul and body were transformed. The change was as great in civil as in religious society" (Henri Pirenne, *Mohammed and Charlemagne,* tr. Bernard Miall [reprinted; New York: Meridian Books, 1961], pp. 151-152).

Those who raised the banner of Islam in the West, in Spain, France, and Italy, were Arabs and Berbers, and those who raised it in the eastern parts of Europe were often Turks and Tartars, peoples who excelled in courage and boldness; yet despite their differences in character, all their annals, from the standpoint of their success in spreading the Message of Muḥammad and their religious forbearance, are covered with glory and deserving of pride. In contrast, both the pious and the wicked among the European nations participated in a chain of sanguinary atrocities over the span of hundreds of years to resist the Message of Muḥammad in Western and Eastern Europe.[2]

What is difficult to explain is that this cruelty which the Europeans exercised in their efforts to put an end to Muslim civilization and religion in Spain, France, and Italy and in Eastern Europe was perpetrated in its ugliest forms even against Christians themselves, whenever there was a sharp quarrel over a religious opinion or a Christian dogma, as well as against Jews.

European nations are not all of one race, nor from one area, nor of one nature. There exist among them the differences in race, language, and temperament that are found among Eastern nations. What, then, unified their methods and rendered violence, murder, treachery, and oppression the most outstanding methods for exalting one religion over another?

What has made desert peoples, such as the Arabs, and peoples whose profession is to wage war, such as the Turks, Tartars, and Berbers, choose to spread their religion by reason and example? For in a long history covering more than a thousand years and including Eastern and Western lands, we see no traces of those crushing atrocities repeatedly committed for long periods of time by Europeans against other Euro-

2 According to Jane Soames Nickerson, "Her [Spain's] history in the fifteenth and sixteenth centuries is stained by ferocious cruelty which she displayed in eradicating the Moslims from her territory" (*A Short History of North Africa* [New York: The Devin-Adair Company, 1961], p. 75).

peans or against members of other religious communities.

We cannot find for this a reason with which we can arm ourselves, for the Lord Jesus (may peace and prayer be with him) was the victim of violence; he was among the best of those who called to kindness and peace, and his Message forbade war and fighting absolutely. It was not the religion of Christ which spread this despicable spirit of prejudice.

The religion of Islam has sanctioned war, and its Message has appeared in the world accompanied by those conquests before which the heights of no Himalayas or Pyrenees, Atlas or Balkan mountains stood as a barrier. Why, then, were adherents of this religion the ones to display the greatest tolerance toward subjects who belonged to other religions and the most openheartedness toward other nationalities and ethnic groups?

Perhaps the reason stems from differences between Muslims and Christians as pertain to religious ordinances.

The Christians have a clerical organization or, to use a different expression, an ecclesiastical order which places leaders over them from groups of religious men. Christianity is also not so clear as Islam in its attitude toward worldly matters, and human dissension has thus often predominated. Islam has forbidden this leadership by a clergy, and permits no other liaison with God except that of conscience; and what it has ordained and prohibited concerning worldly matters is also clear. Perhaps the domination of Christianity by a religious body is what brought about that fanatical religious attitude whose manifestations we have witnessed everywhere throughout the ages.

Likewise, the clarity of the religious decrees of the Muslims renders obvious both what is sanctioned and what is forbidden in a revealed Book. Both the select and the average man know that God has forbidden compulsion in religion; they know that He has declared to His Prophet, "And if thy Lord willed, all who are in the earth would have believed together. Wouldst thou [Muḥammad] compel men until they are believers?"[3] The religion which forbids its members to curse other religions makes no allowance for persecution and oppression. Allah says, "Revile not those who pray to other gods beside Allah lest they wrongfully revile Allah through ignorance. Thus unto every nation have We made their deed seem fair. Then unto their Lord is their return, and He will tell them what they used to do."[4]

The simplicity of the Muslim belief may be one of the factors responsible for the creation of this forbearing nature, for this belief is based on the testimony, "There is no God but Allah, and Muḥammad is His Apostle." These two words —*God* and *Muḥammad*—are the binding elements.[5] When men proceeded on the simple premises embodied in these elements and abandoned what lay beyond to the account of God, they accustomed themselves thereby to the exercise of forbearance and magnanimity toward each other as well as toward those of other religious communities who differed with them.

These causes constitute some of the reasons for the essential difference between the religious laws of Muslims and the religious laws of Europeans. We will not narrate a long history to explain the difference to which we are referring, since it is simple for those who seek to learn the truth to do so. However, it would still benefit us to review certain evidence.

When the Arabs entered Spain, the sixth Council of Toledo had decreed that upon the assumption of their reign, Spanish monarchs were to take an oath not to tolerate in their realms anyone who did not adhere to the Catholic faith, and to carry out this law with ultimate severity against those who dissented. Among other things, this law provided for life imprisonment and the confiscation of property of whoever

[3] Koran, 10:100.

[4] *Ibid.*, 6:109.

[5] As long as a Muslim confesses these two beliefs, his life and property will not be violated by the community or the state for other variances in dogmas or thought.

contemplated disputing the decrees of the Church and Catholic teachings. Baudissin maintains,

> The clergy had gained for their order a preponderant influence in the affairs of the state; the bishops and chief ecclesiastics sat in the national councils, which met to settle the most important business of the realm, ratified the election of the king, and claimed the right to depose him if he refused to abide by their decrees. The Christian clergy took advantage of their power to persecute the Jews, who formed a very large community in Spain.[6]

According to Helfferich,

> Edicts of a brutally severe character were passed against such as refused to be baptized; and they consequently hailed the invading Arabs as their deliverers from such cruel oppression. . . . Slaves who had become Christians also rejoiced greatly in the coming of the Arabs, and those who had been subjected to persecution now joined the religion of the Arabs in waves. . . . The nobility as well as the masses were enthusiastic about this new and free religion.[7]

And Sir Thomas Arnold says,

> Having once become Muslims, these Spanish converts showed themselves zealous adherents of their adopted faith, and they and their children joined themselves to the Puritan party of the rigid Muḥammadan theologians as against the careless and luxurious life of the Arab aristocracy.[8]

In the days of the Arab conquest, no cases were reported of any attempt at compulsion in religion or of any persecu-

[6] W. W. Graf von Baudissin, *Eulogius und Alvar. Bin Abschnitt spanischer Kirchen geschichte aus der Zeit der Maurenherrschaft* (Leipzig, 1872), p. 22.

[7] Adolf Helfferich, *Der Westgothische Arianismus und die spanische Ketzergeschichte* (Berlin, 1860), p. 68.

[8] Sir Thomas Arnold, *The Preaching of Islam: A History of the Propagation of the Muslim Faith* (2nd ed.; London: Constable & Co., 1913), p. 132, citing R. P. A. Dozy, *Histoire des Musulmans d'Espagne* (Leyden, 1861), II, 45-46.

tion or oppression for the purpose of changing a belief. Perhaps the primary reason the Muslims came into rapid possession of this western section of Europe was the magnanimity and forbearance which infused their religion. Likewise, the forbearance displayed by Muslim governors, who permitted religious freedom to the Christians, mingled with them, and married from among them, led to a large-scale Arabization of Christian elements, many of whom took Arab names and had themselves circumcised like their Muslim neighbors. Referring to those Christians subject to Arab rule as "Muzarab" or "Arabized" indicates the direction in which they inclined. Arabized Christians' admiration for the language of the Koran became so great that they began to recite it and marvel at it. Moreover, the effect of the Message reached the heads of the church themselves, whose thinking, both inside and outside of Spain, began to emulate the Islamic view.

In brief, the exemplary conduct of the Muslims, combined with the vigor of their Message, was instrumental in the Christians' adopting Islam after only a very short period of acquaintance. The effect of good example and wise preaching reached the point where Christians would not desist from joining Islam even when the defeated Muslims were being treated with barbarous oppression and forced to desert their homelands in Europe. One of the strangest phenomena in this connection comes to light in Sterling Maxwell's account of the events of 1499, seven years after the fall of Granada—that new Muslims who had entered Islam fled with the crowds who were fleeing the sword and fire.

This is no place for a detailed analysis. I have sought to point to the magnanimous conduct of Arab rule in Europe, which multitudes of Christians acknowledged, to the freedom of belief, and to the gains in science, knowledge, and civilization achieved by people in the shadow of the ethics and law of Islam, of its spirit and way of life. The acknowledgment of this truth by the just was exemplified by a scholar who, reflecting on the Battle of Poitiers (732),[9] declared that the defeat of the Arabs was the reason that civilization did not reach Europe until eight centuries later!

The barbarian armies of the Franks defeated the Arabs in the eighth century, and thereby greatly retarded the cultural advancement of Europe. Treacherous and prejudiced forces triumphed once more in a thorough fashion during the fifteenth century, and thus gave a setback to knowledge and civilization. During the time when the courts of the Inquisition and the swords of the state were leading the messengers of civilization to slaughter or to the sea in the West, stripping homelands of their entire populations, and during the time when Granada fell and the vestiges of two hundred thousand Muslims were wiped out (most of whom were of the original inhabitants) through massacre, banishment, and dispersal, the triumphant armies of Islam under another banner, the Turkish, were conquering the Eastern European kingdoms, Christians were enjoying refuge in the shade of a new justice, and people were being blessed with freedom of conscience and religion.

Byzantium, the center of enmity against Muslims and the source whence tempests blew upon Muslim homelands for eight centuries, fell, but religious rights were not abolished; conquerors did not dominate beliefs and religions, nor were people chased out of their homelands, nor were they brought to account for their intentions and consciences.

Let us leave the word to the Christian historians Phrantzes, Finlay, Betzibus, and D'Ohsson, as condensed by Arnold:

> One of the first steps taken by Muḥammad II, after the capture of Constantinople and the re-establishment of order in that city, was to secure the allegiance of the Christians, by proclaiming himself the protector of the Greek Church. Persecution of the Chris-

[9] In this battle, 'Abd-al-Raḥmān Ghāfiqi, the commander of the Islamic forces, was killed, and the armies of Charles Martel triumphed over the Arabs in western France.

tians was strictly forbidden; a decree was granted to the newly elected patriarch which secured to him and his successors and the bishops under him, the enjoyment of the old privileges, revenues and exemptions enjoyed under former rule. Gennadios, the first patriarch after the Turkish conquest, received from the hands of the Sultan himself the pastoral staff, which was the sign of his office, together with a purse of a thousand gold ducats and a horse with gorgeous trappings, on which he was privileged to ride with his train through the city. But not only was the head of the Church treated with all the respect he had been accustomed to receive from the Christian emperors, but further he was invested with extensive civil power. The patriarch's court sat to decide all cases between Greek and Greek: it could impose fines, imprison offenders in a prison provided for its own special use, and in some cases even condemn to capital punishment: while the ministers and officials of the government were directed to enforce its judgments. The complete control of spiritual and ecclesiastical matters (in which the Turkish government, unlike the civil power of the Byzantine empire, never interfered), was left entirely in his hands and those of the grand Synod which he could summon whenever he pleased; and hereby he could decide all matters of faith and dogma without fear of interference on the part of the state. As a recognized officer of the imperial government, he could do much for the alleviation of the oppressed, by bringing the acts of unjust governors to the notice of the sultan. The Greek bishops in the provinces in their turn were treated with great consideration and were entrusted with so much jurisdiction in civil affairs, that up to modern times they have acted in their dioceses almost as if they were Ottoman prefects over the orthodox population, taking the place of the old Christian aristocracy which had been exterminated by the conquerors . . . .[10]

Such were the deeds of the Muslims in the East, and Granada fell to the Spaniards forty years after Constantinople fell to the Turks. Would that the Christians of the West had followed the example of the Muslims! Even if they had not had in their long past an example of unprecedented forbear-

10 Arnold, *op. cit.*, pp. 145-147.

ance—Jesus—to steer them toward equity and mercy, why could they not have taken notice of the lofty example put before their eyes by the Muslims? As I have said previously, their cruel behavior had many causes, some of which have been mentioned; others can certainly refer to still more causes. In my opinion, this cruelty is not inherent in the nature of the Christian religion; for the coming of the Messiah Jesus (peace be upon him) was a mercy to the peoples.

If every historical event indicates that European manners always inclined toward interference in spiritual and moral matters to the extremes of oppression and indulgence in bloodshed, it is not strange that we should behold in the recent world war and in the one previous to it traces of these manners, reflecting scenes from the past, for in our age ideological struggles have replaced the religious struggles of the Middle Ages.

In conclusion, could it not be the destiny of the inhabitants of the East, of both Christians and Muslims, whose souls always aspire to God's mercy and who are constantly seeking His guidance when distress and gloom threaten, to rise once more with their noble heritage, which would set straight ideological, economic, and racial disputes, mitigate the impulse to extremism in the Western temperament, secure human brotherhood, and act in the service of general peace with the sincerity of intention and good inclination which God has firmly established for them in the world?

We ask the Lord of the worlds to hasten preparations for such an eventuality. "Allah is full of pity, Merciful toward mankind." [11]

[11] Koran, 2:143.

# VII

## *On the Causes of World Disturbance*

*

# 22

## *Colonialism*

*

We have considered international relations from the Islamic point of view, and we have touched upon many aspects of the problem. The purpose of such a brief presentation is to arouse an interest among both Muslim and non-Muslim readers in discussing fruitfully the tenets of the Message of Muḥammad, with the anticipation that they will discover in its fundamentals and precepts a formula for salvation from the sufferings of modern civilization and from that turbulence which inflicted two world wars upon mankind within a quarter of a century.

As a result of the last world war and of its widespread evil products, the modern world finds itself in three camps, two of which have been maintaining a hostile struggle against each other while the third tries to remain neutral but knows no immunity from the aggressiveness of these rivals.

What are the three complaining about? Each of the two inimical factions is making demands to which the other cannot possibly acquiesce, and there is no point in discussing them here. Each claims that it has been wronged and attacked while standing for the right and seeking to uphold the edifice of civilization. Let us leave these claimants the merits or falsehoods of their arguments.

As for the third, the uncommitted faction, it consists of neutrals whose sanctities have been violated and others who watch fearfully at night, fully armed lest they be overpowered.

If we take a general look at the causes of strife among nations during the past two centuries, we are struck by the fact that they have become more serious century after century, probably reaching an apex in the most recent world war, which engulfed all five continents. What provoked such excessive evils, and what are the aims of the belligerents, aims of such evident seriousness that they have persisted without being realized?

Are these aims definable as a desire for territorial expansion or competition for control over the destinies and resources of weak nations?

Do they represent a striving to gain special interests and economic advantage, emanating from disputes and contention among classes?

Are they the expression, perhaps, of indulgence in national or racial friction—a yielding to excessive patriotism and racism—leading to a denial of the rights of others, whether neighbors or citizens of countries in the farthest reaches of the world?

Or do they embody a materialistic tyranny and love of extravagance, resulting in a concentration on amassing wealth or on quick gain, which further intensifies the differences among the classes of a single nation and sets them against one another, thereby provoking internal and external strife?

Are these evils the result of the defeat of spiritual forces before the onslaught of materialistic forces, from which in turn derive a confusion in moral character and beliefs, apathy toward the righteous law, a loss of human virtue and a concomitant decrease in brotherliness, and an increasing disregard for pledges and pacts that has bred treachery and deception in international relations and fear in place of security, what with the constant presence of war preparations and the possibility of a sudden holocaust?

Or are they the result of other causes, greater or lesser, or, possibly, the sum of all these reasons?

Other possible causes and events may have a temporary effect; but if one looks searchingly into those I have mentioned, he is led to the belief that in them lie the roots of world corruption and the causes of calamities and grinding wars.

Does the Message of Muḥammad offer any preventive measures and possible cures for such corruption? This is what we shall attempt to discover.

As regards the first definition given of the aims underlying world evils, it may be summed up in the single answer: modern colonialism.[1] Nothing is more indicative of the corrupting influence and the strength of this ill than the fact that wars did not become universal until after it had appeared and spread; as it extended into the five continents and became the pretext for materialistic strife, wars attained the proportions of a universal calamity.

With the expansion of colonialism, more countries reached out for colonies, and all nations began to believe that colonialism was the road to wealth and power; they envied, hated, and vied with each other, and were not restrained by the fact that some nations had fallen prey to their own expansionist greed—some of colonialism's earliest knights, the Spaniards, Portuguese, and French, became its victims. In his *The Wreck of Europe* (*L'Europa senza Pace,* 1921), Francesco Saverio Nitti declares that the Italians spent fourteen billion lire to buy a track of sand.[2] What was the total price paid by fascist Italy in Libya, Ethiopia, and other countries? Italy exhausted her wealth and blood and jeopardized her very existence for the sake of colonialism but achieved only destruction and ruin.

1 The *Risālah al-Khālidah,* of which this book is the translation, was written, for the most part, during World War II; since then, hundreds of millions of colonial peoples have become independent.

2 Nitti, prime minister of Italy in the prefascist years 1920-1921, was referring to Libya.

When these bloody wars, which have dealt civilization such crippling blows, are over with for all time, all nations will have come to realize that colonialism was but a mirage which they pursued and vied for, but which could not replace honest toil and the good life. Like an object thrown at a rock, it bounces back and strikes the thrower.

Colonialism has been the cause of most of the wars of the past two centuries and has left its imprint on all of them. An investigation of the causes of each war must lead back to colonialism somewhere on earth, either in the heritage of a weak nation or in the form of an object of modern worship—petroleum, gold, coal, cotton, minerals, and other fruits of the earth.

In its modern guise, European colonialism is obviously an evil for both the victor and the vanquished, the colonizer and the colonized. On the one hand, the conquering nations gradually are led to a life of reliance upon others, becoming inflicted with a deadly habit of ease; they fall into disputation with those who envy them or seek revenge upon them, thus exposing their previously powerful existence to extinction. And what has happened to certain nations in the past still has its effects on them today. On the other hand, the maintenance of colonies for material exploitation lowers the standard of living of their inhabitants and limits their ability to consume goods. In addition, it stifles their spirit of inventiveness, their initiative and productiveness, and their dignity, placing a significant segment of the world's population in a desperate position; thus they become a problem for mankind.

Stratagems and wars waged by the envious and greedy hasten the decline, even the ruin, of civilization.

Were not the Napoleonic Wars—a blight on the world, not only on France—the outgrowth of hatred and envy resulting from a desire to dominate the weak and acquire their possessions? So were the wars of Russia, Turkey, and Austria. Were not these wars undertaken for self-enrichment at the expense of the weak? The Russo-Japanese War during the early part of this century (1905) would not have taken place, because of the distance that separated these nations, had the two rivals not clashed in their expansionist aims.

Whatever the reasons one might give for the First and Second World Wars, the hatred buried deep in the hearts of those who were defeated and the desire for expansion and for acquisition of the raw materials and properties of the weak were among the fundamental causes of contention among strong, overpowering nations. And because the large nations felt strongly about the evils of colonialism, after the First World War they tried to find a remedy in the theories of the mandate system and the principle of free access to raw materials.

The evils of colonialism will continue to prevail until people discover by trial and sacrifice a solution equally acceptable to the strong and the weak. In the past, wars were limited to neighboring states, but when colonialism became worldwide, so did wars. Therefore, a need exists for common principles that will set straight the problems of the world. The sacrifice of colonialism is necessary for the salvation of present-day civilization. Already the Great Powers are searching for a way through the Atlantic Pact, and like declarations resorted to by other factions indicate that they too realize the evil colonialism has wrought on both victor and victim.

As long as force is the only criterion in the conduct of nations, hardship will persist. One of the virtues of the Message of Muḥammad is its denunciation of colonialism and of the use of force for worldly purposes. It does not sanction war for the expansion of dominion, for securing raw materials, for cornering markets, or for allegedly civilizing people. Nor does it sanction one nation's exalting itself over another, or one monarch over another, or one race over another. "O ye who believe! When ye go forth [to fight] in the way of Allah, make investigation, and say not unto one who offereth you [the salutation of] peace: 'Thou art not a believer,' seeking the chance profits of this life [so that ye may despoil him]. With

Allah there are plenteous gains."[3] The focus of the Islamic view in international relations is clear, for people are as equal as the teeth of a comb, as the Prophet says, with no preference for one race, class, or nation over another except in their piety and love for peace; and as I have said again and again, Islam recognizes no dispute that does not aim at making the word of God supreme and insuring the freedoms of all.

Certain people might say that the history of the Muslims does not conform with what they preach. We preach the Book of God and His religion, not an apology for the actions of certain Muslim states or rulers, which may resemble, more or less, what the Europeans have done. The Muslims have been punished for these actions even as modern nations have been.

There is no doubt that the Message of Muḥammad rejects colonialism in all its forms. The wisdom of its lofty and sublime views now has been affirmed as a result of the impact of colonialism on people in past centuries as well as in recent times; for when the evils of colonialism expanded, its perils took hold, and its plague became universal, it dragged the world through successive global wars.

We pray that people will awaken to guidance, that they will discover in Islamic principles the means for establishing international relations on a basis other than that of colonialism, and that this new attitude will rest on the Islamic spirit of brotherhood, which does not recognize boundaries of race, class, or narrow nationalism, does not measure rights according to knowledge and ignorance or progress and regression, and considers men only as brethren; for they are all descendants of Adam, and Adam is of dust.

[3] Koran, 4:94.

## 23

# *Class Struggle*

*

Class struggle is a by-product of European civilization.[1] Its disease has spread, and its calamities have become universal.

From the beginning of time, people have met with varying fortunes in this world; there have been the poor and the wealthy, the rulers and the ruled, the weak and the strong, the sick and the healthy, living in reasonable cooperation and understanding with each other within the jurisdiction of the tribe, town, city, metropolis, or nation. Through instinct and experience, their natural disposition has been to associate and cooperate.

The early human groupings were like beehives cooperating to produce an order acceptable to all; if they did not accept it as a matter of personal preference, they would consent to it voluntarily or by law and tradition (*'urf*). Such an order would be subjected at times to disturbances. Disorder would arise from aggression by other groups or from internal corruption in the form of exceptional cases of oppression caused by the deviation of a strong group or a strong individual who would undertake acts of tyranny and commit excesses. These troubles would usually subside, however; and the course of affairs would return to normalcy, and cooperation would be

[1] "The home of Bolshevism is Western Europe, and has been ever since the English materialists' world-view" (Oswald Spengler, *The Hour of Decision*, tr. Charles F. Atkinson [New York: Alfred A. Knopf, Inc., 1934], p. 97).

resumed through the interplay of natural instinct and custom.

In earlier times, people were not conscious of class conflict as an element of disturbance as it is today—a bitter, constant struggle between the poor and the wealthy, workers or craftsmen and proprietors or managers—though in the annals of mankind, we might find extremist ideologies, such as that of the Mazdakites in pre-Islamic Persia, advocating complete equality in living. History witnessed in the wake of the Roman Empire the struggle between the masses and the privileged or, in other words, between the slaves and the free. In the early days of Islam, there is the example of such as Abu-Dharr, a Companion of the Prophet's, who migrated from Syria complaining of opulence and objecting to land ownership.

We also learn of the Khawārij, who unsheathed their swords and plunged bravely into social anarchy with the more exalted among them declaring, "There is no rule but Allah's." They denied the necessity of government, claiming that it is corrupt by nature and that to enjoin the right and forbid the wrong through motivations of religion and conscience suffices to regulate the affairs of the people and the social order. They rejected the ruler's right to rule, while the more moderate among them refused the monarch the right of inheritance. The head of state was elected with no regard for his family or tribe; even if he had been a slave, he possessed an equal right to rule. They would abstain from worldly pursuits and call on people to do the same until the means of subsistence were equally shared, although they did not forbid the possession of property.

These ideologies were regarded as deviant, however. Few in history have followed them, and they never reached the level attained by socialism and communism in modern times, either in magnitude or in pretension. For example, Islam did not even advocate equal distribution of property, nor did the Muslims preach class struggle, as between workers and owners; unlike modern times, earlier periods witnessed no bloody conflicts between classes. The communism and socialism that have organized workers today are undoubtedly new, and are a direct result of modern capitalism.[2]

Acting through instinctive simplicity, the Muslim people understood each other. The wealthy neighbor was the friend of his poor neighbor; he knew him and his children personally. Everyone was united by a communal spirit of brotherhood and by ties of blood or protection. No matter how comfortable his living conditions might be or how extensive his power, the chieftain of the tribe or village was the chieftain of the poor and the wealthy alike, having a feeling of close attachment to all. His wealth and possessions were not held selfishly or directed toward ostentation and opulence: he prided himself on his generosity and glorified in giving. His children, despite the comfort they enjoyed, were like all children of the tribe or the village, playing the same games, eating similar food, and wearing the same kind of clothes as other children.

Sentiments of envy and jealousy were not aroused by the wealth and luxury enjoyed by the important and well-to-do. Moreover, fortunes were limited, and most of the people lived on the same modest scale.

In the modern world, with the advent of steam and electricity, fortunes expanded, and so did the influence of the wealthy, whose numbers increased. Machines replaced manual labor, communications advanced and speed increased, trade expanded; the gap between poverty and wealth widened. The world smiled on landowners, traders, and those who controlled the means of transportation. And so the new capitalistic order thrived with all of its accompanying lack of human relations; consequently, people drifted farther and farther apart in their thinking and their ways of life, and grew to be antagonistic toward one another.

It was inevitable that the deprived class, which fell into a

[2] "Capitalism and socialism are catch words for which all this time [since 1848] literature has searched in vain for a definition" (*ibid.*, p. 112).

kind of servitude to the machine and its owner, should seek a way to freedom, for it felt that despite its numbers it hardly possessed a corresponding power. It deplored existing laws and saw in them the implementation of decisions ostensibly merciful but subtly torturous, enabling the wealthy to have their own way and to use the police to their advantage. The controlling few thus triumphed over the deprived multitudes, who then turned to revolution, fostered by dreamers and frustrated leaders and parties, thus creating one of the fundamental causes of world disturbance.

World War I had hardly ended before ungovernable revolutions and bloody riots began. Their victims reached tens of millions in the Russian civil war, the flames of which raged for years. Nor were the remaining European and American regions secure from bloody riots, and the ideology that arose, communism, still impels the poor to vent their anger against the rich, the class of artisans, workers, and peasants against proprietors, thus preparing the ground for new and more dangerous outbursts everywhere.

Governments and peoples have undertaken a search for a remedy and have wandered off in many directions. Some have extirpated the propertied class, as happened in Russia; some have liquidated the spokesmen of workers and communism, as happened in Spain; and some have resorted to force and oppression in order to establish security and equilibrium, suppressing personal freedom, as happened in Italy and Germany, where dictatorial leadership removed all power of decision from the people.

It is very difficult in a rapid exposition such as this to enter into a discussion of what is called the capitalist system, its assets and liabilities, as it is likewise difficult to outline the social problem and the solutions proposed by Europeans and Americans and the ills they suffer from a system that is based on usury and selfishness. We trust to the reader's knowledge of the intricate question of class struggle, its causes and effects.

Let us examine the precepts provided by the Message of

Muḥammad to see whether we can discover a remedy for the social problem of this age.

Poverty is the first problem of society and the primary cause of class strife. We have seen in Chapters 8 and 9, "Solidarity" and "Beneficence," how Islam has treated poverty, and we shall show here that Islam has a flexible system of its own which embraces the general welfare of its classless society in curing poverty. The Sharī'ah advocated two methods to accomplish this end.

First, it gave the deprived a fixed right to a share of the wealth of all people. I say *all* because every able-bodied worker is subject to the poor tax on wealth, property, and productive assets; payment of a poor tax on al-Fitr,[3] for example, is expected of any Muslim who himself possesses what exceeds his needs for a day. In other words, the poor man is taxed to help those even poorer.

The legal taxes on the possessions of people of all classes, levied to resist and eliminate poverty and other social ills, have varied. The proceeds are specially allocated by decrees of the Koran to the needy, and the head of state may not spend them for any purpose other than that stipulated. Those entitled to charity are listed in the Koran, as in this verse: "The alms are only for the poor and the needy, . . . and those whose hearts are to be reconciled, and to free the captives [slaves] and the debtors, and for the cause of Allah, and [for] the wayfarers; a duty imposed by Allah. And Allah is full of knowledge and wisdom." [4]

The Koran does not state in detail the types of possessions that fall within the jurisdiction of the poor tax or the amount that must be paid,[5] but these questions are answered in Islamic tradition (*sunnah*) by a letter the Prophet wrote to those

[3] The day the fast is broken, following the last day of fasting in the month of Ramaḍān.

[4] Koran, 9:60. *Alms* here mean taxes, not voluntary alms.

[5] The Koran says, "In whatever they [all Muslims] possess there is [to be] a recognized part [share] as a right to the poor" (70:24).

whom he placed in charge of distributing all the funds set aside for the poor.

The Koran laid down the principle, then, and the Prophet implemented it; the Koran designated the poor tax (*zakāh*) and considered it the duty of the head of state to allocate the funds collected according to need. In our day, he might discover that little if any money was needed for the liberation of slaves or for "those whose hearts are to be reconciled" or for the wayfarer; in that case, he could increase the share for the poor or assign funds to a social security program, for he could find in the way of Allah many gates to that beneficence which is directed to the common welfare in every age according to the circumstances besetting its inhabitants.

The Sharī'ah was not content with simply stating this known right of the needy to help from those capable of payment. As a second means of doing away with poverty, it also charged the state with the duty of establishing and maintaining social equilibrium. The head of state is responsible for this equilibrium, which he regulates by use of the poor tax; if it does not suffice, he is entitled to make appropriations from the possessions of the people in the interest of the general welfare, as it is his duty to measure out justice in an equitable balance. Wherever this justice exists, it conforms to the decrees and religion of God. If this justice should demand a decision not previously decreed and which cannot be found in Muslim law, then the head of state, after consultation, is entitled to exercise *ijtihād*—that is, independent reasoning.[6]

Let us consider two cases of *ijtihād* by the great Imāms Abu-Bakr and 'Umar (may God be pleased with them).

Abu-Bakr used to divide the incomes from state revenue among his officials, pensioners, soldiers, and others equally,

[6] Independent reasoning (*ijtihād*) recognizes a full knowledge of Muslim law and a thorough acquaintance with the Koran, *ḥadīth* (sayings), and principles of jurisprudence in Islam; all this requires the consultation of the trusted counselors or jurists.

showing no preference for one over the other. He was once asked, "You have divided this wealth equally among people, but of them are there not those who are entitled to more because of their worth, good precedence, and seniority?" He replied, "Truly, I have not been informed of what you have mentioned of good precedence, seniority, and worth; that is something for Allah to reward. This equating is a means of subsistence, and equality in it is better than preference."

Under 'Umar, the caliph after Abu-Bakr, the conquests of Syria and Iraq took place. 'Umar decided upon varied wages and declared, "I will not equate between him who fought the Prophet and him who fought with him," and on that premise he organized the bureau (*dīwān*) of the army. 'Umar, who did not follow the view that equality in subsistence is better than preference, nevertheless had his own interpretation of the Koranic verse concerning spoils (*ghanā'im*); he replied to those who wanted to divide the land among its conquerors and retain only the *khums*[7] for the general welfare, "How will it be with those Muslims who are to follow when they discover that the land, together with its *'ulūj*,[8] has been divided and inherited for generations? This is not a fair law." 'Abd-al-Raḥmān ibn-'Awf, a respected Companion of the Prophet, then said to him, "What is the just procedure? The land and its *'ulūj* are but what Allah has bestowed upon the Muslims." 'Umar replied, "There is truth in what you say, but I do not see it [this way]. By Allah, no conquest will take place hereafter in which such great gains are to be had, and future conquests may even be a liability on all Muslims. Now, if the land of Iraq and the land of Syria should be divided together with their *'ulūj*, then what will be left to guard the *thughūr*?[9] What will become of the progenies and wid-

7 The *khums* consisted of the one-fifth of the booty which went to the Islamic community's treasury.

8 *'Ulūj* is the term by which non-Muslim non-Arabs settled on the land were known.

9 *Thughūr* were the Byzantine posts set up on the periphery of the empire for defense against the attacks of the enemy.

ows of the people of Iraq and Syria in this and other towns?" Yet they kept pressing 'Umar, saying, "Will you grant to a people that neither was present at nor witnessed battle and to the sons of a people and the sons of their sons who were not present what Allah has bestowed upon us by our swords?" But 'Umar would not add to his words, and said only, "This is my view."

'Umar was then asked to seek counsel, and he consulted the early Immigrants (Muhājirūn), but they differed. As for 'Abd-al-Raḥmān ibn-'Awf, he suggested that their rights be divided among them; the opinions of 'Uthmān, 'Ali, Ṭalḥah, and the son of 'Umar were identical with 'Umar's. 'Umar then sent for ten of the elders and notables of the Anṣār, five from the Aws and five from the Khazraj; once they had convened, he addressed them, saying, "I have disturbed you only that you may share in this trust over your affairs which I have been made to shoulder. I am like one of you, and today you will affirm the right. Disagree with me, whoever will, and agree with me, whoever will. And I do not desire that you follow what I desire. You have from Allah a Book which bespeaks the truth. By Allah, if I have stated something I desire, I desire not but the right."

The Anṣār then said, "Speak and we shall listen, O Commander of the Believers." He then described to them the nature of the dispute, and they confirmed his view, whereupon he decided to keep the land in the hands of its owners but to place on it the land tax (*kharāj*); and the dissenters were silent out of respect for the dominant view.[10]

This is an example of the conduct of a disciple and successor of the Prophet in a matter which ended in the issuance of a major decree, which 'Umar steadfastly upheld. 'Umar

10 'Umar was not acting solely according to *ijtihād,* as some have alleged. His action was also based on legal precedents, as that of the Prophet's handing part of the land of Khybar back to its people after its conquest by the Muslims, and on other Koranic verses than the one on which 'Abd-al-Raḥmān ibn-'Awf was basing his objection.

made the view prevail which was demanded for the general welfare and upon which he and the majority of the sages and men of counsel (*ahl al-shūrā*) of Islam agreed.

The Islamic Sharī'ah does not stand as an obstacle once the general welfare becomes known, for the Sharī'ah will not controvert the aims of welfare and justice.

The establishment of a social balance to insure that the burden of privation is lifted from the needy and that justice and social security prevail is one of the most important duties of the Islamic state. The responsibility of the imām and *ahl al-shūrā* in this matter is clear.

The propagator of the Message and his followers did not hesitate to set up the balance of social justice on the basis of the general welfare, for the Message permits of no contention among its adherents over worldly sectarian interests. It recognizes that the general welfare is indivisible, and that sects and classes are nonexistent when all are the servants of God and thus equal; in sum, the welfare of all is above the welfare of any class.

It could be ascertained that most differences are based on the claim that each represents the general welfare. Preponderant support for the general welfare, as preached in the Message of Muḥammad, is not sufficient to prevent dissension; the word *justice* does not convey the same meaning to all people so that a fixed measure exists. It would constitute a justified objection if this welfare were left free and uncontrolled and if this justice were abandoned to untested opinion. The Message of Muḥammad does not cater to irresponsible desires.

The Islamic Sharī'ah draws its instructions from belief in the Lord of all peoples, Who knows what deceives the eye and what hearts conceal, and from the right-doing (*iḥsān*) that cannot be questioned and through which the blessings of Allah are sought. Believers cannot depend on their private wishes, therefore; to them, the general welfare is of singular importance and thrives on deeds satisfactory to the Creator, namely, deeds sanctioned by His Islamic Law. Believers also enjoy a discipline in the exercise of their pure and guileless conscience. The general welfare is adjudged in terms of the brotherhood that religion has decreed and has made a condition for the perfection of faith: "Truly, none of you believes if he does not desire for his brother what he desires for himself." And "You are all of Adam, and Adam is of dust," says the Prophet. For this reason, discrimination of any sort is nullified in belief, and in belief lies the greatest guarantee of the public good.

The general welfare likewise is not entrusted to chance because there is an account for deeds that is adjudicated by a God Who has the knowledge of this world and the next. He will punish the nations that squander and indulge in excesses in this world and will award men their just due for their deeds on the Day of Judgment. Justice consists of dealing equitably and rightly, with actions weighed in terms of brotherhood and equality. That which disagrees with brotherhood and equality does not constitute justice.

Accordingly, the Islamic state, in which the imām guarantees a social balance based on the words of the Almighty, "And weigh with a right balance," [11] and in which the view of 'Umar, accepted under a specific set of circumstances, formed the basis of a decree enunciated in the interests of the general welfare and within the spirit as well as the meaning of the law, permits no room or access for class struggle.

It might be said that this understanding would apply as long as fear of and obedience to God are basic to the consideration of the general welfare; but what can be said when faith is lost and conscience becomes corrupt? The answer lies in the fact that this tragedy, which has come to pass, has upset the world and imposed calamities on European civilization and, of course, on Muslims and Orientals as well.

11 Koran, 17:35.

Because of its broad horizon and careful evaluation, the Islamic Sharīʿah also takes into account the possibility of this condition of corruption. It provides for reprimand and compulsion as means of leading people back to the right path, and it even sanctions combat to assist the oppressed, entrusting the head of state with the power to establish the right by force if necessary. When upon the death of the Prophet some Arabs apostatized and refused to render to the poor their rights, Abu-Bakr declared, "May Allah be my witness, if they should withhold from me even the tether of a camel which they used to render to the Prophet, I would fight them for it!" He did not relegate the question of the poor to the conscience of men but took up arms instead.

Because the Islamic Sharīʿah, following the decree of the Koran, stipulated the levy of the alms tax (*ṣadaqah*) to insure social security against diverse needs, the community did not have to depend on the conscience of the imām or the nation. In addition, it empowered the imām to levy taxes in the amount considered necessary to insure against needs, and placed unavoidable obligations on him toward every inflicted segment of society referred to in the Koran. Through analogical deduction (*qiyās*), which is the fourth source of Muslim law, one might add to the list in the Koran of the categories of those in need; for example, the imām is responsible for providing medication to the destitute patient, nourishment to a child whose mother cannot provide it, a home to the homeless, and food and the opportunity to work to the man who is capable of working but unemployed.

To sum up, the *ṣadaqah* is an instrument for resisting poverty and consequently a cure for social ills. The imām has the right to sponsor legislation and to further interpret the law upon consultation with wise, learned jurists and distinguished men of judgment (*ahl al-ra'y*). It is his duty to act in behalf of the general welfare and to intercede in disputes among classes and sects, seeking to prevent dissension, envy, and hatred.

The Message places a great deal of stress on conscience and makes Paradise the reward of right-doers. One discovers that the expenditure of resources for those who need them is urged in the verses of the Koran upon every suitable occasion as well as in the sayings of the Prophet. This is no place to recite dozens of Koranic verses and *ḥadīth;* it suffices to relate Allah's saying: "Tell My bondsmen who believe to establish worship and spend of that which We have given them, secretly and publicly, before a day cometh wherein there will be neither traffic nor befriending." [12]

The Muslim ethic is based on social cooperation and makes beneficence the goal of work and life. "Lo! Allah enjoineth justice and kindness, and giving to kinsfolk . . . ." [13] Every person who is properly brought up is thoroughly prepared for social service; this preparation is the most effective method for resisting social ills and for bringing people together and preventing strife.

If we consider the methods discussed for combating social problems as positive factors in preventing class warfare, then taken in the same context, the negative factors are of no less significance. It can be seen that the Islamic state, led by the imām and guided by a consultative body, which acts like a board of directors, is the greatest institution for insuring social security; it can also be seen that this state acts to raise the standard of living of the deprived class. At the same time, the Message of Muḥammad resists extravagance with the weapons of piety, faith, and religion in order to reduce false pride and luxury to a level where they will not excite envy and malice. It also conveys a death message to those who are given to extravagance and lustful indulgence, warning them that they will meet an ill journey's end, suffer the tortures of Allah, be barred from entrance into the next and better world. The Message, moreover, warns the whole of society of catastrophes

[12] *Ibid.*, 14:31.
[13] *Ibid.*, 16:90

for not admonishing and restraining its prodigals and those given to profligacy:

> And guard yourselves against a chastisement [in this world] which cannot fall exclusively on those of you who are wrong-doers . . . .[14]
>
> . . . and eat and drink, but be not prodigal. Lo! He loveth not the prodigals.[15]
>
> And how many a community have We destroyed that was thankless for its means of livelihood! And yonder are their dwellings, which have not been inhabited after them save a little. And We, even We, were the inheritors.[16]

At the root of social ruin is abundance in a nation softened by ease: "And when We would destroy a township We send commandment to its folk who live at ease [in luxury], and afterward they commit abomination therein, and so the Word [of doom] hath effect for it, and We annihilate it with complete annihilation." [17]

The Message permitted enjoyment of the niceties of property and life, but prohibited men from wearing silk and gold as a sign of its disapproval of luxury and false ornament; it permitted women to wear ornaments (silk, gold, jewels, and so forth), but curtailed their tendencies to excess by granting authority in such questions to their husbands and by prohibiting them from appearing in public dressed or acting in a provocative manner.

The Sharī'ah placed further limitations on extravagance, ease, and the display of pride, and people came to think that there was no way for the wealthy to enter the Kingdom of Heaven without parting with their wealth. Austerity thus became the symbol of piety. The Apostle of Allah himself, de-

14 *Ibid.*, 8:25.
15 *Ibid.*, 7:31.
16 *Ibid.*, 28:58.
17 *Ibid.*, 17:16.

spite the authority he was given, was one of the greatest ascetics. Says Ibn-Masʿūd:[18]

> I entered upon the Apostle of Allah while he lay on a mat that had left its marks on his side, and I said to him: "O Messenger of Allah, what would you say if we secured a carpet for you and placed it between you and the mat, protecting you from it?" And the Prophet answered: "What need I of this world! I am to the world but a rider who rests in the shade of a tree, then departs and leaves it."

Ibn-Hishām,[19] citing Zayd ibn-Aslām,[20] relates:

> When the Prophet made ʿAttāb ibn-Asīd governor of Mecca, he granted him a dirham every day. Ibn-Asīd stood up and addressed the gathering: "O people, Allah starves a belly that hungers for a dirham! The Prophet of Allah has bestowed upon me a dirham each day, and I am therefore in need of no one."

It has been told that Muḥammad came upon his daughter Fāṭimah holding in her hand a golden chain which she had been displaying to a woman in her company, saying, "This was presented to me by Abu-al-Ḥasan"—meaning ʿAli, her husband. The Prophet thereupon said, "O Fāṭimah, will it please you if people say the daughter of the Prophet displays a chain of fire!" He then went out depressed. Fāṭimah disposed of the chain by having it sold and purchased with its price a slave, whom she then freed. When the Prophet learned about it, he declared, "Praise be to Allah Who has saved Fāṭimah from fire."

The Prophet's invocation was, "O Allah, grant the family of Muḥammad what suffices it," that is, what does not exceed its needs.

The Message of Muḥammad has resisted poverty and lux-

18 A Companion of the Prophet and a famous writer on the Prophet's life.
19 The first and perhaps most authoritative of the Prophet's biographers.
20 A Companion of the Prophet.

ury, hatred and envy, and with it class struggle has become impossible. It has debased pride in wealth and ancestry and elevated the worth of piety and contentment, and it has redeemed many of the worldly belongings of people with spiritual ones. There is no doubt that Fāṭimah, having sold the chain and freed the slave, experienced a greater feeling of happiness and joy every time she remembered what she had done than if she had kept possession of the golden chain. And was 'Umar, in his patched garment, the conqueror of the Khosraus and the Caesars, of lesser possessions with his contented self than the mighty ones who were given to ease in the palaces of the Caesars and Khosraus?

The Message of Muḥammad achieved greater success in remedying social problems with methods based on self-denial and on conscience than with its positive methods utilizing *ṣadaqah* and state guarantees for the needy. And the Message was capable of bringing together law and conscience in order that both might rule at the same time and follow one course toward one objective. The call to struggle against the ills of society will endure throughout the ages.

# 24

## *Racial and National Strife*

*

Let us now consider another cause of world disturbance, namely, indulgence in racial and national strife. The resulting discrimination, conscienceless pursuit of glory and power, and disregard for the rights of others lead to arming and war.

Men in earlier ages competed with each other as tribes, envied each other as rulers, and differed over their concepts of God and the ways of God, but neither obsession for national homeland nor pride of race formed a decisive barrier between groups, as is the case with modern culture and civilization. The history of the Arabs, Turks, Berbers, and other Muslim peoples is replete with tribal strife, but all were innocent of racial strife; and such was the situation in Europe, for the ruling dynasties gathered under their standards in the name of loyalty either to the monarch or to religion various races, tribes, and nations which differed in origin and language and sometimes also beliefs. Quite often this ruling family would be of foreign origin or of a national minority from within the state. Under its banner would be organized an aggregation of peoples bound to each other by ties of law and incorporating numerous minorities, all partaking of the sorrows and happiness that befell all alike; very often these minorities were more enthusiastic and loyal toward this banner than the peoples and elements closest to them racially and linguistically who followed a different leader.

This was the situation in many of the states we have known in our century, such as the Austro-Hungarian state under the Hapsburgs; and we have seen Arab peoples more loyal and faithful to the Ottomans than to their own Arab rulers. Such was the case also in ancient states and in those of the Middle Ages, as the 'Abbāsid, Holy Roman, and Byzantine Empires. And we know of like situations in which Slavs under Austrian rule, for example, were more loyal to the Austrian ruler than to their Russian cousins.

All were equal under the triumphant monarch, who was supreme over all. And those who through talent or proper attributes climbed the ladder of rank were loyal to that monarch, not to the race or nation. Thus you find the Persian Barmakids[1] and Ṭāhirites[2] occupying the highest positions during the caliphates of the Arabian Hāshimites ('Abbāsids); so did the Köprülü family,[3] which came from the Albanian highlands during the caliphates of the Ottoman Turks. More slaves have climbed this ladder, moreover, than their numerical proportion would indicate. Dozens of Mamlūks[4] reached the height of power in Islamic states stretching from Egypt to India; they have been immortalized in monuments in Delhi and Cairo, and throughout that great Islamic territory reaching from the Atlantic to the Pacific.

People did not ask about race or origin but about deeds, character, and religiousness. Among the Mamlūks who at-

1 A vizerial family, flourished *c.* A.D. 752-903, the most powerful administrators of the Empire, ranking next to the caliphs in authority and opulence.

2 Ṭāhir ibn-al-Ḥusain of Khurāsān, descendant of a Persian slave, was rewarded with the governorship of all Muslim lands east of Baghdad stretching beyond the Oxus by the Caliph al-Ma'mūn in A.D. 820.

3 Grand viziers who upheld the structure and prestige of the Ottoman Empire in the face of manifest weaknesses in the late sixteenth and early seventeenth centuries.

4 The Mamlūks, originally slaves brought to Egypt in the tenth century, founded two dynasties in Egypt (the first in the mid-thirteenth century), which lasted 250 years. They checked the hitherto unrestrained Mongol conquests in West Asia and exerted a controlling influence over Palestine, Lebanon, and Syria as well.

tained the highest state positions we find Armenian, Russian, Sicilian, Georgian, Circassian, Tartar, Turk, Frank, Sudanese, and Ethiopian. If we should trace their pedigrees, we would discover that they represented all the colors of mankind.

Patriotism and nationalism in their present-day connotations have not helped maintain stability, unfortunately, but have rather increased world disturbance and served as a new cause for additional disputes, broader in scope and more difficult to solve. In its geographical aspect, the concept of the fatherland as an abode for a given nation has failed to define boundaries; nations overlap the territory of other nations and collide with their expansion. Nature has very rarely assisted in defining a specific area for a specific people: in the whole of Europe, only the British Isles enjoy a boundary surrounded by water—and even so, Ireland has disputed with England over the province of Ulster in the north. In places where nature did not accidentally decide the matter by an untraversable ocean or an impassable mountain range, such as the Himalayas between India and China, disputes have inevitably arisen.

At least two centuries have elapsed since Europe began drowning itself in its own blood as a result of wars aimed at regulating boundaries and liberating minorities—wars between the French and Germans and the Germans and Austrians; the Austrians, Germans, and Slavs, and the Austrians and Italians; wars between all the Balkan states; the Ottoman state and the European states; Russia and her neighbors to the west, the east, and the south; the Czechs and the Poles and the Magyars and Romanians. Thus, we find that disputes over what is termed the *fatherland* and its boundaries are ever rampant. They do not subside but increase over the years in proportion to the intensity of racism and nationalism.

This defiant European trouble, with its concomitant struggles over boundaries and race and minority questions, soon began to spread to the East from the West; when the East became indoctrinated with Western culture, it adopted Western concepts of fatherland and nationalism. The resulting problems that have arisen in recent years in the province of Alexandretta between Syria and Turkey and along the Shatt-al-'Arab River and the rest of the boundary between Iraq and Iran have resembled those of the Balkans. Because of their Muḥammadan training, Muslims did not quarrel over racial and nationalistic questions in the past, but these are now becoming the cause of calamities in the East, even as they have precipitated bloody wars in the West. Disputes of such a nature are coming to dominate the relationships of Arabs and Turks, Kurds and Circassions, Azerbaidzhanians and Iranians, Afghans and Indians,[5] Uzbeks and Chinese, Mongols, and others; it seems that all will quarrel over boundaries and minorities until the East enters the pit of hatred which the West has so long occupied.

In its modern form, nationalism is a new evil, and racism is worse still; and there is no cure for either except to uproot tens of millions from their present places of residence and confine them to specific geographic areas.

Some Europeans recently became so ardent in their particular brand of racism that they laid claims to membership in one master race of pure blood. This is an empty, unfounded assumption that serves only to increase disturbances and contentions in the world.[6] Who is capable of distinguishing between nations by analyzing their blood? It is sufficient that a people be plagued by the evils of extremist ideologies, prejudicial treatment of linguistic and national minorities, and calamities over boundaries that neither belief nor understanding comprehends.

Both the Turks and the Greeks have attempted compulsory repatriation,[7] and neither people has benefited therefrom;

[5] This was written before the partition of India. The present dispute is between Pakistan and Afghanistan over the Pathans, and between India and Pakistan over Kashmir.

[6] The theory of racial *superiority*, of course, is considerably more widespread than the master race notion ever became.

[7] As a result of the Greco-Turkish War of 1919-1923.

we need not even mention what both have experienced in the way of cruelty and disturbances that accompanied the uprooting of people from their homes and places of birth. However, this example of repatriation, which was both circumscribed and assisted by special circumstances, cannot be expanded into a general rule. Moreover, let us assume that we were able to guarantee a generation of people this change in peace; coming generations are certain to break the peace, for the nature of living necessitates mobility—interests change, nations grow and become extinct, new fusions and expansions are inevitable, and, consequently, there follows a return to cruelty and forcible expatriation.

The League of Nations attempted to solve the problems of minorities. Did it succeed? Was not this problem in the Sudetenland, Lorraine, Danzig, Transylvania, and Bessarabia one of the causes and magnifying factors of the last world war?

Extremism in patriotism or national loyalty has been a basic cause of the increase of world disturbances and the gradual expansion of wars from local struggles to universal holocausts; no corner of the globe is secure from war's dreadful reach: its growth in scope, in other words, has been consonant, along with the great expansion of nations and the modern facility of movement, with the exaggeration of the ideas of nationalism and patriotism.

The Message of Muḥammad recognizes neither nationalism nor racism in their modern contexts; the fatherland of the Muslim admits of no geographic delimitations—it coextends with the faith.[8] In reality, it is a spiritual fatherland, just as religion is a spiritual matter. "O my bondsmen who believe! Lo! My earth is spacious. Therefore serve Me only." [9] And the Muslim is brother to the Muslim wherever he may be, in his own neighborhood or in the most distant parts of the

[8] Lamartine has summed it up in a few words: "Muḥammad created a spiritual nationality which blended together people of every tongue and every race" (see *Histoire de la Turquie* [Paris, 1854], II, 276-277).

[9] Koran, 29:56.

earth. Wherever the Muslim settles in an Islamic state, he settles in his fatherland; and if he should find himself in a belligerent land (*dār al-ḥarb*)[10] among a people inimical to Muslims and consequently be relieved of certain responsibilities or rights, he resumes all his rights and obligations upon his departure from this territory or when, should circumstances change, its inhabitants enter a truce or a pact with the Muslims.

Racism, or a fanatic attachment to tribe, nation, color, language, or culture, is rejected by the Message as a product of pre-Islamic idolatry. The Prophet declares, "He is not of us who preaches bigotry." Islam rejects every form of bigotry. All loyalties are directed to the word of God, and no relation above the spiritual is recognized.

> We . . . have made you nations and tribes that ye may know one another [and be friends]. Lo! The noblest of you, in the sight of Allah, is the best in conduct.[11]
>
> Say: If your fathers, and your sons, and your brethren, and your wives, and your tribe, and the wealth ye have acquired, and merchandise for which ye fear that there will be no sale, and dwellings ye desire are dearer to you than Allah and His Messenger and striving in His way: then wait till Allah bringeth His command to pass. Allah guideth not wrongdoing folk.[12]

This is a concept that has laid the foundation of human relations on unity of thought and spiritual goals; it is without doubt nobler than the modern philosophy, which has made nationality and materialistic interests and ideologies the bases of human relations. The Islamic view elevates humanity and honors it with mind and spirit, while the modern view reduces it to the level of materialism and emphasizes its animalistic side. Concern for spiritual necessities is more conducive to peace, stability, and the exercise of mercy than is concern for bodily needs.

10 See Chapter 13.
11 Koran, 49:13.
12 *Ibid.*, 9:24.

It might be argued that in effect this assertion tacitly admits that there is strife among people over beliefs and opinions as well as over petroleum and cotton, but this scarcely would alter the fact that strife exists or minimize the consequent evils or disturbances that lead to world wars. This distinction between causes of disagreement might appear valid at first glance, but an insight into human nature reveals to us that people react more readily and are more inclined toward violence when discordant situations involve tangible objects and physical needs. The peasant might kill his neighbor over water for the irrigation of his field, or over its boundaries, but he would not be inclined to contend with this neighbor over differences of faith. Further, I have not heard of a case in which such disagreements led to assassination; if this does happen, it is rare and exceptional.[13]

Ideological missions may be accompanied by severe suppressions in the beginning, but they usually end in stability, the triumph of reason, and the prevalence of tolerance, because human beings cannot bring themselves to attack and injure others except in response to a constant incitement, an inducement related to a daily need tied to materialistic demands. And very often their enthusiasm, followed by their cruel acts, results from the pursuit of a noble idea mingled with a hidden material desire.

Nevertheless, the Message of Muḥammad has taken precautionary measures against such evils, for it forbids its partisans to use force in disseminating the Message. The Almighty decrees, "There is no compulsion in religion. The right direction is henceforth distinct from error." [14] Islam does not sanction the employment of force except to guarantee freedom in the expression and practice of faith to all people.

Therefore, we may conclude that world disturbances based on nationalistic and racist claims and on demands for material

[13] This is well known to me from my personal experience with the peasants and nomads of the Middle East.

[14] Koran, 2:256.

advantage for a nation, class, or race would be minimized if we adopted the principles of the Message of Muḥammad in human relations by assuring the triumph of the spirit which Islam, with the other revealed religions, preaches.

Perhaps mankind will find guidance in these principles; perhaps in the organization of the world following this latest terrible world war man will discover a philosophy of brotherhood, that noble, far-reaching concept that made 'Umar ibn-al-Khaṭṭāb say, after he had shed his narrow pre-Islamic loyalties and had become indoctrinated in the Muḥammadan school, "Were Sālim, the slave of Abu-Ḥudhayfah, alive, a successor would I make of him." [15] This concept the Prophet expressed in these moving words: "Truly, I am the brother of every pious man, even if he is a slave from Abyssinia, and opposed to every villain, even if he is a noble Qurayshi."

[15] When 'Umar said this, he was already caliph and had conquered the greater part of the world's two greatest empires, the Roman and the Persian —and still he would have made a liberated slave his successor!

## 25

## *The Defeat of Spiritual Forces*

*

Another cause of world disturbance is the failure of spiritual forces to counterbalance the sudden rise to prominence of materialistic life.

In the beginning, man exercised only limited control over matter; he coveted the conquest of nature far less than in the period following the discovery of steam and electricity, the uses of the atom, and the very elements that constitute matter and the transformation of their composition. When he became skillful in the application of chemical and mechanical forces, he turned his back on the metaphysical and spiritual; the investigation of nature and its rewarding victories attracted his attention over every other field of endeavor.

Within a few generations, the physical world has changed and ways of thinking have reversed themselves; if our ancestors should rise from their tombs, they would repudiate the life of modern civilization in the same manner as cave-dwellers would repudiate the very notion of skyscrapers. The modes and aims of living have changed, and man has turned to the speed he seeks and the perpetual motion he enjoys, shunning stability and tranquillity as much as his ancestors shunned clatter and speed.

The modes of life have changed suddenly, and they have yet to become stabilized; life is in perpetual flux. The gap between my father and myself is one generation, but the differences between us are greater than between my father and his forefathers dozens of generations before him.

This continual material change and this speed, which continue to multiply without finding their ultimate limitations, have caused man, in his pursuit of the new materialistic life, to be unmindful or incapable of sustaining a suitable spiritual life. He is unable to keep pace with the explosion of ideas and new concepts, which resembles the explosion of matter, to the extent necessary to preserve his spiritual heritage. The spiritual life which man has gained from the trials of thousands of years has lagged behind the new materialistic life he has acquired in one century. As this life accelerated, man felt himself weighed down with a huge spiritual inheritance that would not move with him, and so he abandoned it.

People living in various lands differ greatly in their ways of life today, while previously they were bound by spiritual and traditional ties through their attitudes toward life and their manner of personal conduct. Material and intellectual differences between members of the same generation, even the same family, in many parts of the world are greater today than they were between a man in Northern Europe and another in Central Asia several centuries ago. When Ibn-Baṭṭūṭah[1] made his famous travels around the world, I do not think that the differences among human beings whom he visited in the fourteenth century were so great as those encountered today by a peasant from Upper Egypt when visiting Cairo for the first time. In the same nation, there are diverse communities whose ideas, customs, and characteristics vary in direct relation to their ability to pursue the new materialistic life: there are those who ride on the bandwagon of the new way, those who hang on to it tenaciously, those who run after it, those who look on in bewilderment, and those who have despaired, conceded defeat, and been left stranded.

Countries that have been affected by material civilization display an external homogeneity, although their spiritual ties

[1] See Chapter 6, footnote 13.

are much weaker than they used to be; and they are quite different from those countries that are called underdeveloped.

Every nation has seen the development of unrelated classes of people; human beings have been dispersed in a world which does not recognize its members and in which classes, sects, and peoples have disavowed one another. Thoughts have become troubled, human laws adulterated, the colors of material life diversified, new ideas more numerous. The different ways of living have become remote from each other, and man's goals have increased in number and diversity. If this transition period continues, it will become increasingly difficult for men to return to a form of life acceptable to everyone or at least to the large groups, the hundreds of millions of human beings, who once were united by strong spiritual ties and shared common religious outlooks.

The belief that a materialistic life based on speed can serve as a unified concept of life, an ideological foundation acceptable to all, as hundreds of millions of Chinese and Indians accept their ancient law and religion, may perhaps be realized, though the goal remains very far off. The world will continue to face the terrors of change and instability, and people cannot cast off their spiritual and mental inheritance as they would their clothes. In the resulting confusion and indecision we first witness the diversity of thoughts, views, and ideologies, and the insistent disturbances of life.

It is imperative that we think quickly and act rapidly in order to harmonize as completely as possible our inherited spiritual life with the sudden growth in importance of materialistic life, for without this harmony the world will continue to suffer from the friction and strife that generate dreadful explosions among nations and between classes within a nation. We must, if we are to enjoy the fruits of machine civilization and exploit its benefits to the fullest, resurrect the spiritual life in consonance with the new materialistic life. There are unlimited bounties in this material civilization, for man has triumphed through the machine over many difficulties and mishaps. He has increased his products, facilitated his movements, overcome the terrors of many diseases, and learned to guard against drought. The sources of his pleasures and amusements have become numerous; and he has made the earth appear gayer, and its embellishments have proved captivating. In one century, he has progressed materially to an extent unequaled in former centuries. But also in one century, he has come close to discarding entirely the spiritual heritage that he has gained over thousands of years.

The Koran says, "They have forgotten God and God caused them to forget themselves." [2] In a few generations, spiritual life has been dealt a formidable defeat by the forces of materialistic life, aided by the deaf machine which has come to dominate man; and man has wrought havoc aimlessly, unrestrained by religion, moral character, or law. Mankind's spiritual heritage has been of no avail. People question its value and look upon it skeptically. Some are sympathetic, with the sympathy of the living toward the dead; others rejoice over its misfortune as a conqueror rejoices over the misfortune of the conquered; still others are faithful to it, but since they are preoccupied with themselves, they have lagged behind the procession of civilization, which advances with the glory and splendor of the victor.

Without any apparent reflection, we seem to have adopted a course that has turned the benefits we enjoy into tools of destruction for ourselves and our civilization. Rather than supporting spiritual forces by giving them the zeal and energy we give materialistic forces, we undertake to forge new opinions and to invent new theories and concepts to give them value. As we advocate and implement such dangerous ideas, we march on to ruin.

In the name of freedom for women, we destroy the serenity of the home; in the name of freedom for the fatherland, we tear nations asunder. In the name of freedom for labor or capital, we shall wipe out capitalism and oppress all classes;

[2] Koran, 59:19.

and on the contrary, in the name of resistance to abuse of these freedoms, we shall lose the freedom of the individual and the group as well as freedom of opinion. Men of judgment and intelligence, scholars and philosophers, have never exercised less influence on human society than in the age of the triumphant machine, the age in which we live today.

Yet the complete defeat of religion and the traditional law and ethics based on the trials of thousands of years has not been achieved. If they disappear without being replaced by something to bolster spiritual life and ethical standards, what restraint will then remain upon these exploding forces released from nature and these ungovernable machines which man has failed to direct exclusively toward the public good? The thinking of sane minds must not be drowned out by the noise of the machine; men must be patient and strive on behalf of the spiritual life to keep spiritual values abreast of material values so that both will unite as one family and not contest each other.

The view of Islam was farsighted when it called for the marriage of both conditions, thereby enhancing its heritage, in this saying: "Build for yourself in this world as if you would live forever, and build for your afterlife as if you would die tomorrow." This world is but the means (*maṭiyah*) to the next.[3] Let materialistic life, which has taken on so many forms in one century, serve as a vehicle (*maṭiyah*) to the eternal life that remains, the life of virtue, the merciful life.

It may appear that I am denying the ethical and spiritual exaltation that has accompanied this sudden prevalence of materialism and am condemning the favors of this new civilization. Regarding the latter, I do not reject these favors, although one worries about the ground lost by intelligence before the progress of the deaf machine, which seems to carry us with it; the value of things lies in how men use them and

[3] Life, worship, society, and state are but a vehicle (*maṭiyah*) for the eternal life; Islam's Kingdom of God on earth is intended as a means to His Kingdom in Heaven.

in what men accomplish with them. Regarding the spiritual "gains" of the machine age, we who have witnessed the horror of world war twice within a quarter of a century are most entitled to question the true value of a civilization encompassing these wars as part of its manifestation; and we have every right to stop, reflect, and reconsider the spiritual force of religion. Perhaps we may draw from it the weapon of human conscience to use against the tyranny of the deaf machine. Let us return to that spiritual force which used to direct us toward the common welfare with the words of the Almighty, "Ye are the best community that hath been raised up for mankind. Ye enjoin right conduct and forbid indecency . . . ,"[4] and which restricted the aims of life to right-doing and resistance of evil.

When life is aimed at struggling over markets for the distribution of the products of the machine and wringing new or artificial markets out of nations for new products, opening the land for its buried ores and then fighting over the raw materials in order that the machine may continue to run, turning men into slaves of the machine who strive to outrace each other in catering to its demands, and finally instigating world wars in which the entire forces of the machine prevail for its self-destruction and that of human civilization, we have a situation that cannot last. It appears to result from the lack of development of moral strength and men's failure to support the moral good because they are giving their full attention to material things.

Let there be a return to religious guidance, and let there be harmony among religions that man may derive strength from them. The spiritual and material forces of life must achieve an equilibrium in which the former directs the latter toward the general welfare in accordance with the duty laid upon man by the Almighty: "He hath ordained for you that religion which He commended unto Noah, and that which We revealed unto thee [Muḥammad], and that which We

[4] Koran, 3:110.

commended unto Abraham and Moses and Jesus, saying: Establish the religion, and be not divided therein." [5]

The present-day domination of materialism threatens the defeat of the spiritual forces of intelligence, manly virtue, faithfulness, chivalry, piety, mercy, and contentment. And if these qualities are defeated, then ignorance, faithlessness, treachery, selfishness, deception, and cruelty will take their place, nourishing the sources of disturbance in the world order.

Because the Message of Muḥammad expresses concern for the spirit and its purification, because it strikes a balance between the demands of this world and those of the next and sets the Sharī'ah upon the scales of justice, weighing the needs of the spirit against the needs of the body, it resists materialistic tyranny and stands strong against that cause of world disturbance. "[He] who perfected [a soul] inspired it [with conscience of] what is wrong for it and [what is] right for it. He is indeed successful who causeth it to grow, and he is indeed a failure who stunteth it." [6]

[5] *Ibid.*, 42:13.
[6] *Ibid.*, 91:7-10.

# 26

## *The Triangular Forces of Corruption*

*

Besides those discussed, other causes of world disturbance exist, less significant perhaps but still important, particularly as they concern the achievement of a durable peace and good relations between peoples and nations.

Of the many causes related to world disorder, treachery, deception, and hypocrisy, which disturb man's moral character, have left the worst marks on human society. While introducing evil and harm into the lives of individuals, these forces have also had far-reaching consequences, damaging relations among nations. For this reason, the Message of Muḥammad urges men repeatedly to resist the manifestations of such forces in their manners and relationships. Most regrettably, blameworthy traits like these have flourished to a degree that reflects the weakening of spiritual life and the growing strength of materialism; and men today resort to evil behavior that would have been shunned by their forefathers as out of keeping with honor and dignity. Many men have begun to look upon a traitor as they would upon a man of intelligence who excels in good conduct and to measure his worth in terms of his success, while they remain unconcerned by the methods he has utilized, however debased they may be. When self-respect and the honor accorded to virtue weaken, treachery thrives in international relations and international ties become seriously endangered.

Anyone who has followed closely the course of world politics during the past half-century can point to countless treacherous actions, and very rarely will he find a pure link in the chain of repugnant double-dealing. Unanticipated attacks and the violation of pacts have become almost the rule, whereas formerly, as following the introduction of the etiquette of chivalry in the Middle Ages by the Arabs when Islam was expanding, and even in the days of the Jāhilīyah, such acts were looked upon as debasing the value of individuals and nations and were generally disapproved of.

The venerable Book constantly excoriates traitors and incites men to faithfulness, and the sanctity of an agreement is placed above that of religion: ". . . but if they seek help from you in the matter of religion then it is your duty to help [them] except against a folk between whom and you there is a treaty." [1] To honor an agreement and sanctify fidelity has been a matter of pride to Muslims throughout the ages. The Koran disparages traitors in the words of the Almighty:

> Fulfill the covenant of Allah when ye have covenanted, and break not your oaths [pacts] after the asseveration of them, and after ye have made Allah surety over you. Lo! Allah knoweth what ye do. And be not like unto her who unraveleth the thread, after she hath made it strong, to thin filaments, making your oaths a deceit between you because of a nation being more numerous [and dominant] than [another] nation. Allah only trieth you thereby . . . .[2]

The likening of the traitor to a woman who unravels the thread after she has spun it is of significance to those who toy with their pledges, hurling them into the abyss of imprudence; when treachery replaces the fulfillment of pacts and pledges, it results in universal discontent. "Truly, for every traitor a standard will be established on the day of resurrec-

1 Koran, 8:72.
2 *Ibid.*, 16:91-92.

tion in proportion to his treachery, and no treachery is greater than that committed by an imām," says the Apostle of God.

During his entire life, the Prophet himself set the highest example of loyalty in his relationships with individuals and groups. An example is found in the history of his long regard for a pagan enemy, the Quraysh nobleman al-Muṭ'im ibn-'Adiy, the same man who safeguarded Muḥammad's entry into Mecca on his return from al-Ṭā'if. Al-Muṭ'im was among the enemy's dead at the Battle of Badr. Though he was a polytheist who lost his life while fighting against the Prophet, he was eulogized in a poem composed by the Prophet's poet, Ḥassān ibn-Thābit, who recited it in the presence of Muḥammad himself. The Prophet listened without voicing any objection. This is strong evidence of the value of loyalty in the eyes of the Messenger of Allah, a value unmarred by religious differences or war.

At first glance, treachery may appear to be a means of attaining victory since men have long talked about war as justifying deception. However, there is a marked difference between treachery, a surprise attack, and the betrayal of an oath on the one hand and deception in combat on the other. Deception in battle is a trick. The opponent realizes that he is being exposed to it, and that he has no promise that it will not be resorted to; consequently, it falls within the province of legitimate war. If you should lead your enemy to believe that you will approach him with all your forces from one direction and then send only a few, deploying most of your men in another direction, this does not constitute treachery; it is merely the art of war, which is not incompatible with moral behavior as long as human beings regard war as consistent with manly virtue and ethical conduct.

On the other hand, treachery is frowned upon even by villains. When a bedouin chief whom I once knew betrayed a criminal to the government after promising him help, justifying himself with the saying *"Al-khawn 'awn,"* "To betray is to assist [oneself]," he was roundly condemned by his own men, although they had been engaged in a life of feuding with the tribe of the betrayed man. The saying acquires a special significance and danger, furthermore, when we consider relationships among the great nations of the world.

Betrayal, the use of surprise attacks, and the perpetration of cruel deeds on innocent victims who are unaware of what is happening, in complete disregard of pledges or of human virtue, are not uncommon. It is as true among contemporary nations as it was in ancient times that treachery is a source of constant turmoil and insecurity. Yet recourse to treachery as a means of obtaining victory scarcely yields any special benefits to traitors at any time; they may win the first battle, but inevitably they wind up as victims, for "Allah guideth not the snare of the betrayers." [3]

Treachery among nations leads ultimately to conspiracy and suspicion. Men are then deprived of the blessing of security in peace as in war. We behold the present generation seething in the midst of calamities from which it will graduate into an atmosphere of fear and preparation for new wars; indeed, such is the promise of punishment from Heaven. For this reason, Islam insists on the fulfillment of pledges, even when made to a betrayer—it is preferable that one carry out his pledge in exchange for treachery than that he return treachery for treachery.

As regards lying and hypocrisy, it cannot be said that people are more inclined to veracity than they used to be; nor can it be said that lying is an ethical characteristic that has emerged in its worst form in the machine age. Honesty is no more respected today than in former times. What we lament in this age is prevarication in politics and international relations. We can assert that lying and deception do more to upset international relations today than they did in the past.

In *The Prince*, for example, Machiavelli sets forth views that are deemed unacceptable in the light of standards of ethical character and virtuous behavior; although today peo-

[3] *Ibid.*, 12:52.

ple conform to Machiavelli's views, they do not display his honesty when declaring themselves. *The Prince* would appear to indicate that people in the Middle Ages showed greater veracity than do men today, who denounce Machiavellism while at the same time making use of it.

Islam deplores and shuns lying and hypocrisy in politics, which people consider so justifiable and such necessary tools of diplomacy that they skillfully develop their use. The annals of early Islamic conquests are living testimony to the honesty and truth exercised in relationships between friends and foes alike. The biographies of the early caliphs who promulgated the Message of Muḥammad are redolent with the simplicity of truth and the clarity of right-dealing; when they, their emissaries, or their representatives spoke, wrote, or gave pledges, it was with an explicitness entirely free of double meanings. Their words were lucid, unembellished, and simple. "I am host of a home in the suburbs of Paradise," said the Prophet, "for him who resorts not to disputation, even though he be right, and of a home in the middle of Paradise for him who resorts not to lying even in gesture, and of a home in the heights of Paradise for him whose moral character has been purified."

Anyone reading the Book of Allah and learning the traditions of the Prophet will come to the conclusion that lying and hypocrisy are more debased than blasphemy, for Allah has cursed liars and placed hypocrites on the lowest level of the Inferno. At first one might not appreciate the wisdom of this strict attitude, but if he should consider the far-reaching general effects of hypocrisy, even ignoring for a moment its effects on the hypocrite, he would discover that it forms an essential element of the corruption prevalent in the world today. More specifically, on reflecting upon the turmoil that engulfs the modern world, would not one discover that hypocrisy is one of the primary causes of world disturbance? If the organizers of the League of Nations had established that organization on a foundation of honesty and fidelity, would it have collapsed as it did? Would its failure have led to the widespread corruption that manifested itself during World War II? If those who preach respect for the general welfare and the sanctity of human rights were sincere, truthful, and free of deception, would men dispute the meaning of such rights and of the general welfare as they do today?

Indeed, hypocrisy has forged the pattern for men; if one utters the beloved expressions *freedom, equality,* and *justice* and speaks of the right of all to live in happiness and perpetual peace, men suspect an ulterior motive and think that truth has taken on the garb of falsehood.

The effect of hypocrisy, however insignificant in the relationships of individuals, grows many times stronger, becoming a rampant evil, when nations and their rulers adopt it as a tool in domestic and foreign relations. Basing a policy on treachery, lying, and hypocrisy is forbidden by the Message of Muḥammad and rejected by all the religions of God because it nourishes world conflict and contributes to the destruction of civilization.

# VIII

## *In Search of a Spiritual Bulwark for Civilization*

*

## 27

## *Trusteeship over Civilization*

*

Whereas the foundations of Islamic civilization are moral and spiritual, those of materialistic civilization are utilitarian. The question to consider is which of the two deserves to serve as the stabilizing influence or bulwark. While analyzing this question, we may well uncover certain hidden factors working for the downfall of civilization and come upon an explanation for certain causes of turmoil in the world today.

What do we understand by "the right," and whose prerogative is it, that of the most powerful or the most pious? Several thousand years of history teach us that civilization does not confine itself to any particular area, nor is it the monopoly of any one people. As a matter of fact, it may be compared to a commodity, like gold, circulating from hand to hand the globe over and ultimately returning to its point of origin.

Civilization therefore belongs to no one race in particular; it benefits those who are able to sustain it until such time when, through failure to shoulder its responsibilities, they relinquish it to others more worthy of marching forward with it. History amply testifies to the fact that no one people or race has had exclusive possession of civilization or been especially endowed with unique capacities for discernment.

Anthropology, the science of man, refers to types of human species and, in spite of its ambiguities and limitations, differentiates between one people and another in physical terms, but it does not measure differences in mind and spirit. When attempting to establish categories on the basis of inherent and spiritual differences between peoples and thus to discover the merits of one race over another for bearing the message of civilization and culture, we must move on from true science to speculation.

Indeed, modern anthropological studies might help us measure the intelligential capacities of certain human groups as distinct from others, but it cannot help us delineate the multiple facets of moral and spiritual traits and instincts and their manifestations. To say it another way, as a science anthropology can guide us to an understanding of certain spiritual elements which we regard of some significance in determining the merits of a race to bear the message of civilization; however, this role requires a number of varied spiritual and moral forces and a balance between such forces.

Let us look into the racial differences existing among peoples of the world, beginning with the time when the Pharaohs raised the pyramids in witness of their far-reaching ambitions and as an expression of the civilization attained by the ancient Egyptians.

Egypt played the first and most important role in the development of civilization; it was she who taught man agriculture, building, and writing. Next came the Sumerians, Babylonians, Phoenicians, Assyrians, Chaldeans, Persians, Greeks, Carthaginians, Chinese, Indians, Romans, and Arabs; they were in turn followed by the nations of Europe and, in recent times, of America, all of whom added to and improved upon civilization.

If we assume that civilization had its origins in Egypt and has reached its highest material expression in America today, and if we leave aside for the moment the fate of the yellow race and its influence on our part of the globe, we will be able to confine the area of the civilizations we are dealing with to Western Asia, North Africa, Europe, and America.

Anthropologists seem to agree that what they call the Caucasian race consists of three racial subdivisions, distinguished by clearly defined physical differences, whose habitat stretches from West to East. To the extreme north we have the "Northerners" or Nordics, to the south of them the Alpines, and to the south of the latter the Mediterraneans. The Nordics are tall, blue-eyed, and long-headed; the Alpines are round-headed, and the Mediterraneans are long-headed and shorter in body than the Nordics, with black hair and dark eyes.

There is no need to dwell upon the physical differences by which anthropologists have distinguished among these racial elements or to go into tracing their past and present, as we derive no particular assistance from these data in reconstructing ancient civilization. We possess no absolute standards of truth for the peoples who carried the torch of civilization before the Arabs or for the Arabs themselves. The same scientific research that has pointed to physical differences among the three elements of the so-called Caucasian race shows also that no one nation is populated uniquely with any one element. As insulated as Britain is, still she contains all three racial types, and in proportions that have no specific relation to distance from lands of origin; in the British Isles, the Mediterraneans are proportionally greater in number than are the Alpines. All that we can affirm confidently is the predominance of the physical traits of a given racial element in one nation over its other racial traits.

Even if we were able to measure the physical differences mentioned with accuracy, we would still be far from able to measure spiritual forces and influences in any one people; nor could we obtain a better knowledge of these influences even if we were to consider them the outcome of the interaction of blood inheritances from different peoples. Consequently, we are justified in asking, whose civilization is this? Can we attribute it to any one race or deny it to any other?

Were not ancient nations, the Pharaonic Egyptians notwithstanding, like those of today, a mixture of races in which the Mediterranean predominated? What are the few thousand years about which we know a little when compared to the tens of thousands of years in human history about which we know nothing? Whether the ancient civilizations were shouldered by one of the three racial elements in the Western world or by peoples born of an intermingling of the three, there is one consideration which we cannot escape: civilization is not specifically or exclusively related to any one set of racial traits, that is, it does not necessarily either reside with or bear the stamp of a single race's characteristics. Civilization is not the product of natural hereditary forces, nor is it the rightful possession, so to speak, of the physically most powerful under any circumstances.

With all its materialistic and cultural offshoots, civilization is a product of spiritual conditions which do not necessarily accompany the physical traits that distinguish one people from another. No matter how much effort we might put into an attempt to find evidence that certain physical traits point to certain spiritual peculiarities, we would still be far from an understanding of the mystery, for we cannot alter the truth that no set of distinct racial traits with which we are familiar possessed at any time in human history a monopoly over intelligence, knowledge, and originality. What is clear is that the spirit alone illuminates the obscurities of human life once the ground has been prepared for it. The bulwark of civilization is spirit and moral character, not materialistic force. How true Koranic law is in this respect, as revealed in the words of the Almighty: "Lo! Allah changeth not the condition of a folk until they [first] change that which is in their hearts . . . ."[1]

Even if we were to assume that spiritual traits, like physical, can be inherited, still there would be no doubt that other intangible influences shape and mold spiritual forces and that strong beliefs and ethics are what initiate and safeguard civilization.

We are as ignorant of the nature and depth of the spirit as

1 Koran, 13:11.

we are of the causes and effects, the sources and consequences of spiritual action, which prevents us from establishing scientific principles by which to distinguish among the spiritual traits of races as we do among the physical. All we are able to determine from observing and reading about the present or the past is that peoples of varying racial strains are equally ready to acquire knowledge and pursue ethical conduct, and that in general they can adopt a civilization and a culture regardless of its form or source.

If we overlook certain limited differences based on climate and other circumstances in given situations, we are on safe ground when we speak of the complete equality of human spirits; at least, we know of no evidence to the contrary. The transmission of knowledge and initiative or of ignorance and corruption throughout the ages reflects a common and equal proclivity on the part of all men for good or evil. And if the differences we note can be considered as the result of living under varying conditions, then we can claim that they also are indicative of a common spiritual capacity; in other words, the mental resources of all men are similar.

This suffices to negate the theory that certain physical racial traits automatically imply certain spiritual characteristics and thus give one race perpetual predominance over others. We are justified in saying that there is no indication of differences either in physical or in spiritual traits that would make a civilization a monopoly of a segment of mankind or would prevent the universal acceptance of the obligations set forth in the Islamic Sharī'ah. Once this becomes clear, racial doctrines crumble, as does the principle of force *qua* force as a basis for civilization. For if on the other hand it could be proved that nature chooses and prepares a certain people to lead in knowledge and progress, then this people would have the right to compel others to imitate them; that is, this compulsion would be justified.

Experience, science, and knowledge do not assure predominance to any one people. Moreover, the conduct of nations shows that they tend to utilize the forces granted them to benefit themselves at the expense of those they have temporarily defeated. The desire to become the master race does not originate from traits inherent in any one race. History has shown that defeated nations do not necessarily benefit from their conquerors; on the contrary, they can be obliterated as a result of subjugation.

To say that might makes right is to show preference for some nations over others for no natural reason and to sanction tyranny for those capable of exercising it to wipe out the rights of the weak. This the Islamic Sharī'ah vehemently rejects; the Sharī'ah requires the same obligations of all before the law, trusts the most pious and beneficent, and decrees that people constitute one family with the kindest among them the favored of God.

The faithful Messenger declares, "There is no preference for an Arab over a non-Arab except for his piety and what Allah has given him of love for human welfare and peace." The noblest is not the strongest physically or the one who possesses the largest inheritance or the most learned but rather the kindest spiritually, for the kind spirit is enshrined in piety, which prevents it from perpetrating evil and moves it to do good.

## 28

# *The Maintenance and Perpetuation of Civilization*

*

The bulwark of Islamic civilization is spirituality, and the proper guardians of civilization are thus the most pious and most beneficent. I have just said that men are equal, that the science of man falls short in explaining the truth concerning mental capacities and responsiveness to impulses, and that the external racial differences manifest in human beings do not render one race any more qualified than the next to create civilization or give to any one people as distinct from another a monopoly over civilization.

The history of mankind indicates that civilization is a torch passed on from age to age and shows how the nations that produced the greatest civilizations eventually fell from the apogee to the perigee of their glory.

If we were to trace history back nation by nation over the span of five thousand years, we would discover that one unchangeable rule applies: a nation rises and falls like a stone thrown up in the air, rising to the height of its range, hovering momentarily, then falling straight to the ground. The nation that rises, however, is somewhat different from the nation that falls and disintegrates. For some of the nations that have survived seem to have left their descendants unaware of their glory, as if no ties exist between them and their forefathers!

How can we explain the causes of the rise and fall of nations? Those who adhere to the economic interpretation of history attribute them to material factors, of which the Koran gives a more concise explanation in these words of the Almighty: "These are [only] the vicissitudes which We cause to follow one another for mankind . . . ." [1] These men explain the rise and fall of societies in terms of matter—as the fructification or transformation of land from natural causes like rain and climate, the discovery of new routes, the invention of a tool, the output of a mine, or similar developments which enrich and increase the materialistic elements of life. They claim that these are the forces that impel a people to become civilized and to achieve progress, even as the loss of such economic forces is followed by downfall and deterioration.

Others see the reason for the emergence of a certain nation as inherent in the race itself—in the strengths derived from its racial heritage and from intermingling with peoples of like background; out of this is born a stronger racial strain which is directed toward loftier heights and which adds growth, knowledge, and culture to the human heritage.

These assertions alone are insufficient to explain the enigma; many a time a people has succeeded and failed, its civilization has risen and fallen, without economic conditions accounting for its appearance and disappearance. The ancient Egyptians and Babylonians, who stood at the head of civilization, were the ones who planted the desert; it was not the desert that planted them. They rose and fell in a land always fertile.

The egress of the Arabs from the peninsula and their expansion, their bridging of old and modern civilization, and their innovations in and cultivation of sciences and industries were not due to local economic reasons, even as the fall of the Arabs, the Romans, the Egyptians, and the Babylonians was not due to barren lands, changing climates, or new routes and newly discovered lands.

[1] Koran, 3:140. Opportunities for races rotate throughout history; no one nation has been eternally endowed by God with superior gifts.

Very often material deprivation was a seeming cause of emergence—a people achieved control over their surroundings and won difficult goals by crusading efforts, and in the process created mighty civilizations for the world; this was the case, for example, with the Greeks, Arabs, and Phoenicians. The resources of America and Central Africa did not produce a vigorous civilization for thousands of years, but American civilization was made by the disinherited, heirs of European culture.

Furthermore, there is no scientific proof that the integral self-perpetuation of a people, that is, their refraining from intermarriage with others, results in their deterioration—the contrary seems to apply. Indeed, it has been said that the emergence of the ancient Egyptian civilization was the result of the incursion of alien peoples, the predecessors of the Arabs, who mixed with the inhabitants of the Nile Valley to produce the ancient Egyptians who built the pyramids. It does not necessarily follow, however, that the reinvigoration of a people is a prerequisite for their continued ascendancy.

In sum, neither the economic nor the anthropological theory is sufficient to explain the causes for the emergence or disappearance of a civilization. Either view may throw light on a given situation, but not in all cases.

If we want to be specific in our views, we will discover that spiritual and moral causes have always contributed substantially to the emergence or disappearance of a civilization, and that ethical factors are always the determining elements among all peoples. The Koran yields numerous verses in confirmation:

> Lo! Allah changeth not the condition of a folk until they [first] change that which is in their hearts . . . .[2]
>
> Like Pharaoh's folk and those who were before them, they disbelieved Our revelations and so Allah seized them for their sins. And Allah is severe in punishment.[3]

[2] *Ibid.*, 13:11.
[3] *Ibid.*, 3:11.

That is because Allah never changeth grace He hath bestowed on any people until they first change that which is in their hearts . . . .[4]

And if the people of the townships had believed and kept from evil, surely We should have opened for them blessings from the sky and from the earth. But [unto every messenger] they gave the lie, and so We seized them on account of what they used to earn.[5]

And verily We have written in the Scripture, after the Reminder: My righteous slaves will inherit the earth.[6]

Allah hath promised such of you as believe and do good works that He will surely make them to succeed [the present rulers] in the earth even as He caused those who were before them to succeed [others]; and that He will surely establish for them their religion which He hath approved for them . . . .[7]

Allah coineth a similitude: a township . . . dwelt secure and well content, its provision coming to it in abundance from every side, but it disbelieved in Allah's favors, so Allah made it experience the garb of dearth and fear because of what they used to do.[8]

How many a community that dealt unjustly have We shattered, and raised up after them another folk! And, when they felt Our might, behold them fleeing from it! [But it was said unto them:] Flee not, but return to that [existence] which emasculated you and to your dwellings, that ye may be questioned. They cried: Alas for us! Lo! we were wrongdoers. And this their crying ceased not till We made them as reaped corn, extinct.[9]

No people went out into the world with a message of knowledge and civilization without having been prepared for it by a strong faith, a strong culture, and a strong calling; and no nation's beliefs lessen, ethical conduct deteriorates, or existence wavers without its being struck as others before it and falling as if it had never existed. True belief, sound moral

[4] *Ibid.*, 8:53.
[5] *Ibid.*, 7:96.
[6] *Ibid.*, 21:105.
[7] *Ibid.*, 24:55.
[8] *Ibid.*, 16:112.
[9] *Ibid.*, 21:11-15.

conduct, and righteous laws can be compared to the power of fuel in a missile, propelling a nation forward to the extent permitted by the power and righteousness of its beliefs.

If the general culture and customs of a people are considered as moral forces, then it is these that push a nation forward. If these elements deteriorate, a civilized nation will remain for a time in its present state and then fall to the ground, a lifeless society. History attests to the fact that the decline of every nation begins when materialism gains control over its life, leading it and replacing spiritual and moral values in predominance; in other words, when a lust for luxury replaces spiritual desire, that is the decisive point of demarcation between progress and regression.

Some consider Western civilization as having reached this stage undeceived by the power displayed by materialistic forces; but not wealth nor knowledge nor airplanes, tanks, and cannons nor any of the instruments for the control of materialistic life can avert the defeat of civilization and the obliteration of peoples whose beliefs have shrunk, whose conduct has deviated, and whose laws have become perverted.

Learned men do not consider brilliant mental powers as necessary for material advancement. Such advancement may continue for some time even though man may lack brilliance and proper perspective; a people may continue to prosper until the judgment of God, reserved for the overluxurious, ends a civilization: ". . . when the earth hath taken on her ornaments and is embellished, and her people deem that they are masters of her, Our commandment cometh by night or by day and We make it as reaped corn as if it had not flourished yesterday."[10]

The coming of the commandment by night or by day refers to the element of surprise; for the decline of a civilization and the downfall of those who maintain it would not be detailed by any apparent evidence but would be subtle and difficult to perceive, as are the forces of mind and spirit that are the real

10 *Ibid.*, 10:25.

and fundamental causes of the continuation or the downfall.

It is very difficult for us to explore deeply the causes, effects, and speed of the decline and extinction of a civilization, but that does not prevent us from pointing to two factors which might be agreed upon: the life of ease, and the loss of faith.

Once a righteous spiritual home has been prepared for a nation, it grows and advances to achieve knowledge and better itself. It produces, and things go well for it because of the faith and ethical behavior that unite it, set its course, prevent it from deviating, and preserve it from faltering and despairing. Before long, this nation finds itself enjoying the bounties of life with the niceties of material possessions within its reach. Preoccupied with such niceties and indulging in them, a nation may then begin to live for these pleasures and to compete with other nations in its lusts. The message of truth then becomes burdensome to it because of its loss of patience and the delights it finds. Next it begins to doubt the origin of its civilization, to question every aspect of its ethical heritage, and to turn its attention away from the mission of truth. Soon the traditions that bind it are lost; the forces that sustain its existence crumble; sterility begins to play havoc, and turmoil sets in. Allah now appoints as trustees over civilization other peoples who are "empty-bellied," in the Prophet's phrase, and who love the truth at least as much as the materialistic love their luxurious life.

The life of ease engenders the second cause of deterioration. The message to earlier people is simple because they master it by devoting themselves to it; but to their successors, the burdens of the message increase with the natural growth of civilization itself and its demand for greater efforts, clear-sightedness, and unceasing vigilance. The cavalry captain in the army of an early conqueror is replaced after a generation in a new empire that has attained new standards of civilization by the commander of an army, the manager of an industry controlling tens of thousands of workers, and the director of a bank handling billions in currency.

At such a juncture, civilization requires from its partisans unoccupied hearts, pure minds, and healthy bodies, as its load has become heavier. But in the meantime, the life of pleasure will have deprived men of their reason; delight will have put an end to simplicity, for "Allah hath created not two hearts in the hollow of man." [11] The new generations become incapable of assuming the burden of the culture originated by their ancestors, lose their faith, and collapse, stripped of their spirit, victims of their own crooked ways. In their ascendancy, the forefathers were martyrs to truth, virtue, and chivalrous action; they met death with some satisfaction. They will be remembered with gratitude while their descendants, who loved material things, will be forgotten.

There is no doubt that righteous belief clothed in piety is the primary force that builds a civilization; the loss of righteous belief presages civilization's doom. Furthermore, the faith that rests on a set of beliefs suitable for progress engenders and gives power to righteous laws and ethical behavior. These are the forces that organize civilization and are the prelude to the decisive phase of a civilization's growth. The ordinances of Allah are based on the assumption that man's soul delights in possessions, in success, and in the benefits and niceties of the earth; if these are prepared for man, then he is relieved of the necessity of striving for them, an effort which in turn tends to render him iniquitous and to lead him to the fate of former like-minded nations.

It is a cause of grief that we should behold in the world today a foreshadowing of God's pending judgment. There is no evidence that much piety exists either among Muslim nations, considered regressive, or among the Christians and Jews, who are regarded as progressive. Beliefs seem to have deteriorated and beneficence to have departed; love of this world's goods has prevailed, and ingratitude has arisen everywhere. Has the promise of God approached? We pray to God to entrust

11 *Ibid.*, 33:4. The meaning of the verse is that man can devote his loyalties to only one cause at a time.

the care of civilization to "empty-bellied people" who love the right as those who claim to be civilized love possessions and wealth—to a people who would inherit civilization, add knowledge to it, progress with it, and restore to this world the intelligence and faith of which it has been deprived.

Those who inquire will find in the Message of Muḥammad what the pioneers found: spirituality, enlightenment, piety, and guidance. Indeed, they will discover the guidance which the Qurayshis once derided, saying, "If we were to follow the right path with thee [Muḥammad], we should be torn out of our land." [12] But when the Qurayshis followed Muḥammad, they were seized and dispersed from their land not for a servile life but for their honor and glory in the world!

12 *Ibid.*, 28:57.

# 29

## *A New Order for the World*

*

Let us endeavor as best we can to discover those bases which we consider appropriate for a new order acceptable to individuals, communities, and nations alike. In so doing, we shall avoid opinionated declarations made by spokesmen the world over, and we shall seek to free ourselves from the biases of others regarding any one creed. Should we succeed, it would be all to the better; should we fail, then it is hoped that our efforts in the search for truth and guidance will lead to similar attempts in the future.

We must be willing to eschew those theories which some time ago were looked upon as realities but which through the evolution of social life and the rapid increase in the speed of communication have become damaging to the course of civilization. There is no doubt that the world is going through a trial the like of which has not been seen before; from our knowledge of history, we do not know of anything similar to the events that have astounded the modern world in one generation. The Tartar raids, still referred to as catastrophes, are unworthy of mention in comparison with the widespread destruction and killing wrought by air weapons and the mass extermination made possible through the misuse of modern knowledge. It is urgent, therefore, that we seek a new order for this world to rescue it from downfall and ruin.

What will the nature of this order be? This is a problem

that interests people everywhere. If we approach the subject as would a doctor searching for the cause of an illness, we may hit upon a method of diagnosis and cure.

The first question that comes to mind is why our modern civilization is accompanied by such prevalent evil, regardless of man's advances in science and general knowledge.

A striking element of modern civilization is *speed.* Let us examine this for a moment. How many centuries did man spend in learning how to use animals as means of transportation? How many additional centuries lapsed before he discovered the wheel so that an animal could move it, and before he used a sail on a boat and made use of the wind? And during all these centuries, to what extent did the speed of his movement increase? When we compare that progress with the utilization of steam in trains and ships, we realize the startling suddenness with which our present civilization leaped forward a century and a half ago. If we add to that the harnessing of electricity, the invention of telegraphic and wireless communication, and the domination of the skies by airplanes, and if we examine the increase in the speed of movement during the past twenty years, we will also gain some notion of what the difference will be between the civilization of this generation and the next. The maximum speed of man's movement in most countries two hundred years ago was some hundred miles a day, while it is possible today to far surpass the speed of sound; and we may safely postulate that man's travel speed will continue to increase by leaps and bounds.[1]

If speed is a distinguishing criterion, then the difference between the speeds achieved in our age and in that of our forefathers will be the standard by which we measure civilization. And even as steam separated the old from the modern world,

[1] In 1923, when I was returning to Cairo from Garian in Tripolitania (Libya) by a caravan of camels and horses, I made the journey in sixty-three days (eight to ten hours' march each day). In 1947 I made the trip by plane in seven hours on my way to the United States. Today, the trip can be accomplished in three hours by jet. Astronaut John Glenn circled the globe twice in three hours and observed two sunrises.

so will electronics and ever-increasing speeds separate the next age from our own.

It is the misfortune of my generation that, serving as the link between these two worlds as it does, it should have to sacrifice its customs to such cruel changes. Accordingly, are we members of this generation actually qualified to bequeath a world order to our successors? The order that would satisfy our successors might be as different as ours has been from the thinking of the pre-steam era! From another point of view, men are still in ignorance of themselves, unable to penetrate the realities of their bodies and souls and hardly able to master their mental and spiritual forces; it will always be difficult for a given generation to establish an order for a world that is not of its making, for man is but an animal endowed with enough strength to allow him freedom of action within a limited sphere only.

The world has pursued a singularly uniform path for thousands of years. Civilization has advanced slowly and moved on slowly from one land to another, and it took hundreds of years to degenerate among one people and centuries more before it flourished anew among another. Within the range of its capacity, human intelligence was able to keep pace with and guide civilization to a considerable extent; but when the powers of modern science exploded suddenly, the earth quaked and threw out from its depths all sorts of new things. Man, struck with awe, was overwhelmed, and wanted to understand what was happening.

In a few generations, the countenance of this civilization has changed; the old and the new hardly recognize each other. By way of example, let us look at a village chieftain in the vicinity of Thebes in Upper Egypt. This man still lives as his forefathers lived in ancient times. During the early part of this century, he sent his son to America to be educated; the son married and returned with his family to his village. There he found his father alive, plowing his land with a plow used in the days of the Pharaohs, living in a dwelling in the style of those of the Hyksos, and thinking as men thought in the days of Khufu. Unquestionably, son and father did not recognize each other when they met again; it was as if the son had descended on his father from another planet. They were unable to live with each other or to cooperate.

Let us assume that during the hour of meeting Allah resurrected one of the former inhabitants of Thebes, say, the head of the village during the days of the Ramses, an ancestor who was made to witness the family celebration over the son's return from America. Would citizens find the present chieftain closer to the head of the village resurrected from his grave after almost three thousand years or to the son born in the twentieth century and absent for less than thirty years?

Those present at the celebration would find the father closer to the ancestor, to his mentality and mode of living, than to the son born in their midst and just returned from the New World.

Thirty years succeeded in altering the pattern of one family where thirty centuries had failed to do so. This enormous change has occurred not only in Egypt but through the entire world. Like an earthquake, one century has so changed the surface of the earth and has so widened the gap between us and the past that we appear to have been transplanted to another planet.

Can it be said that we who are the victims of this sudden change, who have dominated the machine and have been dominated by it, who have directed it toward the unknown and have been transported by it to greater unknowns, are actually capable of propounding a new order for the future? Were we to believe so, then we should receive the reward of our pretensions. It may prove more beneficial and sensible for us to be satisfied with a negative approach to a new order —to refrain completely from using the forces we control for destruction and ruin and from multiplying those conditions which have agitated our entire existence. In essence, our objective in what we call the "new order" should be to minimize the troubles attending our age of change.

We were witnesses to World War I, and we heard and grew excited over proposals of new principles of organization for the world; then we witnessed the greater conflagration of World War II and listened to more inspiring talk. But does there appear to be much difference between the mentality that supervised the instruments of destruction during the four years 1914-1918 and the mentality that supervised them for the more than four years 1939-1945? It is indeed the same handicapped mind, captive of the past and the present, enmeshed in the machine, in matter, in transportation, in communication, and in ever-increasing speed, which have staggered it and caused it to bend under the weight it has borne.

In our youth, we listened to discussions concerning a new world order with great enthusiasm; but when we hear about such plans today, we are more skeptical and fearful because of the deceptions and failures they reveal.

The past civilization of man progressed in slow evolution through hundreds of centuries, thus enabling the human mind to digest it; it will take more time than we have yet had for the human mind to digest modern civilization.

I have little confidence that the world's leaders are able enough and the common man mature enough to bear the huge and renewed responsibilities of our day, but I have great faith in that transcendent power which directs this world! For in nature all our hopes may be realized. Man was born with sufficient strength to recover from shock, and he possesses the ingenuity, competence, and adaptability needed to guarantee the survival of the species and the continuation of its progress. Through fearful and harsh trials and through his instinctive drive for survival, man will discover a suitable and renewable world order which will keep pace with the era of the machine, the era of ever-increasing speed. I say a suitable and renewable order because it does not appear sensible in any way to attempt to dictate a perfect and stable order which would not admit of change, for by their very nature all forms, situations, and innovations bear the seeds of change, decay, and obliteration.

Most of the catastrophes besetting man are the result of presumption and ignorance; and most of the evils that befall him redound from his own hostility and provocative pretensions.

Were we to attempt to endow the world with an exemplary order and ignore the love of recognition, power, and exaltation deeply entrenched in the human ego, we would be attempting to cap a bursting volcano of uncontrollable instincts. Every proposed order that is not built on the requirements of human nature will therefore be destroyed by human nature itself, for it is the way of man to upset every exemplary order and to form it anew if this order is not to become intolerable in his eyes.

Nothing bears out this assertion more clearly than the history of the systems of thought and the religions that have preached a noble ideology. Take, for example, the cases of Christianity and communism, separated by two thousand years: what has the primitive animal instinct of man done to them? Has not each sought to propound a noble, exemplary order? What has remained of high example in them? Only long historical sufferings!

In the name of Christianity and for the sake of Christianity, which forbids war, more blood has been shed than for any other message in the history of mankind. Moreover, the European Continent, which is the seat of Christianity, has been the vortex of wars and destruction throughout the last thousand years. What has become of the noble, merciful, and humble inheritance of Christ? Has it not been desecrated by man's instinct for domination, suppression, and self-exaltation? Is it not used to satisfy the low desires of human nature?

As regards communism, its message is not new to this world; in many respects it is an ideological sister of the Persian Mazdakite program, which ruined Persia in the past. In the name of communism, more blood has been spilled than was shed by barbarians for loot in previous ages. What remains of communism?

It would seem, therefore, that the exemplary or perfect order is to remain a dream for this world because human nature rejects it. Is it desirable for us to insist on searching for it? Or is it not preferable to remain content with an order that suits this world, that would serve nations and groups in the way common law serves individuals, that would limit the reaches of evil, perpetuate peace, circumscribe the harmfulness of war, and direct human instincts into acceptable channels which would satisfy temporary needs without recourse to hostility? Such an order should insure a better living for all, and should be sustained by common interests involving the individual, the community, and the nation in a world which, through the new means of transportation, has become one.

In other words, the new order would encompass a set of regulations that are universally applicable, and would acquire in time the force of tradition and common law; it would thus become acceptable to all people, and would be observed throughout the world.

30

# *Duty Before Right*

*

Before World War I, as in the years since, many of the world's serious thinkers tried to formulate an order acceptable to man, an order that would spare him the misery and pains brought about by the causes of world turmoil that I have previously discussed.

One of the many organizations concerned with this task was a group of noteworthy men from London publicized by the well-known writer H. G. Wells. After debating and corresponding at length, the group presented a program which enunciated the rights of man, and proposed that this program become a constitution for the world in the postwar era.

The constitution consisted of eleven articles which, in the opinion of the group, embodied the rights of man, and asserted that these rights should not be contradicted by any existing law, constitution, or local custom of tribe or nation; for this constitution was to be the fundamental law which would abrogate every law that disagreed with it.

The most important of these articles dealt with the sanctity of property, the right to education, freedom of belief, personal freedom, the right to work, and the right of the weak to protection from the community.

The group sent the program to two of the great thinkers of the East, Mahatma Gandhi and Jawaharlal Nehru, seeking their advice. Their responses were very different.

Gandhi answered by first asking a question: what were the practical results of declaring such rights, and who would watch over them and safeguard them? He suggested that the group had begun at the wrong end of the problem, that what the world needed rather was a conviction concerning human *duties*. This reply provoked Wells's anger, and the latter unleashed a shameful attack on the great leader for having refused to cooperate because of his passive faith, accusing him of retrogression and lack of appreciation of the necessities of the age.

But did Wells do justice to Gandhi? Does his response not deserve consideration and reflection?

As for Jawaharlal Nehru, his answer pleased Wells, who considered it practical and worthy of concerted attention, although he disagreed with him over a few minor issues. Nehru declared that, like the Kellogg-Briand Pact outlawing war, the proposed declaration might end in nothing because it did not incorporate specific methods for its realization. He said that the blame for the sufferings of the world of our time could be laid to the corruption of its imperialistic and capitalistic political and economic system, and that the system had to be altered before men could enjoy the rights outlined in the declaration. A new world order based on socialism was the answer, in Nehru's view, to the problem of assuring all men their basic rights and liberties.

I would agree that the rights of man have been frequently declared and as often violated; but I would depart sharply from Nehru's standpoint and cleave to Gandhi's in this: that as long as men of power are not motivated by ethical conduct, laws, and conscience—by the perception of their *duties*—the rights of man will remain in their present state: impossible of realization.

It is proper that we try a new system of ethical conduct and a new approach, with a new order based on duty; instead of attempting to equate people on the basis of rights, we should make duty the basis of equality—perhaps that would be more effective in repelling aggression and more conducive to respect for the rights of others.

If through training we can accustom people to honoring the person who fulfills his duty rather than the one who demands his rights, we might succeed in making duty the source of ethical and social relations and thereby initiate a new order for a better world. For the training which focuses on duty as the goal of the refined human being leads to a form of respect for the rights of others which is more protective and beneficial than the employment of force in establishing and safeguarding those rights. Such training is more in conformity with the history of human reform inasmuch as it has always been the method of prophets and reformers. It would not be difficult to return to this method or to create a new attitude that dwells on praising those who fulfill their duty toward the rest of mankind.

Prophets have forbidden killing, stealing, betraying, and deceiving, and have expounded upon the importance of one's duties to others, not one's rights. Should we become accustomed to denying ourselves that which is harmful to others and make our example universal, we would be taking a positive and decisive step in the direction of establishing a new order, although on the surface this might appear to constitute a negative message.

By way of example, let us suppose that men were trained not to make distinctions between killing and warring because duty obliges the cultured and self-respecting man to refrain from depriving others of their lives when no crime has been committed and no law has been trespassed upon. This training could dissuade people from warring; the duty of the soldier fighting in a legitimate war would be regarded in the same light as the duty of the executioner is regarded by the public almost everywhere. Such training, and the ethics and law it would engender, would be more effective in preventing wars than all the pacts and charters mankind might draw up.

Transforming the human concept of life is indeed a strenuous task, but then have not many views changed completely in a generation or two? Why should it not be possible to create, through proper upbringing and training, fundamental universal customs based on a respect for duty in all situations and circumstances? Perhaps it is feasible to direct those human instincts which we regard as sources of corruption toward the realization of pride in the fulfillment of duty.

Man boasts when he saves someone from drowning or exposes himself to danger in extinguishing a fire. Now, if he could accustom himself to regarding nonviolence and self-sacrifice—even martydom—in duty as deeds deserving the highest awards of society and as constituting perfect heroism, he would be employing his instincts for self-exaltation and boastfulness in the service of the general welfare.

Why not immortalize the memory of those who have displayed virtue in fulfilling their duty rather than the memory of those who have exhibited their power in devouring and destroying others? To teach what constitutes duty and to sanctify it would be to erect and immortalize the citadel of the right. Thus, we would attain to reform through our natural disposition and refrain from disturbing such a disposition as we direct it toward the maintenance of the new order.

It is difficult to believe that any member of my generation who has witnessed two world wars and who concedes that it is possible to achieve a new world order worthy of perpetuation would not advocate that war be completely outlawed. Can there be a way to this end more righteous than the way of the prophets—the abolition of crime through instruction in the precepts of duty?

Why not teach people, therefore, to loathe war as they loathe murder? Is it possible to guarantee peace by disarming nations or by appointing certain armed nations as custodians of peace? What is there to prevent the armed custodians from warring against each other in a greedy desire to devour their charge if they do not have the self-discipline that ethical training based on the sanctity of duty instills?

Such training is not impossible, nor are its fruits undependable; in the early times of man's experience he had considerable pride in his self-control and self-restraint. The history of human virtue is a long one, attending man in every generation, and the self-denial contingent on such virtue was acquired by man through social custom and religion. It became part of man's instinctive behavior because the instincts that serve human virtue are the same as those that suit man's sense of aggressiveness.

When men take pride in being generous, they are satisfying their instinct to excel by expending and giving; but when they pride themselves on their material acquisitions, they are exercising the same innate power with selfishness and egotism.

If, for example, we were to teach our children that their pleasure and self-admiration should not depend on donning new clothes on a holiday when the children of their cousins and neighbors cannot do the same, accustoming them to take pride rather in voluntarily refraining from putting them on as a form of self-respect, then the instinctive love for ostentation would be trained to satisfy its ends through restraint and would discover its fulfillment in duty.

This would not be a new experience in the annals of mankind as it would conform with the spirit of the religions that have dominated man's history.

Any natural disposition of man is universal, but its manifestations are many and various inasmuch as the human ego is shaped according to precepts of training and particular customs that aim at appeasing man's secret drives. There is no denying the fact that those who purport to organize the world should always have the natural instincts in mind. The way of the prophets, who directed instincts in a manner satisfactory to the standards of virtue and the common welfare, is the righteous way. If today, instead of announcing the rights of man, we enunciated his duties and clothed these duties in robes of honor and sanctity, we might succeed in arriving at a new order of righteousness. Let the law and customs fundamental for this order define the duties of man toward members of his household, his neighbors, and his country, toward his own kind and other beings. This practice may prove more enduring and more stable for future generations.

# Index

*

'Abbās, 186
'Abbāsid (Hāshimite) caliphs, 106, 195, 237
'Abd-Allah, 6, 7*n*
'Abd-Allah ibn-Jud'ān, 7*n*
'Abd-Allah ibn-Rawāḥah, 182
'Abd-al-'Azīz ibn-Su'ūd (ibn-Saud), 6
'Abd-al-Malik, 75
'Abd-al-Malik ibn-Hishām, 181*n*, 234
'Abd-Manāf, 13
'Abd-al-Muṭṭalib, 6, 7*n*, 13, 154
'Abd-al-Raḥmān Ghāfiqi, 210*n*
'Abd-al-Raḥmān ibn-'Awf, 227-8
Abraham, 25-6, 34, 37, 41, 42, 64, 250
*abu,* defined, 14*n*
Abu-Bakr (first caliph), 4*n*, 10, 17, 20, 52*n*, 97, 98, 103-4, 115*n*, 116-17, 165-6, 226-7, 231
Abu-Dharr, 91, 222
Abu-al-Ḥasan, *see* 'Ali
Abu-Ḥazm, 75-6
Abu-Ḥudhayfah, 243
Abu-Isḥāq al-Shīrāzi, 61
Abu-Jandal ibn-Suhayl, 141-2
Abu-Lahab, 17
Abu-Sufyān ibn-al-Ḥārith, 4, 25, 168, 186
Abu-Ṭālib, 6-7, 8, 10, 16-17, 18, 36
Abu-'Ubaydah, 52*n*, 136
Abu-al-Walīd, *see* 'Utbah ibn-Rabī'ah
Abyssinia (Ethiopia), 15-16, 18-20, 100, 127-8, 178, 238
acts of worship, 23, 33, 54-6, 61, 79
Adam, 42, 102, 220, 230
'Adiy ibn-Ḥātim, 61
'Aḍūd al-Dawlah, 193
Afghanistan, 58, 67-8, 239
aggression, as cause of war, 130-1, 134, 140, 158; Message on, 65, 144, 149, 151, 153, 159, 171; *see also* compulsion; tyranny and oppression; war, legitimate
*ahl al-dhimmah, see* protected peoples
Aḥzāb (confederacy), 25, 166*n*, 171; *see also* Quraysh
al-, *see first element of name or next element of title or word*
Albania, 66-7, 237
alcoholic beverages, *see* intoxicants
Alexander, 4
Algeria, 67, 192
'Ali (fourth caliph), 4*n*, 8*n*, 9-10, 20, 48, 106*n*, 228, 234
'Alids, 106, 195
Allah, defined, 35*n*; *see also* God
allies, lands of, as abode of peace (*dār al-ṣulh*), 132, 134; Message on, 105, 132, 136; relations with Islam, 105, 141, 154-5
alms, 93, 97, 98, 103; tax (*ṣadaqah*), 195, 231, 235; *see also* beneficence; poor tax; poverty
Āminah, 6
amīr, defined, 76, 80, 116; *see also* Islam, leaders of